RSAC

JUN 2007

THE STORY OF GOLF IN OKLAHOMA

THE STORY OF
GOLF
IN OKLAHOMA

DEL LEMON
FOREWORD BY SUSIE MAXWELL BERNING

UNIVERSITY OF OKLAHOMA PRESS • NORMAN

This book is published with the generous assistance of the Wallace C. Thompson Endowment Fund, University of Oklahoma Foundation. The paper in this book meets the guidelines for permanence and durability of the Committee on Production Guidelines for Book Longevity of the Council on Library Resources, Inc. ∞

Library of Congress Cataloging-in-Publication Data
Lemon, Del, 1952–
    The story of golf in Oklahoma / Del Lemon; foreword by Susie Maxwell Berning
    p. cm.
    Includes bibliographical references and index.
    ISBN 0-8061-3300-7 (alk. paper)
    1. Golf—Oklahoma—History—20th century. I. Title.

GV982.O55 L46 2001
796.352'09766—dc21

00-062897

1 2 3 4 5 6 7 8 9 10

DEDICATED TO

*L*ESLIE

MY OKLAHOMA GIRL.

"FOREVER AND BEYOND"

CONTENTS

CONTENTS

Color Plates

Following page 128

Tiger Woods at hole No. 1, Southern Hills
Arnold Palmer, Southern Hills, 1994
Dale Fleming McNamara
Dornick Hills Country Club, hole No. 15, Ardmore
Tiger Woods and Fluff Cowan, Southern Hills
Coaches Labron Harris Sr. and Mike Holder
Charles Howell
Jo Jo Robertson
Jimmie Austin–University of Oklahoma Golf Course
hole No. 9, Norman
Hunter Haas
Edward Loar
Mike Holder with Karsten and Louise Solheim
Karsten Creek Golf Club, hole No. 16, Stillwater
Oak Tree Golf Club, hole No. 16, Edmond
Tiger Woods and Treas Nelson

Course Layouts

ILLUSTRATIONS

FIGURES

$\mathcal{I}$ do not hail from Muskogee, but in the words of Merle Haggard's classic country and western song, I'm proud to be an Okie.

Is there some special ingredient in Oklahoma's red soil? I like to think so. Just look at what her people have accomplished in nearly one hundred years of statehood, both in golf and in many other walks of life. You can be sure that all of Oklahoma, including the Muskogee Golf and Country Club, where I won my first professional golf tournament, will forever have a special place in my heart.

With Oklahoma's third U.S. Open set for June of 2001 in Tulsa, Del Lemon's *Story of Golf in Oklahoma* is a timely narrative that depicts our state's distinguished first century of golf, a story I believe the rest of the golf world will find interesting as well.

The book is not just about Oklahomans—it also includes accounts of numerous players from other states who have won championships there. At one time or another almost all the great American golf champions—from Walter Hagen, Babe Didrikson Zaharias, and Gene Sarazen through Sam Snead, Arnold Palmer, Nancy Lopez, and Tiger Woods—have been part of the tapestry that is Oklahoma golf.

Beginning with my earliest golf lessons from U. C. Ferguson (he insisted we call him Fergie) at Oklahoma City's historic Lincoln Park, and through four decades as a tournament professional, I came to realize that Oklahoma's golf teachers, courses, players, and championships were as impressive as those in any state I could think of. I count it a blessing to have learned the fundamentals of the game in that special place in the heartland of our nation.

As a training ground, the courses of Oklahoma, in combination with the ever-changing elements, presented a golfer with most every condition she might encounter on the professional tours. When people ask me how it was that four of my eleven LPGA victories came at major championships, I tell them this can be traced directly back to my youth in Oklahoma City, learning the game at Lincoln Park and later having opportunities to play some of Oklahoma's finest country club courses, such as Twin Hills, Southern Hills, and Oklahoma City Golf and Country Club.

At Lincoln Park I discovered every manner of shot, especially the British style bump and run, often on hardpan conditions, tempered by the prevailing winds. At the country clubs, however, every blade of grass was perfect, the fairways were tight, the bunkers deep, requiring pinpoint drives and high iron shots to the fastest of greens.

For an aspiring professional golfer it did not get any better than that. The shots I manufactured during those golden days would serve me well for all of my tournament career, whether I was competing with the men's team at Oklahoma City University or striking an approach shot during the final round of a U.S. Women's Open.

Since then, travels have separated me from Oklahoma. But I return there each year for the Susie Maxwell Berning Intercollegiate. It is a chance to renew lifelong friendships and give something back to the game that has been so good to me. And now Del's book has successfully captured the feel of what I recall about my years in Oklahoma and my many friends who still reside there. He even relates stories that I had not heard before, and suffice it to say I have heard a few.

In May of 2000, Del interviewed me at the LPGA's Harvey Penick Invitational in Austin. Upon seeing his enthusiasm for this project, I was delighted to accept when he asked me to write a foreword. Del has strong family, university, and professional ties to Oklahoma. And I was pleased to learn that he had interviewed Fergie, several times, in Oklahoma City, because I place Fergie on the same pedestal as Harvey Penick, Byron Nelson, and Ben Hogan.

To me Fergie was Super Okie. If ever there was a walking encyclopedia about Oklahoma golf history, it was U. C. Ferguson. He taught my brothers and me everything about the game, from how to chip and putt to operating the pro shop. Later he presented to me as gifts both the Wilson R-90 sand iron and the Macgregor driver I carried for every major victory of my professional career.

Fergie was a marvelous teacher and a fine player, who instilled in me and in untold legions of other kids the correct fundamentals of golf. His heart was larger than large, his kindnesses never ended, his patience and enthusiasm lasted a lifetime.

To the end of his time, nobody was more passionate or knowledgeable about Oklahoma golf than Fergie. Along with Bill Bentley, Sig Harpman, Wally Wallis, C. B. McDonald, J. W. Barry, and J. I. Everest, he organized the Golf Incorporated scholarship fund that made it possible for so many of us to attend college. And for as long as I can remember, Fergie was outspoken in his conviction that "somebody needs to write a book" about the rich heritage of Oklahoma golf.

With the publication of *The Story of Golf in Oklahoma*, I think we can all rest assured that somewhere Fergie will be smiling. Those who loved him will feel his presence in these pages.

This book taps into the spirit of Oklahoma and Oklahomans. I believe it will help others, whether they be golfers or not, to understand better why so many of us are proud to call ourselves Oklahomans.

Susie Maxwell Berning

THE STORY OF GOLF IN OKLAHOMA

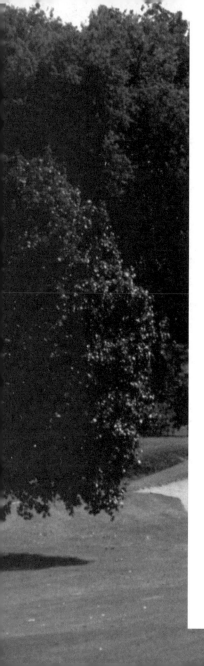

Introduction

In August of 1994, as a freelance writer living in Austin, Texas, I was on assignment for the *Austin American-Statesman* to cover the PGA Championship at Southern Hills Country Club in Tulsa. My job was to report on the play at Southern Hills of Central Texas pros like Ben Crenshaw, Tom Kite, Bob Estes, and J. L. Lewis. In addition to the heightened interest that accompanies any of the four major championships in professional golf, there was a storyline in Tulsa that marked the end of an era. Southern Hills would be the final PGA Championship appearance for one of golf's greatest legends—Arnold Palmer.

Palmer was known worldwide for his heroics in the Masters, U.S. Open, and British Open. But he had never won golf's fourth major, the PGA Championship. On more than one occasion, including at Southern Hills in 1970, he had been tantalizingly close to joining the four-major fraternity of Jack Nicklaus, Gene Sarazen, Ben Hogan, and Gary Player. But the PGA was destined to remain the only one of professional golf's four majors that Palmer would not win.

As it turned out, Palmer could not have chosen a more appropriate venue for his final PGA. Besides the near miss in 1970, he had twice won PGA Tour events in Oklahoma—at the 1959 and 1964 Oklahoma City Opens. I was fairly certain that the second of Palmer's Oklahoma City victories had come at Quail Creek Golf and Country Club. But as my deadline approached, I could not confirm this or where he won in 1959. I filed a story about Palmer's final PGA round at Southern Hills, where he missed the cut by nine strokes. But uncertain of the facts, I made no mention of Arnie's successes at the Oklahoma City Open.

The next morning I returned to Southern Hills and went immediately to the pro shop, anxious to purchase a book about Oklahoma's golf past. However, only a slim volume about the history of Southern Hills was available. It occurred to me that although dozens of books had been written detailing the history of golf in Texas, a book about Oklahoma golf history might not exist, which indeed proved to be the case. At that moment the research for this book began.

As an Oklahoma State University graduate married to a native Oklahoman, I have had many occasions during the past twenty-five years to visit Oklahoma, play golf there, and read about golf in the state's two largest daily newspapers. I was always struck by the substantive golf writing in the sports pages of the *Daily Oklahoman* and *Tulsa World*, writing which would later supply much of the background research for this book. As a kid growing up in the Texas Panhandle town of Perryton (closer to six other state capitals than to my birthplace in Austin and well within the *Daily Oklahoman's* circulation area), I had pored over the *Oklahoman* sports pages each morning before school.

If there were keener sportswriters in those years than Frank Boggs, Volney Meece, John Cronley, Vernon Snell, and Bob Hurt, we were not exposed to them in Perryton. Not only could I revel in tales of the never-ending Bedlam series, between the Cowboys and Sooners, and the Friday night exploits of our interstate high school football rivals Woodward and Guymon, but I was also reading the golf articles of Wally Wallis, as he profiled Oklahoma champions Tommy Bolt, Charlie Coe, Jimmie Gauntt, and Bo Wininger with nicknames like "Ol 'Thunder,'" "Thin Man," and "Bwana."

Outside Augusta, Georgia, few media outlets cover professional and amateur golf with more intensity than newspapers, radio, and television in Oklahoma City and Tulsa. Typical of the Oklahoma media's interest in golf was coverage of the odyssey of Oklahoma City amateur Jake Engel. On December 16, 1996, Engel, a retired hatchery owner, putted out on a hole at Oklahoma City's Lincoln Park West—not unusual in itself, except that he had done the same thing earlier, 10,075 times during 1996 alone. In the process, Engel broke South Carolinian Ollie Bowers's twenty-seven-year-old world record for most holes of golf played in one year.

Walking almost every step of the way, Engel, aged sixty-four, wore out five pairs of shoes and one Bag Boy pullcart. His final totals at the close of 1996 were 332 days played and 10,374 holes completed, most of them at Lincoln Park. The *Daily Oklahoman* covered Engel's feat. So did the *Tulsa World* and *South Central Golf* magazine. Local television aired the story, and Engel said later that the publicity inspired him.

Typical Oklahoma golf reporting appeared on page 15 of the *Daily Oklahoman* on July 2, 1961. Clockwise, beginning with Wallis's column "Golf Shop" on the upper left corner of the page, the headlines read:

> Lawton Golfers Shine in Chickasha Pro-Am
> Carter Quits Post as PGA Tourney Chief
> Three Still Share Lead at Flint
> Autrey Shades Harris with 68

Texan's 66 Wins Medal at Elk City
Nagle's Finishing 68 Wins English Tourney
Lawton Tourney Next for Golfers
Golf Clinic Set at Hefner Today

and there is a photograph of fifteen-year-old Howard Bowens (scorecard in hand), a caddie at Lincoln Park and a member of the Douglas High School golf team. While playing in a junior tournament at Lake Hefner the day before, Bowens had aced the 165-yard twelfth hole with a 7-iron, reportedly becoming the first African American in Oklahoma City golf history to score a competitive hole in one.

The owners of more than a few nationally recognized bylines jumpstarted sportswriting careers with golf beats in Oklahoma. Nick Seitz, Doug Ferguson, Jay Cronley, Mac Bentley, Bill Connors, Ross Goodner, Berry Tramel, John Rohde, Dan O'Kane, John Klein, Ken MacLeod, Jay Upchurch, Jenk Jones, Tom Lobaugh, Bus Ham, and Bill Inglish have all written extensively about Oklahoma golf. So respected was Inglish, a long-time *Daily Oklahoman* editor and fifty-year member of the Golf Writers Association of America, that he was commissioned by Augusta National cofounders Clifford Roberts and Bob Jones to serve as the official Masters Tournament historian, a position he held from 1964 until his death in 1998.

During the 1996 Tour Championship, the state's two largest dailies, multiple radio stations, and a half dozen network affiliates covered the tournament like an Oklahoma blue norther. For seven consecutive days the *Tulsa World* published six-page special sections, plus a thirty-page Sunday supplement and dozens of golf-related features throughout the rest of the paper. For the week, the *World* and *Oklahoman* had twenty-two stories and eight columns about Tiger Woods alone.

"We like Tulsa and appreciate all the attention—from both the media and the community," PGA Tour Commissioner Tim Finchem told the press. "Southern Hills, Olympic, and Pinehurst are in a league by themselves. We'd come back here in a heartbeat."

The PGA Tour, PGA of America, and the USGA have returned to Oklahoma time and again. The 2001 U.S. Open at Southern Hills marks the sixteenth USGA championship in Oklahoma, two fewer than in neighboring Texas, which has five times as many golf courses. Oklahoma's attractiveness as a major championship destination is a product of several factors, none more significant than its splendid array of courses and a climate survivable for bentgrass greens. Across its five-hundred-mile breadth, stretching from the 4,973 feet of elevation at Black Mesa in the northwest to the Southern Pine Forest near Broken Bow in the southeast, Oklahoma is blessed with a topography of mountains, hills, bluffs, rivers, lakes, prairies, saltflats, forests, and dunes—much of it well-suited for golf.

"Were I to set out looking for classic terrain on which to build a great golf course," wrote architectural critic Tom Doak in 1996 (*Confidential Guide*, 46), "the Great Plains of America are certainly not the first region of the country I would think to explore, but even I can be wrong sometimes. For one thing it is the windiest region of the USA, an important element if we wish to pose the classical problems of the great British links; there are wide-open vistas, as on the great seaside courses; and in isolated pockets there exists some great terrain."

None is better suited for golf than that in Oklahoma. Nearly 10 percent of the state's more than 220 golf courses are of championship caliber, and many of these are open to the public, making the state a prime destination for both recreational and tournament golfers. In March of 1999, *Golf Digest* came out with its biennial rankings of the top ten courses in each state. Courses *omitted* from the list of Oklahoma's ten best include Cedar Ridge (1983 U.S. Women's Open); Muskogee Country Club (1970

U.S. Women's Open); Twin Hills (1935 PGA Championship); Quail Creek (ten PGA and Senior Tour events); Tulsa Country Club (1960 U.S. Women's Amateur, 1984 Roy Clark Senior Open, 1999 Women's NCAA Championship); Oaks Country Club (1960 U.S. Girls' Junior); Stillwater Country Club (1973 NCAA Championship, 1979 Women's AIAW Championship); Lincoln Park (1955 LPGA Oklahoma City Open); and two classic Maxwell courses that have hosted numerous Oklahoma Opens and PGA section championships (Hillcrest Country Club in Bartlesville and Oakwood Country Club in Enid).

The climate is temperate enough to average more than three hundred golfing days per year, yet far enough north and west for virtually every course in the state to be able to grow the smoothest putting surfaces in the game—bentgrass greens. Bentgrass, native to the Scottish linksland, is a cool-weather turf. Most states south and east of Oklahoma are plagued with enough heat and nighttime humidity to suffocate the fine blades of bentgrass. Oklahoma's midsummer nighttime temperatures average eight to twelve degrees cooler than in states in the deep South, which allows Oklahoma's bentgrass to survive.

But as impressive as are Oklahoma's golf courses, climate, agronomy, and media interest in the game, it was a century's worth of stories about the determination, talent, and generosity of Oklahoma golfers themselves that brought this book to life.

In 1959, a group of Oklahoma Citians, headed by longtime Lincoln Park professional U. C. Ferguson, founded the Golf Incorporated Scholarship Fund. By 1980, Golf Incorporated had raised more than $100,000, which helped seventy-seven Oklahoma youngsters attend college. The scholarships were awarded based on "merit, ability, character and some contribution to golf." Among the early Golf Incorporated scholarship recipients were two future USGA champions—Susie Maxwell Berning and

Bob Dickson—along with Shelby Futch, Roger Maxwell (Susie's brother), Greg Lambert, and Dean York, one of five sons of an Oklahoma City auto mechanic.

York used his Golf Incorporated scholarship to attend the University of Oklahoma and earn a degree in accounting. He later served as chairman of the Golf Incorporated scholarship fund. Money was raised by hosting tournaments, two of which were the Susie Maxwell Berning Women's All-College and the U. C. Ferguson Men's All-College. Tournament organizers in other parts of the state followed the example set by Golf Incorporated and have raised hundreds of thousands of dollars for noble causes ever since.

Contributions by Oklahomans to golf have not been limited to scholarships and charitable causes. In 1961, the courage of one Oklahoman, Tishomingo native Bill Spiller, breached the previously impenetrable wall of professional golf's racial divide. Spiller's story was first documented in a 1986 anthology, *Gettin' to the Dance Floor*, by Al Barkow, longtime writer and editor for Tulsa-based *Golf Illustrated* magazine.

Bill Spiller was born in Tishomingo in 1913, the great grandson of a full-blood Cherokee. Since his mother was African American, Spiller was required to attend segregated elementary and high schools in Tulsa. A track star, he went on to all-black Wiley College in Marshall, Texas, where he won three national championships in track and field. After college, Spiller took a job helping his father, an employee at Hillcrest Country Club in Bartlesville.

As African-American lockerroom attendants, Spiller and his father had limited access to the course. Once around 1932, Spiller played five holes at Hillcrest with his dad, later recalling, "I whiffed eight times." It was not until ten years later that Spiller played again, this time in southern California. Like Larry Nelson and Calvin Peete of another era, Spiller bloomed late. He won the 5–7 handicap flight of the first California tournament he ever entered, good enough for a seventy-five-dollar war bond. By 1946, Spiller had won all the black tournaments up and down the Pacific Coast.

Despite his successes, any time Spiller attempted to enter PGA Tour events, he was shown a copy of Article III of the PGA of America's Constitution and its "Caucasians only" membership clause, which read: "Professional golfers of the Caucasian Race, over the age of eighteen (18) years, residing in North or South America, who can qualify under the terms and conditions thereinafter specified, shall be eligible for membership."

Spiller would never be permitted to join the PGA. Instead, his dream of playing golf for a living was derailed by institutional racism. Joined by fellow black professionals Charlie Sifford and Teddy Rhodes, Spiller embarked upon a fifteen-year crusade to overthrow the Caucasian clause. Finally, in 1959, attorney Stanley Mosk, a champion of civil rights in California, filed suit against the PGA, documenting discrimination against African-American golf professionals.

After two years of legal wrangling and denial, and the threat by Mosk of an injunction to halt the 1962 PGA Championship, the PGA finally realized that their position was untenable and dropped the Caucasian clause from their bylaws. Spiller never won another tournament, instead sacrificing his competitive career to champion a cause. But thanks in part to the doggedness of this one man from Tishomingo, Oklahoma, some walls came tumbling down, opening the PGA's doors to everyone, regardless of skin pigment. Fittingly, it was at Burneyville, Oklahoma, in 1964 that Mississippian Pete Brown became the first African-American PGA pro to win an official PGA Tour event.

The stories of Spiller and Brown, and those of so many other Oklahomans, made researching and writing this history a most fascinating journey. Books I consulted in the process are listed in the bibliography; newspaper and magazine articles are given in the notes. People quoted without formal citation are those I interviewed in the course of the research or during other freelance work. Profiles of many championship players, tabulations of their wins, and a chronology of Oklahoma tournament golf are presented in the appendices.

Investigation turned up much about golf course design and politics, the competetive intangibles that a simple listing of winners cannot reveal, the key importance of a single individual or event in the careers of some notable golfers—and even a death threat during championship play. The research indeed confirmed, as shown in appendix 3, that Arnold Palmer's wins in the Oklahoma City Open were at Twin Hills Golf and Country Club in 1959, with a fifteen-under-par score of 273, and at Quail Creek Golf and Country Club in 1964.

When the Bostonian first starts for Indian Territory, he is filled with fear and trembling, armed to the hilt. But for a subsequent visit he finds the tennis racket and driver better suited to his needs, furnishing all the protection he requires. Instead of the unwelcome challenge of "hands up," he is met with the more genteel suggestion, "tee off."

Sturm's Statehood Magazine,
October 1905

ONE
First Tee

To newcomers in the spring of 1900, laying eyes for the first time on the Oklahoma Territory capital of Guthrie, perhaps the acreage east of the Atchison, Topeka and Santa Fe depot more closely resembled a deserted battleground, or an overstaked claim from the Land Run of 1889, than a rudimentary new golf course that would still be in the business of pars and birdies a hundred years later.

According to *Harper's Official Golf Guide of 1901*, there existed only one golf course in pre-statehood Oklahoma, and that was in Guthrie: "Guthrie Golf Club—One mile from the Atchison, Topeka and Santa Fe Railroad station. Post office address: Guthrie, Oklahoma. Organized May 10, 1900. Annual dues, $6. Open all year. Membership: 22."[1]

This account, with Guthrie Golf Club named as territorial Oklahoma's only course at the turn of the century, was corroborated by a 1980 *Guthrie Daily News* article that quoted from golf historian Harry B. Martin's *Fifty Years of American Golf*, published in

1936: "In 1900 every state in the Union had its golf course, New York state leading the procession with the proud total of 165." Martin then listed each state and its corresponding number of courses, concluding with those states claiming just one apiece: Louisiana, Arizona, New Mexico, Wyoming, Oregon, Nevada, Utah, and Oklahoma. "The total count of U.S. golf courses at the turn of the century numbered 1,040, *but did not represent all the clubs that had been constructed*" (italics added).[2]

There is evidence to suggest that at least one other golf club, and one social club, were operating by 1900 in territorial Oklahoma. According to *Spalding's Athletic Library Official Golf Guide of 1925*, Bartlesville Country Club (today known as Hillcrest Country Club) was founded as a social club in 1900, but golf was not played there until 1912. Furthermore, W. F. Kerr and Ina Gainer, in their 1922 *Story of Oklahoma City, Oklahoma*, wrote: "Not until 1900 did Oklahoma City begin to take an interest in golf. The first course was laid out east of the city, just beyond the Maywood addition."[3] Kerr and Gainer's account of the earliest golf course in Oklahoma City—the city that would became the state capital in 1910—is corroborated in 1958 and 1985 *Daily Oklahoman* articles by staffers Wilbur Johnson and Jim Hamilton. "In 1900 a nine-hole course was built on the Jordan farm in what is now northeast Oklahoma City," wrote Johnson.[4] Hamilton reported: "Golf came to Oklahoma City in 1900 when a crude nine-hole course was laid out and built in the vicinity of NE 12th and Stiles. Dr. R. T. Edwards, R. J. Edwards, and Fred E. Petterson were among those instrumental in building the course, and the first golf club in Oklahoma City was created at that time."[5]

Some of the earliest photographs of golfers in Oklahoma are of Tulsans. Two such photos appeared in the October 1905 issue of *Sturm's Statehood Magazine*. A full-page photo inside the cover of the magazine depicted Mrs. M. C. Hale at the top of her backswing, wearing a full-length white dress. A second, wide-angle photograph showed seven golfers and four spectators on the front porch of "the country club house and grounds at Tulsa, I.T."[6] According to Clarence Douglas, in *The History of Tulsa*, the Tulsa club was "organized in 1903, with a small number of members" and opened to golfers in 1904.[7]

As with Oklahoma City's first golf course, the name of the designer of Tulsa's first course, if other than a committee of members, remains a mystery.

Sturm noted: "The site is one mile southeast of Tulsa, commanding a splendid view of the city and surrounding country. Its clubhouse is modest in dimensions, being designed for convenience and comfort rather than display. The ground floor plan providing a large reception room; 50 lockers are for men, a less number for women. Two rooms on the first floor are reserved for the use of the keeper of the grounds, and the entire second story provides a comfortable home for himself and family.

"The golf links extend over the entire 60 acres and consist of the regulation nine holes, the actual distance being 2,306 yards. The shortest hole measures 133 yards and the longest 384. Bogey for the course is 43 strokes. A large spring in a picturesque ravine about 250 yards south of the clubhouse supplies an abundance of pure water."[8]

Early courses in Oklahoma and elsewhere were routed in, or paced off, in the method of the times: "18 stakes on a Sunday afternoon." According to Cornish and Whitten, in *The Architects of Golf*, few early courses had more than nine holes. But even then, a course builder might require dozens or hundreds of wooden stakes to mark the perimeters of all the tees, fairways, and greens accurately, then "grade, shape and contour by teams of men and flat horse-drawn metal scoops known as pans or scrapers."[9]

In Guthrie, a group of twenty-two citizens with the blessing of officials of the railroad commissioned a Scottish immigrant, Alexander H. Findlay, to lay out the golf course. In that Findlay was considered by golf historians to be one of the first half dozen or so people ever to play the game in the United States, his selection to design Oklahoma's first course set a high standard for subsequent golf course architects in the state.

Findlay was born in 1865 at Montrose, Scotland, a spacious coastal village halfway between St. Andrews and Aberdeen, on the North Sea. Like other Scottish seaports—Carnoustie, Leith, Dornoch, North Berwick, Musselburgh, and St. Andrews—Findlay's hometown was situated on linksland, the barren strips of coastline left behind when the seas receded after the last ice age.

By the mid-nineteenth century at Montrose, as at other seaside courses, the game of golf had become so popular as to have created a demand for the services of players knowledgeable about all facets of the game. These players, who became the first professional golfers, charged fees and derived income, paltry though it was, from their expertise at instruction, caddying, clubmaking, agronomy, and repair. They also competed in tournaments, which offered cash prizes. The most renowned competition, attracting players from all over Scotland, was the Open Championship, then played annually at Prestwick, St. Andrews, or Musselburgh.

As a teenager in Montrose, Findlay earned repute as an accomplished player and clubmaker. He also designed golf courses. Sometime in his late teens Findlay left Scotland for the United States, where his first job was as a ranch hand. According to a 1980 newspaper article by his grandson, Findlay moved to Nance County, Nebraska, in the early 1880s, ostensibly to work on a ranch, but could not get out of his system the game that became his homeland's national pastime. On April 4, 1887, Findlay laid out a crude golf course at the ranch and soon after gave up the life of a cowboy.

After routing in a handful of courses in Massachusetts, New Hampshire, New Jersey, and Florida, Findlay came to Guthrie in early 1900 and staked off the nine-hole Guthrie Golf Club. On May 10, 1900, the new course opened for play.[10] A century later, the 3,278-yard course, renamed Guthrie Country Club, is still in operation.

"We have small, English-style, bentgrass greens," said club manager Brian Branch, whose late grandfather, Howard Smith, purchased the club in the 1950s. "There are fourteen bunkers on the nine holes, with three par 3s and two par 5s. We have a membership of 220 families and average about twelve thousand rounds per year," Branch said in a 1998 interview.

Situated a half mile east of Guthrie, where Bird Creek flows into the old Santa Fe Lake, Guthrie Country Club was constructed on a site with excellent drainage and an abundance of hardwoods. In the late 1990s, Branch and head pro Jack Rhinehart have attempted to replace what attrition and a century's worth of Oklahoma weather had worn away. "During the past decade we've probably lost fifty mature oaks and cottonwoods to wind, lightning, thunderstorms, and disease," said Branch. "But we've replanted at least five hundred trees. In another ten years I think people will be amazed."

Arguably, the success of Guthrie Country Club can be attributed in part to Findlay's incorporating some classic design elements of Scottish links courses. Instead of using the omnipresent "push-up" greens typical of the era, Findlay was a minimalist, preferring to disturb the land as little as possible. Whenever he could, he chose greensites with natural drainage and esthetics.

In addition to being a prolific course architect (Findlay ultimately designed more than a hundred courses from Montana to the Bahamas), the Scotsman was a golfer of considerable note. He established dozens of course records and put on a series of American exhibitions with the great Englishman Harry Vardon. Findlay's sons—Norman, Ronald, and Richard —who were his construction team, once estimated that their dad played twenty-four hundred courses in his lifetime. Later in life Findlay was associated in clubmaking and course development with Wright-Ditson and Wanamaker's, both prominent East Coast sporting goods firms. He also planned, constructed, and operated courses for the Florida East Coast Railroad.

Always, Findlay kept his Scottish sense of humor. In 1926, he sent word to Pope Pius XI that in his opinion, there was just enough room at the Vatican for a six-hole golf course. But the Pontiff declined. Pius put in a broadcast station instead.

Fifty of Findlay's courses, most of them private, are still in operation today. In addition to Guthrie Golf Club, two of the best examples of his work are a public course, Galen Hall Golf Club in Wernersville, Pennsylvania, and the private San Antonio (Texas) Country Club, where 1981 British Open champion Bill Rogers became director of golf. Findlay also designed Beaumont (Texas) Country Club and the original nine holes at Fort Smith (Arkansas) Country Club. Of the 111 courses he designed, only seven were west of the Mississippi River. Five remain open today, four of which are in Oklahoma, Texas, and Arkansas. Findlay died in Philadelphia in 1942, at age seventy-six.

ALWAYS, FINDLAY KEPT HIS SCOTTISH SENSE OF HUMOR. IN 1926, HE SENT WORD TO POPE PIUS XI THAT IN HIS OPINION, THERE WAS JUST ENOUGH ROOM AT THE VATICAN FOR A SIX-HOLE GOLF COURSE. BUT THE PONTIFF DECLINED. PIUS PUT IN A BROADCAST STATION INSTEAD.

After Findlay completed his work at Guthrie Golf Club, other Scottish pros immigrated to territorial Oklahoma, bringing with them an abundance of knowledge about building golf courses. Leslie Brownlee of Edinburgh was the next architect of note in Oklahoma, designing a nine-hole course at Muskogee Town and Country Club, which opened March 10, 1903, and Oklahoma City's Lakeview Country Club, which opened in 1907.

On November 16, 1907, Oklahoma became the forty-sixth state admitted to the Union. Brownlee's successes brought other Scottish pros to the new state, including William Nichols (who became pro at Muskogee Golf and Country Club), Arthur Jackson, J. G. "Jock" Collins, Jack Taylor, John Gatherum, O. S. "Sandy" Baxter, Phil Hessler, and William Creavy.

In 1910, Oklahoma City's Lakeview Country Club, the forerunner to Oklahoma City Golf and Country Club, hired Brownlee as the first full-time golf professional in Oklahoma. His assistant was his stepbrother, Jackson, who had arrived in Oklahoma as a teenager in 1909. Jackson was born in 1894 and grew up in the tiny Scottish village of North Berwick, in an era when golfers still used gutta-percha balls (called "gutties") and an assortment of weapons variously referred to as mashie, niblick, mashie-niblick, mid-iron, driver, brassie, spoon, baffy, wooden cleek, plain old un-wooden cleek, and putter.

The guttie ball, made from the sap of trees native to India, was so hard that it shattered clubs and jarred bones. If you got good cleek on the ball, it might go 175 yards. "It sounded just like you'd hit a rock," Jackson told sportswriter Frank Boggs.[11]

By all accounts Jackson was a dedicated tournament competitor with modest talent. He won few if any championships; however, his legacy to golf in Oklahoma transcended any trophies he might have won. Jackson eventually designed all thirty-six holes at Oklahoma City's Lincoln Park, the state's first great municipal course. For his efforts, Jackson has been called the "father of public golf" in Oklahoma.

"Art Jackson was a hero as far as I was concerned," said the late U. C. Ferguson, who succeeded Jackson as Lincoln Park head pro. "He was real quiet, easy-going, serious, and, most important of all, he wanted to see you succeed. He had talent to be a good player, but he seldom won. I'm quite certain it was because he hated to see anybody lose. He would rather get beat by you than beat you. But he never got upset, never showed any temper. To this day he is the finest all-around man I ever met in my life."

Before settling permanently in Oklahoma City, Jackson served as professional at other courses in the state, including McAlester Country Club. While working at Tulsa Country Club, just before World War I, he was hired to design a course on the Ponca City estate of E. W. Marland, oil magnate and later governor of Oklahoma.

The nine-hole Marland Estate Golf Course, constructed in 1915, is no longer in existence. But in 1920, Jackson used what he learned at Marland to lay out the first nine holes at Lincoln Park in Oklahoma City. Lincoln Park Golf Course officially opened for play on July 4, 1922. Like most of the private courses in the state, this one opened with sand greens.[12] With Jackson as the head professional, Lincoln Park flourished. Jackson established a caddie program and, borrowing a page from private clubs, offered golfers an annual pass for fifteen dollars. Otherwise greens fees were fifty cents a day.

Within the next three years, two other public courses came on line in the state, giving Oklahoma sixty-eight country clubs and three public courses by 1925, of which only ten had grass greens. In Tulsa, four-time state amateur winner J. A. Kennedy established Tulsa's first public course —6,075-yard Kennedy Golf Club—which played to a par of 71. Like Lincoln Park, Kennedy's Tulsa course had sand greens in 1925.

Edgemere Golf Course in Oklahoma City is believed to have been the first public course in the state with grass greens. Opened in 1925 by brothers Bert and Paul Blakeney, Edgemere had greens fees of fifty cents on weekdays and one dollar on Saturdays and Sundays. Though Edgemere and Kennedy eventually were closed, Lincoln Park survived. A second eighteen holes at Lincoln were added in 1932.

"The city of Oklahoma City appropriated $20,000 and Mr. Jackson built the second eighteen holes out there," recalled Ferguson, who assisted in the construction process. "It was about the same time Floyd Farley built Woodlawn. I was a just a little old bitty kid, but Mr. Jackson let me hold up the survey stick. The land was just packed with trees. I'd get out there in those old tall trees and hold that flag up there. And he'd survey it."

If Jackson saw promise in a youngster, as he did with Ferguson, he would invite him to caddie. Jackson's caddie program at Lincoln Park became the model for other public courses in the Southwest. Ferguson later rose to be vice president of the Professional Golfers' Association of America and was winner in 1978 of the first-ever PGA Merchandiser of the Year Award. He said going to work for Jackson changed his life.

"I grew up at Fourth and Stiles, which was the toughest neighborhood in the whole city," said Ferguson, who had seven siblings and whose parents were divorced. "Back then, everybody was segregated. Black families didn't live any further north than Third Street. But all the kids played together anyway, beating each other out of marbles. I wanted to get a job, so one of the other kids said, 'You can caddie.'"

As a Lincoln Park caddie, Ferguson was a quick study. With Jackson as his mentor, Ferguson met all kinds of people. He left Lincoln for a few months one summer to chauffeur a wealthy couple around in their Packard. But soon Ferguson returned to Lincoln Park for good and was promoted to caddiemaster.

When the 1935 PGA Championship was held at Oklahoma City's Twin Hills Golf and Country Club, Ferguson got his first look at the pro game. "I tell you Walter Hagen was the man," Ferguson said of the five-time PGA and four-time British Open champion, who made his only Oklahoma City appearance ever in that year. "He outdrew everybody. I went to several parties that week where Hagen was. They said he drank a ton, but I didn't see that. By that time, I think age was catching up with him. At Twin Hills he was qualifying medalist but got upset in the first round, one up, by [eventual champion Johnny] Revolta."

In the spring of 1937 professional golf came to Lincoln Park in the form of an exhibition match between the teams of Harry Cooper–Horton Smith and Lawson Little–Jimmy Thomson. Smith, a native of nearby Joplin, Missouri, and Englishman Cooper, both future Hall of Famers, got beaten that day by Little and Thomson. But something about the pairing clicked. The following October, Smith and Cooper returned to Oklahoma City and paired to defeat a strong field in the Oklahoma Four Ball, which that year was considered an official PGA event.

In the 1937 exhibition, Ferguson, already in his ninth year as Jackson's assistant, had his pick of the players, and he chose to loop for Smith, who had already won two of the first three Masters Tournaments. "Horton paid me $1.25 for caddying for him, which was a good tip back then; 85 cents was the usual," said Ferguson. "He gave me the three golf balls he used that day. But, oh, Lord, I would have paid him to get to caddy for him."[13]

According to an account by Bob Hersom in the *Daily Oklahoman*, four or five thousand "swarming natives" witnessed the exhibition at Lincoln Park. At the end of the match, Thomson, a Scot who was runner-up in the 1935 U.S. Open, and Little, a champion of both the U.S. Amateur and the U.S. Open, defeated Cooper and Smith, two up. Highlights of the match were a 25-foot eagle putt by Thomson at No. 1 and a 45-footer for eagle by Little at the thirteenth.

"Besides the PGA, it was the biggest day in golf in Oklahoma up to that point," recalled the late Bill Inglish, former editor/reporter at the *Daily Oklahoman* and official historian of the Masters Tournament. "Earl Jones, the Spalding man in Oklahoma City then, drove around in a 1937 version of a sound truck and announced what club the player was using before each swing.

"After 18 holes, the golfers were whisked away by police escort to the WKY studios. I still remember seeing them zooming down Eastern Avenue to make that interview on time. It's still very vivid to me, even 50 years later."[14]

When Jackson retired from Lincoln in 1952, after thirty years as professional, he handpicked Ferguson as his successor. "Fergie," as he was called by those who knew him, stayed on as Lincoln Park pro for the next thirty-eight years. Counting his years as caddie, caddie master, maintenance man, starter, shop boy, club fitter, instructor, mentor, guidance counselor, confidant, father figure, second assistant, first assistant, and head pro, Fergie served a total of sixty-one years at the storied links.[15]

The caddie program and other projects Jackson had started at Lincoln Park continued under Ferguson. And Ferguson sought new ways to promote golf in Oklahoma City. In 1955, Ferguson brought the first Ladies Professional Golf Association–sanctioned tournament to Oklahoma City and Lincoln Park.

When Louise Suggs, a powerful player from Georgia, arrived at Lincoln Park in April of 1955, her nickname of "Miss Sluggs" was already familiar to Oklahoma City golf fans. Suggs, the first woman ever elected to the Georgia Athletic Hall of Fame, had six years earlier dominated the 1949 Women's Western Open at Oklahoma City Golf and Country Club. In 1955 at Lincoln Park, Suggs shot three under par for fifty-four holes, winning the $1,000 first prize. Jacqueline Pung and Alice Bauer tied for second.

As professional at one of the few municipal courses in the United States to host an LPGA Tour event, Ferguson was elected national vice president of the Professional Golfers' Association, a position he held for three years. Fergie was a favorite among the general public because he implemented many of the same amenities at Lincoln Park that upscale players had come to expect at their private clubs. Most important, Ferguson was a tireless promoter of golf in Oklahoma City. "Anytime anybody wanted to get something done to promote golf, they went to him," said Ross Goodner, who departed the *Daily Oklahoman* in 1962 to work for the *New York Times*, *Golf Magazine*, and *Golf Digest*. "He had boundless enthusiasm and boundless energy. He never quit working for the game. He put in untold hours."[16]

Throughout his career, Ferguson maintained a keen interest in Golf Incorporated, which provided college scholarship money for deserving youngsters. He also founded the Oklahoma City–Texas Matches, between Pro-Am teams from Oklahoma and Texas. In 1995, six years retired, Ferguson, at age eighty, helped organize the Senior PGA Tour benefit tournament at Quail Creek, to benefit victims of the Oklahoma City bombing.

Fergie's work with kids was the stuff of legend. Mark Hayes, a Stillwater native who won the 1977 Players Championship, was introduced to the business end of golf at the Lincoln Park pro shop, working for Ferguson. Three-time U.S. Women's Open champion Susie Maxwell Berning, the only woman in Oklahoma history to be awarded a full golf scholarship onto a college men's team, learned the game from Ferguson; she was a three-time Oklahoma state high school champion. So appreciative was Maxwell Berning, who played at Oklahoma City University and took lessons from Ferguson, that she later returned to Ferguson the driver she used to win the three U.S. Women's Opens.

"He took care of the kids," said Maxwell Berning. "If they didn't have a golf club, Fergie made sure they got one. He was always there regardless of who you were. He treated everybody the same."[17]

In turn, Ferguson never forgot the old Scotsman who had built Lincoln Park's thirty-six holes among the wooded hills of north Oklahoma City and had set him up for a lifetime in the game. "Besides the golf course, Art Jackson's main gift to the game was teaching kids the values of life," said Ferguson. "Caddying, if you could prove yourself to Mr. Jackson, taught responsibility. I tried to carry that on. If a kid turns out to be a good caddy, you think you won't recommend that kid if a business friend of yours is looking for someone? You take kids that grow up playing at Lincoln Park. Nothing could please me more than to see them go on to be members at the Oklahoma City Golf and Country Club, Twin Hills, Quail Creek, or Oak Tree. That was a win for me."

Unlike Jackson, who spent most of his life in Oklahoma (he died in 1981), course architect Arthur W. Tillinghast spent only a couple of brief stints in the state, both times in Tulsa: once immediately after World War I to design and build Tulsa Country Club and again in 1923 to oversee construction of the Oaks Country Club. Nonetheless, Tillinghast's designs at Tulsa Country Club and the Oaks complemented the efforts of Findlay and Jackson. Simply having Tillinghast's name associated with a club gave a project immediate credibility. When the United States Golf Association announced that the 2002 U.S. Open would be held at New York's Bethpage Black Course, it added another page to the major championship pedigree of the course architect variously known as "the Mad Master" and "Tillie the Terror." Few professionals in any field matched the bombast and brilliance of Tillinghast.

"HE TOOK CARE OF THE KIDS. IF THEY DIDN'T HAVE A GOLF CLUB, FERGIE MADE SURE THEY GOT ONE. HE WAS ALWAYS THERE REGARDLESS OF WHO YOU WERE. HE TREATED EVERYBODY THE SAME."

In a 1997 *Sports Illustrated* article, Ron Fimrite described Tillinghast as "a regal figure in three-piece tweed suit and hunting boots, perched atop a shooting stick with a flask of bootleg gin at the ready, barking commands to, as a contemporary writer put it, 'an affable elderly laborer and a morose mule tugging at a Fresno scoop.' Gesturing theatrically, he bellows, 'Green here! Bunker there!' From time to time, it was written, 'the laborer and the mule would get a sniff of his richly flavored 100-proof exhaust and knew they were working for a man of great power and artistry.'"[18]

A native of Frankfort, Pennsylvania, Tillinghast, who lived from 1874 to 1942, is perhaps best known for his designs at private major championship venues like Winged Foot, Baltusrol, Quaker Ridge, Shawnee (Pennsylvania) Country Club, and San Francisco Golf Club. All told, sixty of his courses have hosted national and international championships. And he designed public courses as well, including former PGA Tour sites like Cedar Crest Municipal in Dallas (site of the 1927 PGA Championship) and Brackenridge Park in San Antonio (site of twenty-one Texas Opens between 1922 and 1959).

Tillinghast made numerous pilgrimages to Scotland, but as his greensites at Tulsa Country Club and the Oaks would attest, he was not overly enamored of the gargantuan putting surfaces at some linksland courses, which he said gave rise to slow play. So Tillie implemented well-placed bunkers and slender greens as his favored means of protecting par. "I think that I will always adhere to my old theory that a controlled shot to a closely guarded green is the surest test of any man's golf," wrote Tillinghast, who had skill enough at the game to finish twenty-fifth in the 1910 U.S. Open at Philadelphia Cricket Club. "Extremely large greens breed slovenly play."[19]

Tulsa Country Club's original nine holes opened in 1907, but it was not until a decade later, on land leased from Dr. S. G. Kennedy, that the club expanded to eighteen holes. Tillinghast was commissioned to design the new nine and remodel the original. Chicago amateur Chick Evans, the only golfer besides Bobby Jones to win the U.S. Open and U.S. Amateur in the same year, played an exhibition at the unfinished Tulsa Country Club course in September of 1919 and later was consulted during construction of the new bunkers. Since 1920, Tulsa Country Club has played host to eight Oklahoma Opens, a U.S. Women's Amateur, a Women's NCAA Championship, and a Senior PGA Tour event.

Tillinghast's other Tulsa course, the Oaks, was completed in 1924. Like Tulsa Country Club, the Oaks also hosted a USGA Championship in 1960, the U.S. Girls' Junior. For its first seventy-five years the Oaks had just four head professionals: Jack Guild, Marion Askew, Larry Crummett, and Rick Reed. The only alterations to the course have been for a new watering system and a 1993 renovation of the greens. According to Crummett, head pro from 1967 to 1997, if Tillinghast were still alive he would be proud of the Oaks. "When former club members or students of mine come back to Tulsa, they all want to play the Oaks," said Crummett. "They still have fond memories. We are so blessed in this part of the country. Some of the greatest courses in the world are right here."[20]

Remarkable as the Oklahoma designs of Tillinghast, Findlay, and Jackson have proven to be, if the legacy of the state's earliest golf courses were defined only by the Oaks, Tulsa Country Club, Guthrie Country Club, and Lincoln Park, it is improbable that Crummett or anyone else could boast of Oklahoma as home to some of the greatest golf courses in the world. And the Sooner State certainly would not have hosted fifteen U.S. Golf Association national championships during the twentieth century, plus a fifth USGA National Open in 2001.

But evidence suggests that Crummett did not exaggerate. He was only echoing sentiment first expressed seven decades earlier, when, in a span of nine years, Grand Slam winner Robert T. Jones Jr., Dr. Alister Mac-Kenzie, and the boards of directors at Pine Valley, Colonial, Merion, Westchester Country Club, Saucon Valley, and Philadelphia Country Club were so impressed by a handful of courses in Oklahoma that they procured the architectural expertise of a heartbroken banker from Ardmore.

Perry Duke Maxwell, born in Princeton, Kentucky, to Scottish parents in 1879, had two attempts at college interrupted by bouts with tuberculosis. On a physician's recommendation he moved to Ardmore in 1897, with the hope that the drier, warmer climate of southern Oklahoma would help him fight the disease. In 1902, Maxwell married Ray Woods, his high school sweetheart from Kentucky. They remained in Ardmore, where Perry worked as a cashier and later as vice president of Ardmore National Bank.

Ray sensed an artistic bent in her husband and in 1909 showed him an article by H. J. Whigham, a two-time U.S. Amateur champion and the son-in-law of golf course architect extraordinaire Charles Blair Macdonald. Whigham's article, which appeared in *Scribner's* magazine, chronicled the development of Macdonald's masterpiece, the National Golf Links on Long Island, New York. Intrigued, Maxwell traveled to New York to see the National Golf Links. In 1913, with the assistance of his wife and four children, Maxwell laid out a rudimentary nine-hole course on their farm north of Ardmore. He called the course Dornick Hills, naming it with the Gaelic word for "small rock," because thousands of these had to be cleared off the property when the course was built.[21]

Perhaps nine holes at Ardmore would have sated Maxwell's creative bent but for Ray's untimely death in 1919. To blunt his grief at losing her, Maxwell took Ray's advice to heart and poured himself into the study of golf course architecture. He not only visited the best courses in the United States but traveled to his ancestral homeland in Scotland, the birthplace of golf.

In 1921 Maxwell completed Shawnee (Oklahoma) Country Club and Rollingwood Hills Country Club (later renamed Indian Hills, then Spunky Creek) in Catoosa. Those were followed in succession by the second nine at Dornick Hills in Ardmore (1923); Muskogee Country Club (1924); Hillcrest Country Club in Bartlesville (1926); Twin Hills Golf and Country Club in Oklahoma City (1926); Ponca City Country Club (1928); and Oklahoma City Golf and Country Club (1929). By the end of the decade Oklahomans were enjoying golf at eight Maxwell courses.

With only nine holes of previous design experience, Maxwell quietly brought to life such a remarkable sequence of eighteen-hole courses in Oklahoma that his work came to the attention of Jones and Mackenzie, who were about to undertake construction of Georgia's Augusta National Golf Club. After Mackenzie toured Ardmore and Oklahoma City with Maxwell in 1931, the Scottish-born architect invited the Oklahoman to become his associate. Maxwell readily accepted. Thereafter, Mackenzie was not reluctant to extoll the talents of his understudy.

"Mr. Maxwell speaks of my ability to make a good fairway or develop a worthy green," Mackenzie told historian Charles Evans. "But I wish to tell you that in laying out a golf course and to give it everything that the science and art of golf demand, Mr. Maxwell is not second to anyone I know."[22]

On his visit to Dornick Hills, Mackenzie saw virtually all the characteristics he prized in a course: esthetics, minimal disturbance to the land, and the proper blend of hole lengths and tee sites so as to be equally challenging and interesting for both handicap and expert players. Both men preferred that wherever possible, the lie of the land, not the requirements of a mule team or a dump wagon, should determine the location of greensites. Fairways and bunkers were positioned to direct traffic. Perhaps most significant, each believed that par was best protected nearer the hole, test-

ing the short games of handicap players and experts alike. They generally favored broad fairways, shallow bunkers, bounce-and-run aprons, and
undulating greens.

They made a good team. Mackenzie, his talents in enormous demand, sometimes took on more work than he could handle. He occasionally did "paper jobs," leaving the actual construction to others. Maxwell's
approach was more "hands-on," with site selection paramount. A favorite
story about Maxwell was that after arriving at a job site, he would disappear into the woods for a few days with nothing but a sack of fruit and a
jug of water. Upon his return he would proclaim, "There are dozens of
good holes out there. We just need to eliminate all but eighteen."

In 1932–33, while Mackenzie completed Augusta National, Maxwell's role in the partnership was to work on site at projects for the University of Michigan, Ohio State University, Iowa State University, and Crystal
Downs in Frankfort, Michigan. In 1933, Maxwell also did remodeling work
at Pine Valley Golf Club at Clementon, New Jersey, regarded by many en-
thusiasts as the world's best inland course.

After Mackenzie's death in early 1934, prior to the first Masters
Tournament, Maxwell's presence at Augusta National escalated, as did his
friendship with Augusta cofounders Jones and Clifford Roberts. Wrote
Jones's biographer O. B. Keeler: "Bobby Jones was ably assisted in the (Augusta National) program of improvement by Perry Maxwell, an architect
who can be said to be a disciple of Mackenzie's."[23]

By the mid-1930s Maxwell had come into his own and was considered the preeminent American golf architect of the Depression era.
Even as hundreds of country clubs fell victim to the economy, Maxwell's
talents were in demand. In addition to the work at Augusta National, Maxwell completed Crystal Downs, Vencker Memorial in Ames, Iowa, and
Southern Hills Country Club in Tulsa, three of the few courses of note to

be built during the Great Depression. In 1935 a Maxwell course hosted its first major championship—the PGA Championship at Oklahoma City's Twin Hills Golf and Country Club.

In 1937, Jones and Roberts brought in Maxwell to relocate two of Augusta's greens and modify two others. Today, the "Maxwell rolls" make greens at Augusta's first and fourteenth holes two of the toughest putting holes at the Masters. By moving the seventh and tenth greens to their present locations, Maxwell stretched the length of both holes: the seventh to 360 yards, the tenth to a formidable 485 yards. Augusta's famous crow-foot cross-bunker, short of the tenth green, was the original green-side bunker designed by Dr. Mackenzie. Maxwell left it intact.

Also in 1937, Maxwell laid out the first nine holes at Prairie Dunes Country Club, in Hutchinson, Kansas, a sandhills course, considered by many to be Maxwell's finest work. By the time the Ohio State Gray and Scarlet Courses opened in 1939, Maxwell had national respect. Soon after, he was hired for remodeling work at Merion Golf Club (in Ardmore, Pennsylvania) and at Colonial Country Club (in Fort Worth, Texas) prior to the 1941 U.S. Open.

At Colonial, Maxwell's resdesign of holes three to five along the Trinity River came to be called the "terrible horseshoe," the heart of the golf course. As a designer, Maxwell had hit full stride. "We considered him both an artist and a salesman," said retired golf architect Floyd Farley, designer of Oklahoma City's Quail Creek Country Club. "He reminded me a lot of Will Rogers." Farley moved to Oklahoma from Kansas in the 1930s and built courses at the same time as Maxwell. "Perry would smell a golf course coming, hear someone talking about it, and he'd just go there and camp out

BY THE MID-1930S MAXWELL HAD COME INTO HIS OWN AND WAS CONSIDERED THE PREEMINENT AMERICAN GOLF ARCHITECT OF THE DEPRESSION ERA. EVEN AS HUNDREDS OF COUNTRY CLUBS FELL VICTIM TO THE ECONOMY, MAXWELL'S TALENTS WERE IN DEMAND.

and sell himself, get the job. He didn't need a set of plans. He'd just go out there and plot it in, by waving his arms and hands," said Farley.[24]

In the 1940s Maxwell developed cancer in his leg, which led to an amputation. He never mastered the prosthesis and during his later years it hindered his work. Maxwell's son, Press Maxwell, assisted his father on several of his final courses, including Lake Hefner Municipal in Oklahoma City and the University of Oklahoma Golf Course in Norman.

Like those of Findlay, Jackson, and Tillinghast before him, Maxwell's designs have stood the test of time. "The thing about Maxwell courses is that they're shotmaker courses," said Jerry Cozby, golf professional for thirty years at the Maxwell-designed Hillcrest Country Club in Bartlesville. "You can't go around the courses and just overpower them. It's not just power golf.

"And back in those days they had to use what they saw. To me, that's what makes them so good. I don't have much respect for a course where it looks as if somebody had a war, you know what I mean? Maxwell took the natural terrain of what he found and he built a golf course around it."

TWO
Oklahoma Open

From a humble beginning in 1910 with only two competitors to its turn-of-the-millennium status as a tradition-steeped championship for some 350 professionals and low handicap amateurs, the Oklahoma Open evolved into one of the premier state open golf championships in the United States. The Massachusetts Open, founded in 1905, is believed to be the only on-going state championship to predate the Oklahoma Open. And for almost a century, few state opens have consistently attracted stronger fields, offered larger purses, drawn bigger galleries, or featured better courses than the Oklahoma Open.

"The Oklahoma Open has always been a favorite of mine, one of the most competitive, best-administered state opens in the nation," says former Oklahoma State University All-American Danny Edwards, a three-time Oklahoma Open champion. "When guys are out on the PGA Tour," Edwards said in a 1998 interview, "they don't have that many opportunities to play in their home state. So it's always special to get back to Oklahoma and tee it up against old friends."

Unlike most statewide golf competitions, which are usually limited to amateur players residing in the host state, state opens are for the most part open to professionals and amateurs alike, regardless of residence. In a state open, professionals normally constitute a majority of the entrants and compete for cash prizes. Amateurs, on the other hand, must meet certain handicap requirements and are permitted by the U.S. Golf Association's rules of amateur status to compete only for trophies or golf merchandise valued at five hundred dollars or less. If an amateur competes in an open championship without declaring himself an amateur, the player forfeits status as a nonprofessional.

Historically, entry fees have made up the bulk of the professional prize money at most state opens—which is hardly an appearance incentive for the game's top stars, who compete annually for millions on the PGA, Senior PGA, and Nike tours. So how has the Oklahoma Open consistently been able to secure entries from PGA Tour winners such as Edwards, his brother David, Bob Tway, Gil Morgan, Doug Martin, Scott Verplank, and Mark Hayes? And how has the tournament increased its purse from less than $100 in 1910 to $150,000 in 1997, a record for state open golf championships?

The success of the Oklahoma Open since its inception can be traced directly to the efforts of its sponsoring organization, the Oklahoma Golf Association, and its twenty thousand members across the state. Even so, there were a couple of decades after World War II when the OGA was less than efficient at administering its statewide competitions, particularly the Oklahoma Open. Contestants unleashed a litany of complaints, from paltry purses and bad pairings to poorly maintained courses and slow play. However, the OGA never wavered from its primary objectives: conducting the statewide competitions and enforcing the USGA's rules of play and amateur status.

"There were many times when the OGA was in the trunk of someone's car," said former OGA executive director Bill Barrett. "But our prime concern was the amateur golfer and adherence to the rules. We'd butt in if we heard of an instance where rules were compromised or amateur status was being threatened or ignored."[1]

While amateur competitions flourished across the state, the Oklahoma Open struggled. Eventually, it required resuscitation by one of the best-known club pros in the state. "For a while there it was a dull, nothing tournament until Art Proctor got hold of it," said Barrett. "One of the things he did was talk the Oak Tree boys into staying home and supporting it."[2] Since May 1, 1976, the date Joe Walser and Ernie Vossler's dream course opened up north of Edmond, Oak Tree Golf Club had been home to several of Oklahoma's best-known professionals. Edwards, his younger brother David, Morgan, Hayes, and Doug Tewell were all members of the PGA Tour. Hayes and Morgan had had Tour victories. Proctor's mission was to find a permanent home for the Oklahoma Open, preferably close to Edmond, so that the Oak Tree boys would have one less excuse not to play.

A tournament player himself, Proctor was the head pro at Edmond's Kickingbird Golf Course. At 6,816 yards, par-71 Kickingbird seemed a perfect site. A public course designed by Floyd Farley and located ten miles north of Oklahoma City, Kickingbird featured challenging greens and elevation changes. A 10-acre driving range provided ample space for contestants and the general public. With Kickingbird as his main selling point, Proctor convinced the OGA to bring the championship to Edmond.

But more than a change of venue was needed. Without a title sponsor, the Oklahoma Open purse had been stuck on $10,000, which was little more than entry fees. Increasingly the tournament was beset by slow play, bad starting times, absence of scoreboards and pin sheets, and, according to some professionals, a disproportionate number of unqualified amateurs. It was one thing for a tour pro, out of loyalty to friends and sponsors, to come home and play for peanuts in a state open. But to be paired with players who ignored rules or tournament etiquette, and then have to endure six-hour rounds, was something else again. By 1978 Proctor and other pros were ready to boycott.

As the story goes, Proctor was grouped with David Edwards and Lindy Miller during the first round of the 1978 Oklahoma Open at Broken Arrow's Indian Springs Country Club. Proctor birdied the first two holes, then arrived at the third tee, a long par 3. There were so many groups backed up at the tee that Proctor had to wait nearly an hour to hit his next shot. After the six-hour round, Proctor, Edwards, and Miller vowed if changes were not forthcoming, it would be their last Oklahoma Open as competitors.

As a last resort, Proctor made an offer to the OGA executive committee. He suggested he be allowed to run the tournament the next year. For an event headed nowhere fast, the suggestion came as a godsend. Proctor had the respect of the players, and he had a history of delivering the goods. Once, to secure charitable pledges for the PGA of America's National Golf Day, Proctor played 414 holes of golf in twenty-four hours—twenty-three eighteen-hole rounds. Amazingly, Proctor was 6 under par for the day, with 1,604 strokes, an average score of 69.74. His eighteenth and nineteenth rounds were back-to-back 67s and his twenty-first round was a 66. His high round for the day's work was 75.

"According to the odometer, I rode 98 miles in the golf cart," said Proctor. "I averaged just over two minutes a hole. I changed shoes three times. I was ready to quit at 4 o'clock, but the crowd, which kept growing the longer I played, encouraged me to keep going. They kept me pumped up. It was Cal McLish [former Cincinnati Reds pitcher from Oklahoma] who told me I only think I'm tired and to get back out there."[3]

A man with that kind of energy had little trouble convincing the OGA to let him run the tournament. In 1979 the Oklahoma Open moved to Kickingbird, Proctor's home course, where it remained for seven years. Through 1984, the tournament stabilized, with a slight increase in purses. Then in 1985, Proctor pulled off a coup that promoted the Oklahoma Open to head of the class where state opens were concerned. With help from Barrett and others, Proctor persuaded the *Daily Oklahoman*, the state's largest newspaper, to become title sponsor for the tournament. The name of the tournament was changed to the Daily Oklahoman Open, and the purse jumped to $100,000, tops for any state open. First prize went from $4,000 in 1984 to $15,000 in 1985.

"We're going to work every way we can to make this the premier golf event in Oklahoma," said Howard Hicks, general manager of the *Oklahoman*. "We're very proud to be a sponsor and very pleased with this tournament. I can't say enough about the work done by Art Proctor and his staff."[4]

Bob Tway won the 1985 Daily Oklahoman Open at Kickingbird. A year later the tournament moved up the road to Oak Tree, where it has been held ever since. Certainly the *Daily Oklahoman's* involvement and the move to Oak Tree guaranteed a strong field and the tournament's financial viability for the foreseeable future. But in a game where old-fashioned concepts like rules and honor were supposed to mean something, other decisions crucial to the integrity of the competitions had already been put into practice. During the turbulent 1960s, which finally saw the dissolution of the PGA's "Caucasians only" membership clause, and the 1970s, the Oklahoma Open was an "open" championship in every sense of the word.

"At that time, golf, especially at country clubs, was sort of a closed shop almost anywhere you went," recalled Bobby Stroble, winner of the 1974 Oklahoma Open, in a 1997 interview. "But as I remember, Oklahoma was really open and they welcomed the black golfers to most of the courses. I don't remember anybody there ever saying anything harsh to me or out of line. It was really a class act."

Stroble, a self-taught player from Albany, Georgia, and a Vietnam veteran, had competed in multiple state opens around the country. The 1964 Civil Rights Act notwithstanding, Stroble said black golfers still faced discrimination at some tournaments. "Most places, the black guys couldn't even get in the clubhouse. But the courses I played in Oklahoma weren't that way. At Lakeside Golf Course in Ponca City, you could charge things at the grill and they would send you a bill later. That's how relaxed it was, very unusual for those days. They were open to us and it felt great."

Stroble said the state opens were often the best chance for minority golfers to break into professional golf. "During that time I was touring, finding state opens to play in, trying to work my way onto the PGA Tour," said Stroble, who earned $312,000 on the 1997 Senior PGA Tour. "A friend of mine, Charlie Lee, was from Muskogee and he told me about the Oklahoma Open. I flew out and entered and was fortunate enough to win it in my first attempt." Besides his victory in 1974, Stroble estimated he played in seven or eight Oklahoma Opens, including a runner-up finish to Danny Edwards in 1975.

"There were always a lot of good players in the Oklahoma Open and the year I won, at least four or five were Tour players. Labron Harris Jr. was playing well. [There were] Spike Kelley, Grier Jones, and several other guys. Labron was pushing me pretty hard and they kept thinking he was going to catch me. But finally I birdied the tenth and twelfth holes to open up about a five- or six-stroke lead, and that did it."

Stroble was a one-time winner of the Oklahoma Open; eighteen others have won it multiple times. The tournament's roster of past champions includes six Scottish pros who came to Oklahoma shortly after the turn of the twentieth century (William Nichols, J. G. "Jock" Collins, Jack Taylor, John Gatherum, William Creavy, O. S. "Sandy" Baxter); six amateurs (Emmett J. Rogers, Walter Emery, Jack Malloy, Billy Simpson, Bob Dickson, Jamie Gough); a college coaching legend and his U.S. Amateur champion son (Labron Harris Sr. and Labron Harris Jr.); a PGA Championship winner (Tway); a Players Championship winner (Hayes); and the first player in history to ever be twelve shots under par in a U.S. Open (Morgan).

The most prolific champion in Oklahoma Open history was Ardmore native Jimmie Gauntt, who captured five titles from 1948 to 1960.

Gauntt got his start in golf as a caddie at Dornick Hills Country Club in his hometown of Ardmore. He later became head professional at Oklahoma City's Twin Hills Country Club, from 1946 to 1951. Both Dornick Hills and Twin Hills, and four of the five courses where Gauntt won Oklahoma Opens, were designed by fellow Ardmoreite Perry Maxwell. Maxwell was a genius at routing in courses to test every facet of a golfer's game. Gauntt's experience at Maxwell courses paid off handsomely in the Oklahoma Open.

"I did it on the greens and off the tee," Gauntt said of his five victories. "Most of the courses Mr. Maxwell designed were tight. He made you wedge the ball and drive it well, which were my strong suits."

Gauntt would retire to Austin, Texas, and his pro career dovetailed with the careers of two notable Texas pros who also had their moments in Oklahoma—Ben Hogan and Byron Nelson. Hogan competed in the 1933 and 1934 Oklahoma Opens, at Bartlesville and Catoosa, finishing second to Scotsman Jimmie Gullane at Hillcrest and fourth to Kansas City's Jug McSpaden at Indian Hills.

Nelson never entered an Oklahoma Open but played in two Ardmore Opens and, in his first amateur event outside Texas, won the 1930 Southwest Invitational Amateur, at Oklahoma City Golf and Country Club (then known as Nichols Hills Country Club). During Nelson's all-time PGA record eleven-victory streak in 1945, Gauntt finished third to Nelson at the Durham (North Carolina) Open.

"He was the best I ever saw," Gauntt said of the one they called Lord Byron. "At that time he could take a driver in the fairway and hit it like a 3- or 4-wood, up in the air. At Durham, he birdied the eighteenth hole each of the last two rounds with a 1-iron, from 190 yards. I made three and four on the hole; Nelson made two twos."

During World War II, Gauntt joined the Civilian Pilot Training Program, in which Hogan also had enlisted. While in the CPT, Gauntt became acquainted with Hogan, and through Hogan with Marvin Leonard, the department store magnate who built Fort Worth's Colonial Country Club. For a few months in 1943, Gauntt had an arrangement with Leonard whereby Gauntt taught a few lessons at Colonial each morning and played golf during the afternoons, often with Hogan. Leonard even provided him a small salary and meals.

"Hogan was always playing and practicing at Colonial," Gauntt recalled. "Once or twice a week, for two or three months, I played golf together with Hogan, his brother Royal, and Raymond Gafford [1946 Oklahoma Open champion], who was pro there." Asked if he ever beat Hogan, winner of four U.S. Opens, Gauntt replied, "Very rarely. The thing about Hogan was, when you got on the

No. 1 tee, he wouldn't make a bet unless you asked. I'd say, 'Ben, I'll play a $1 Nassau with you, but no presses.' On a good day, I'd break even or win $1. But betting didn't interest Hogan much. He just wanted to hit balls and practice."

In the 1933 Oklahoma Open at Bartlesville, Hogan was in the hunt for his first professional title. But he unraveled at the final hole, finishing second to Gullane, who was the host pro."Hogan was in fine shape until the last hole, where five is par for the 585 yards,"reported the *Tulsa World*."Trying to play safe, he got away from the tee, found a bad lie, topped and went into the deep rough. He wound up with seven, for 33-39—72."[5]

The next year, at Catoosa's Indian Hills Country Club (formerly Rollingwood Country Club, later Spunky Creek), Hogan finished in fourth place, six behind Jug McSpaden of Kansas City. During the World War II years, McSpaden and Nelson were dubbed the "Gold Dust Twins" for their lucrative talents."We were classified 4-F,"wrote Nelson, "meaning we couldn't pass the army physical to serve our country in World War II."[6] McSpaden suffered from allergic reactions; Nelson was hemophiliac. Both retired from tournament golf soon after the war.

For the most part, McSpaden stayed away from the tournament scene for almost forty years, returning to competition at age eighty-six in the 1994 Legends of Golf. He played again the next year in the Legends, when it moved from Austin, Texas, to Palm Springs, California. McSpaden's final competition was the Legends of Canada in July 1995.

Interviewed in Austin, McSpaden said three of his proudest accomplishments in golf were shooting a course record 59 in a practice round at the 1939 Texas Open, winning his age division at the

1987 Senior National Tournament, and helping design the longest golf course in the world: par-78, 8,101-yard Dub's Dread Golf Course in Piper, Kansas, in 1963.

McSpaden's reasoning for building the course was decades ahead of the game. "The idea was at that time they were talking about the ball going 400 yards instead of 300," said McSpaden. "So I just figured we better add a few hundred yards."[7] The course has since been shortened to a par 72, around 7,400 yards. McSpaden died as one of the American game's true pioneers, on April 22, 1996, at age eighty-seven.

While pros like Hogan, Nelson, and McSpaden were known primarily for their skills as players, several of the early winners of the Oklahoma Open excelled as both competitors and teachers. So it was with Dick Grout, winner of the Oklahoma Open in 1927 and 1929.

"Grout was but one member of a remarkable golfing family from Oklahoma City, that played alongside golf greats and near-greats, during the Depression years in the Southwest," read a story in the *Daily Oklahoman.* "They left behind an extraordinary legacy of championships and accomplishments."[8] In 1927, Dick Grout left Oklahoma City for the head professional job at Okmulgee Country Club. That year, the Oklahoma Open was just a short trip from Okmulgee, at Tulsa Country Club. Grout entered.

At the end of regulation (thirty-six holes), Grout was tied with Tulsa Country Club pro Clarence Clark. In an eighteen-hole playoff, Grout birdied the final three holes to beat the host pro by two strokes, 75 to 77. "Never in the 18-year history of the State Open has such a brilliant finish been recorded," reported the *Tulsa World.* "Clark was the first to congratulate the state's new champion. Even the most staunch supporters of the Tulsa professional joined the surging crowd that completely surrounded Grout. Then the Okmulgee pro modestly accepted the shower of congratulations and lauded Clark for his sportsmanship and fine golf."[9]

Two years later, at Dornick Hills, Grout won his second Oklahoma Open, by three shots over his nineteen-year-old brother Jack, who had just turned pro. Jack, slight of stature, nonetheless impressed the spectators at Dornick Hills. "Paired with his elder brother and a young amateur, Bob Conliff, Jack played like a Scotch master," reported the Associated Press. "He gave spectators numerous thrills with some beautiful shots. To Jack goes the honor being the only player to birdie No. 16, the treacherous cliff hole."[10]

He later partnered with Nelson. "By 1930 I was playing a lot of local Monday morning pro-ams in Fort Worth with Jack Grout," recalled Nelson of his days as an amateur. "Jack had come to Glen Garden as assistant to his brother Dick. After Dick took a job with Texarkana Country Club, Jack was the best pro around, and I had become one of the best amateurs. We won those pro-ams so many times that the other pros got together and made a rule that a pro could only play with same amateur once a month. That gave the other boys a chance."[11]

Jack Grout played on the PGA circuit from 1931 to 1957. But it was the club pro job he landed in Columbus, Ohio, that made his career. At that city's Scioto Country Club, Grout taught the most famous Jack of them all. Jack Nicklaus was ten years old in 1950 when he signed up for a Grout-taught junior clinic at Scioto.

"He was just another little boy, no different than the other little boys who showed up," Grout said. "He was just out there slamming away like little boys do. But that little rascal learned quick. Some kids forget, but you'd tell Jackie Nicklaus one time and he'd remember. I'd watch him, and he'd be doing all the things I told him."[12]

When Jack Grout died at age seventy-eight, in May of 1989, Nicklaus, the greatest golfer in history, had high praise for his mentor from Oklahoma. "Jack Grout was like a second father to me," Nicklaus said. "Along with my parents and my wife, he has been the biggest and surely one of the best influences in my life. He taught me to play the game and there is no doubt at all that almost everything I've achieved in golf I've done with the techniques taught to me by Jack."[13]

All told there were eight children at the north Oklahoma City household of H. D. and Nellie Grout. Six became golf professionals. The oldest, Jim, started caddying at Oklahoma City Golf and Country Club in 1913. He introduced his siblings to the game. Ray "Dutch" Grout was considered the most talented of the bunch. He taught at old Edgemere Golf Club in northwest Oklahoma City and qualified for both the 1933 and 1934 U.S. Opens. Dutch, who enjoyed a friendly wager when he played, won the Oklahoma Match Play Championship in 1934. Sister Jenny, the youngest sibling, is considered one of the best female golfers in Oklahoma history. She won multiple Oklahoma City championships and the 1937 Oklahoma Women's State Amateur.

By the time Dick Grout won his Oklahoma Opens, a majority of the courses in the state had grass greens. But any pro who learned the game in the early years of the twentieth century was familiar with

"HE WAS JUST ANOTHER LITTLE BOY, NO DIFFERENT THAN THE OTHER LITTLE BOYS WHO SHOWED UP. HE WAS JUST OUT THERE SLAMMING AWAY LIKE LITTLE BOYS DO. BUT THAT LITTLE RASCAL LEARNED QUICK. SOME KIDS FORGET, BUT YOU'D TELL JACKIE NICKLAUS ONE TIME AND HE'D REMEMBER. I'D WATCH HIM, AND HE'D BE DOING ALL THE THINGS I TOLD HIM."

putting surfaces that were sand, dirt, or cottonseed hulls—which produced a generation of players with peculiar putting strokes. And
among the putting strokes of the professionals, the strangest of all
may have belonged to Tulsa Country Club pro William "Wild Bill"
Mehlhorn, winner of the Oklahoma Open in 1920 and 1923.

"I was the world's worst putter," Mehlhorn said matter-of-
factly in 1986.[14] Few who saw him play would argue with that. "The
best I ever saw from tee-to-green was Bill Mehlhorn," said Ben Hogan in 1975. "He was a fantastic hitter of the ball. I played with him
once when he hit his second shot two feet from the hole. He then
played his *fourth* shot out of a bunker. It was inspiring to see this
man hit a ball. But it was pathetic to watch him putt. I've always said
there are two different games: hitting the ball and putting. Well, he
showed me."[15]

In 1920, Mehlhorn, a native of Chicago, moved to Tulsa and
replaced J. G. "Jock" Collins, winner of the 1917 Oklahoma Open, as
head professional at Tulsa Country Club. At the time, Mehlhorn had
not yet been tagged with the nickname "Wild Bill." Instead he was
called "Oklahoma Bill."

"Leo Diegel [winner of two PGA Championships] and I did a
lot of things together," recalled Mehlhorn. "We were the same size,
wore the same hat, shoes, gloves, same everything. Diegel gave me
the name Oklahoma Bill when I went to Tulsa. It stands to reason.
Then we had a cyclone and he changed it to Cyclone Bill."[16]

Mehlhorn was recommended for the job at Tulsa Country Club
by Chick Evans, the brilliant amateur from Chicago. When Mehlhorn
arrived in Tulsa, the club's new Tillinghast course was still being completed. Since there was not any play, Mehlhorn hit balls and gave a
few lessons. In October of 1920, Tulsa Country Club hosted the Okla-

homa Open, for the first time since 1912. At the conclusion of the thirty-six-hole championship, newcomer Mehlhorn was tied at 152 with Tulsa amateur sensation James Kennedy. Kennedy would go on to win four consecutive Oklahoma Amateur titles, still a record. Bad weather postponed the playoff between Kennedy and Mehlhorn for almost a month. Finally, on November 15, 1920, Mehlhorn defeated Kennedy by three shots, 78 to 81.

Despite the putting woes that plagued him throughout his career, Mehlhorn may have known as much about the golf swing as any player ever. His teaching philosophy was simple: swing a golf club like a baseball bat and keep the muscles relaxed.

Mehlhorn spent part of 1921 competing in Scotland, the birthplace of golf, with a group of American pros. The competition, the first of its kind, pitted the "Yanks" against their British counterparts in an international event that would eventually come to be called the Ryder Cup Matches. Twice during the matches, Mehlhorn played with the master, Englishman Harry Vardon. Winner of the 1900 U.S. Open and a six-time winner of the British Open, Vardon was as revered in his time as Jack Nicklaus was in his.

According to Mehlhorn, the rounds with Vardon in Scotland changed him both as a tournament player and as a teacher. "The one significant thing Vardon said to me was to never use more than two-thirds of my effort," Mehlhorn recalled. "And that if you keep the left arm straight, you don't use it, you lock the joint. Vardon bent his left elbow almost at right angles. I started out as a hooker of the ball, but after playing with Vardon, I changed. I worked 13 months at it, to hit the ball from left to right."[17] Mehlhorn said this enabled him to swing more easily and to control the flight of the ball better.

Upon his return to the United States, Mehlhorn's scoring improved dramatically. He said it was his newfound knack for shooting low—not his personality—that earned him the nickname "Wild Bill." Mehlhorn told Al Barkow that some believed his nickname had to do with an incident at the 1927 Texas Open. Mehlhorn said that after he finished the final round, he climbed up in a tree to see over the gallery and watch Bobby Cruikshank finish. "The last hole and Cruikshank had two putts to win," said Mehlhorn. "He four-putts. . . . Bobby pointed to me up in the tree when he came off the green. But he was fifty yards away. . . . All the newspapers around the country had it: 'Mehlhorn causes Cruikshank to Blow Tournament!'"[18]

Mehlhorn actually acquired his nickname six years before the tree incident. In 1921, a year after his first Oklahoma Open win, Mehlhorn and his old pal Diegel were paired together in New Orleans, at a thirty-six-hole exhibition match with Gene Sarazen and Cyril Walker, two of the top players of the era. After the first eighteen holes, Diegel and Mehlhorn were four down. Then Mehlhorn caught fire, playing the first five holes of the afternoon round in fourteen strokes—with a three-putt thrown in for good measure.

"I broke the course record by four shots," said Mehlhorn. "Diegel was writing a guest column for the New Orleans newspaper at the time and he wrote that, 'Bill Mehlhorn went wild.' I tried to stop that 'wild' stuff, because I thought it hurt my image. But that's what made it stick, trying to fight it. Then in the 1927 U.S. Open it comes over the ticker tape that 'Wild Bill Goes Wild.' Because I went out in 32 the last round, when nobody else broke 40. So every time I burned things up they said I was 'Wild Bill.'"[19]

In 1923, Mehlhorn and Kennedy had an Oklahoma Open rematch at the same course where they had dueled in 1920—Tulsa Country Club. The 1923 championship was the first seventy-two-hole Oklahoma Open, which meant it was accredited as an officially sanctioned event of the fledgling Professional Golfers' Association.

Kennedy took an eight-shot lead into the final thirty-six holes but could not shake his old nemesis. Paired together in the final foursome of the final round, Mehlhorn and Kennedy went at it hammer and tongs. Mehlhorn, his professional experience wearing down his amateur counterpart, finally drew even with Kennedy at the sixty-fourth hole and cruised home for a two-shot victory—310 (79-80-75-76) to 312 (75-76-80-81). E. P. Murphy, of St. Joseph, Missouri, was third at 315.

Ironically, it was Kennedy's balky putter that doomed him, much as had been the case in 1920. Mehlhorn, on the other hand, reportedly hit most of the fairways and astonished all by putting the best of any of the eleven entrants. With the win, Mehlhorn racked up his second and last Oklahoma Open title, the first of his twenty official victories on the PGA circuit.

Yet psychologically, the player once known as Oklahoma Bill never overcame his putting woes. The flat stick was a complete mystery to him. More than once he blamed his lack of feel on manual labor he did as a child, in a Chicago suburb, helping his father in the brick business. Whatever the cause, it helped Mehlhorn earn a spot alongside Harry Cooper as two of the greatest players never to have won one of golf's major championships.

"He could strike the ball pure, even when he was eighty-five years old," recalled former Florida International University player Bill Moretti, who became director of the Academy of Golf in Lakeway, Texas. "On rainy days we used to sit around and listen to him talk about the golf swing or tell stories about the early days on tour." Mehlhorn spent his twilight years in Miami assisting Bobby Shave, the golf coach at Florida International. On April 4, 1989, Mehlhorn gave a couple of golf lessons in the morning then drove himself to Miami's Larkin General Hospital, complaining of respiratory problems. He died that night, at age ninety.

Though the Oklahoma Open was always a stroke play tournament, for five of its first seven years, from 1912 to 1916, it evolved into a battle between the two top professional golfers in the state: Scotsmen William Nichols of Muskogee Town and Country Club and Chester Nelson of Oklahoma City Golf and Country Club. Nichols won the first two Oklahoma Opens, in 1910 and 1911, with token opposition. In 1910, at Tulsa Country Club, fellow countryman Leslie Brownlee was the only other competitor in the field. Nichols posted a thirty-six-hole total of 169 (41-43-42-43).

"The course was not in the best condition," reported the *Tulsa World*, "and the greens were far from being conducive to good golf. Nevertheless, Nichols put up some good cards and Brownlee, of the Lakeview Club in Oklahoma City, defaulted the match after the second nine, when Nichols had an eight stroke advantage. The Shawnee Country Club and Tulsa Country Club professionals did not enter the contest."[20]

Research turned up no documentation for the amount of the purse at the 1910 Oklahoma Open, but one year later, at Muskogee Country Club, five pros from three states showed up to compete for a hundred-dollar purse. Playing at his home course, Nichols won again, with a total of 153. A player from Bartlesville, identified only as "Fernie," came in second at 154. Pros from Dallas, Fort Smith, and Oklahoma City rounded out the field.[21]

By the time of the third Oklahoma Open, in 1912, Nichols had attracted a legitimate contender. The Oklahoma Golf Association had originally scheduled the 1912 Oklahoma Open, and the State Amateur, for Oklahoma City's nine-hole Lakeview Country Club, near Fiftieth and Walker. But there was a condition to the OGA's offer: that improvements be made to the course and its overall length be stretched to 3,000 yards. However, a meeting in July 1911—two months after the second Oklahoma Open—canceled those plans. Oklahoma City's quest to host its second state open would have to be postponed.

The July 7, 1911, meeting, presided over by Judge C. B. Ames, was held at the Oklahoma City Chamber of Commerce. With fifty-three Lakeview members in attendance, plans were introduced to build a new course to be called the Oklahoma City Golf and Country Club. J. C. Clark put before the assembly a motion that 160 acres of land, known as the "J. H. Johnston quarter," be acquired adjacent to Lakeview, on which to build a new eighteen-hole course. Three hundred shares of stock, at $125 per share, would finance the debt and establish the membership. The plan was to keep Lakeview open until the new course was completed, then sell Lakeview.[22] This meant that instead of going into improvements to Lakeview, all money and labor would be directed toward the new course, at Thirty-ninth and Western. Therefore, with construction in progress, the plan required the Oklahoma Open return to Tulsa in 1912, for the second time in three years.

With Tulsa getting two of the first three Opens, club members at Oklahoma City Golf and Country Club were anxious for the tournament's return to Oklahoma City. They promised the OGA they would have eighteen holes ready in time for the 1913 State Open, even if it meant using Lakeview's original nine and nine of the new holes. Time was short. The club needed someone to oversee the course construction, preferably a golf professional who could also give lessons and manage the clubhouse. A search committee found their man, albeit half a continent away, in Scottish pro Chester Nelson.

Besides having knowledge of course construction and the business end of managing a golf course, Nelson, employed at a club in Battle Creek, Michigan, was a respected instructor and polished player. He had competed in both the U.S. and Western Opens. Nelson arrived at Oklahoma City in October of 1911. His primary job would be to oversee construction at the new course, but there was also a competitive matter that required his attention. In June of 1912, Nelson showed up at Tulsa Country Club and, much to the delight of his new employers, snatched the title from two-time defender Nichols.

A year later, at the Oklahoma City course he was helping to build, Nelson won it again. That 1913 Oklahoma Open made history in several ways. It was the first Oklahoma Open played over eighteen separate holes, instead of nine; it was the first Oklahoma Open decided by a playoff; it marked the unveiling of one of the longest holes in the U.S., a 612-yard par 6; and three players set a tournament record for the most holes in one day, forty-five, a record unlikely to be broken.

The tournament was contested over nine holes of old Lakeview and nine from the new course. After morning and afternoon rounds of eighteen holes each, Nelson, Nichols, and a seventeen-year-old Oklahoma City junior player named Maury West had thirty-six-hole totals of 157. A coin flip determined that a nine-hole playoff would be held over the new nine holes, which were par 38.

In the playoff, only one stroke separated the three players after three holes, but Nelson birdied three of the final six holes, including the par-6 eighth, for a round of 38. West had two birdies, two triples, and one bogey for 43. Nichols had two bogeys and two double bogeys for a 44.

With Nelson's second consecutive victory, the total for the two rivals stood at two wins apiece. The fifth Oklahoma Open was held in June of 1914 at Oak Hill Country Club in Bartlesville. Once again Nichols and Nelson were the class of the field, with Nichols regaining his title in a three-stroke victory. A year later, at Oklahoma City Golf and Country Club, Nelson won his third Open title, rather easily, with a six-stroke margin over runner-up Bob Peebles of Topeka, Kansas. Nichols, by then a pro at Lakewood Country Club in Dallas, did not enter the 1915 tournament.

The decisive match took place on June 17, 1916, at Muskogee Town and Country Club. Returning to his old club, Nichols captured his fourth and final Oklahoma Open, with rounds of 71-70. First prize was fifty dollars. Runner-up was Ivan Miller of Ardmore. Nelson finished third, at 149, eight strokes behind his rival.

Golf Rash

Heat Rash, Chafings, Irritations, Tan, Sunburn, Bites and Stings, Too Free or Offensive Perspiration, Red, Rough, Blistered Hands, Tired, Lamed, Strained Muscles, Soothed, Cooled and Healed by Baths with

Cuticura SOAP

ABOVE: By the time this advertisement appeared in July 1900, Oklahomans were itching to tee off.

Guthrie News Leader.

LEFT: Mrs. M. C. Hale of Tulsa, in good form, two years before Oklahoma became a state.

Sturm's Statehood Magazine, October 1905.

Scotsman Art Jackson,
the father of public golf in Oklahoma.
Courtesy U. C. Ferguson.

"Old Stone Face": the notorious cliff hole at Dornick Hills.
Courtesy Jep Wille.

Savoring the silver: low amateur Charlie Coe (right) toasts Waco and Opie Turner,
golf's giveaway couple, at the 1953 Ardmore Open.

Fonville Studio, Ardmore. Courtesy Barbara Sessions.

This golden gift horse from Waco Turner (right) to Byron Nelson had some Texas cowboys seeing red.

Fonville Studio, Ardmore. Courtesy Beryle Moore.

When Babe Didrikson Zaharias heard about Nelson's palomino, she asked Waco and Opie Turner, "Where's mine?"

Photo: Bill and Vick Vickers. Courtesy Barbara Sessions.

ABOVE: Claude Duffy Martin opened eight courses in Logan and Oklahoma counties and brought his wife, children, and grandchildren into the business. "I build 'em, they run 'em," explained Martin.

Photo: Wally Wallis. Courtesy Duffy Martin.

LEFT: U.S. Open Champion Orville Moody and his mother Sarah, in the Wichita Mountains near Lawton, Christmas 1969.

Photo: Bill Dixon. Courtesy Reggie (Moody) Harrison.

ABOVE: The great Ben Hogan at Lawton Municipal Golf Course, April 1956.
Photo: Bill Dixon. Courtesy Jackie Greer.

ABOVE: Family style: the 1985 Moody Pro-Am at El Reno Country Club. Left to right: Sam Moody, Leon Moody Jr., U.S. Open champion Orville Moody (note the long putter), Lloyd Moody, Jay Moody, Leon "Spanky" Moody, Teddy Harrison.
Photo: Brenda Moody. Courtesy Reggie (Moody) Harrison.

RIGHT: During the World War II years, Orville (lower left, aged eleven) and his brother Lloyd (upper left, aged fourteen) could not afford golf shoes, but even so they barefooted away with their share of trophies.
Courtesy Lloyd and Betty Moody.

"Wild Bill" Mehlhorn, ball
striker extraordinaire and
head pro at Tulsa Country
Club in the early 1920s, won
twenty-one events during his
professional career, including
the Oklahoma Open in 1920
and 1923.

Courtesy Al Barkow.

Institutional racism gutted the professional golf career of Tishomingo native Bill Spiller, but his reward came through the judicial process when he helped overturn the PGA's exclusionary "Caucasians only" clause in the early 1960s.

Courtesy Al Barkow.

"The Man": five-time champion Walter Hagen was qualifying medalist of the 1935 PGA Championship at Oklahoma City's Twin Hills Golf and Country Club but lost to Johnny Revolta, one up, in the first round.

Betty Dodd, who learned to
play at Lawton's Fort Sill
course, returned to
Oklahoma in 1956 and
captured the Lawton Open.

Photo: Bill Dixon,
Lawton Constitution.

ABOVE: Hawaiian Jacqueline Pung checks her tally at the 1957 Lawton Open.
Photo: Bill Dixon, *Lawton Constitution*.

LEFT: Marlene Bauer Hagge arrives at Lawton in style on April 17, five days before winning the 1957 Lawton Open.
Photo: Bill Dixon, *Lawton Constitution*.

ABOVE: Champion Beverly Hanson, putter and prize in hand, after winning the 1958 Lawton Open.

Photo: Bill Dixon, *Lawton Constitution.*

LEFT: Sisters Alice Bauer (left) and Marlene Bauer Hagge admire the trophy Marlene won at the 1957 Lawton Open.

Photo: Bill Dixon, *Lawton Constitution.*

THREE
The Man

Ever since Oklahoma's first PGA event was held at Tulsa Country Club in 1923, Oklahoma golfers have demonstrated time and again their support for tournament golf, both amateur and professional. Through the 2001 U.S. Open at Southern Hills, Oklahoma has hosted a combined fifty-six PGA Tour, LPGA Tour, Nike Tour, and USGA professional championships. And that does not include eighty-six Oklahoma Opens, three NCAA Championships, eleven USGA amateur championships, and numerous Western, Southern, Trans-Mississippi, Trans-National, and intercollegiate tournaments.

Prior to 1923, the state's only pro event—the Oklahoma Open—had been administered by the Oklahoma Golf Association and was held in conjunction with the Oklahoma Amateur, as a one-day, thirty-six-hole affair. But taking a cue from Texan Jack O'Brien's successful $6,000 San Antonio Open in 1922, members of the fledgling Professional Golfers' Association, who had created a Winter Tour, were invited to play seventy-two-hole events at Tulsa Country Club and Dornick Hills Country Club in Ardmore, in 1923 and 1924, as officially sanctioned PGA events. By this

time Bill Mehlhorn, formerly at Tulsa Country Club, had moved to St. Louis, but he returned to win the 1923 Oklahoma Open. A year later, Kansas City pro William Creavy, previously of Oklahoma City, won at Dornick Hills in Ardmore.

Four of the best amateurs in the state during the 1920s were James A. Kennedy of Tulsa, who would later own and operate that city's first public course, and three Oklahoma Citians: Gus Mattson, Keefe Carter, and Robert Conliff Jr. All but Conliff won at least one Oklahoma Amateur, Kennedy winning four times in a row. Conliff made his mark as winner of three of the first four Oklahoma City Amateur Championships. None of the four ever turned pro, but all were instrumental in bringing professional tournament golf to Oklahoma. From the efforts of these men, a healthy rivalry evolved between golf promoters in the state's two largest cities, raising the bar both in terms of golf course architecture and in the level of play.

Through the efforts of Kennedy's father (Dr. S. G. Kennedy) and others, Tulsa could lay claim to hosting the first Oklahoma Open Championship (in 1910) and bringing the first PGA event to the state. But Oklahoma City was gaining ground. At Lincoln Park, the capital city of Oklahoma could already pride itself in having the state's first public course. Now it looked to build a first-class private course.

By 1923, Carter and Conliff had seen A. W. Tillinghast's handiwork at Tulsa Country Club and the Oaks. They recognized that if Oklahoma City was to attract championships, it needed an equally challenging course. After organizing a board of directors, Conliff and Carter turned their attention to hiring an experienced but affordable architect who could design and build a championship course in Oklahoma City. As it turned out, they needed to look no farther than a hundred miles to the south, to Ardmore's Perry Maxwell.

In 1923 Carter, Conliff, and four others formed a syndicate to finance construction of a new course—Twin Hills Golf and Country Club. Maxwell, who had seen the linksland courses of Scotland and studied C. B. Macdonald's National Golf Links on Long Island, was hired as architect. From the start Maxwell oversaw every facet of the project. Upon its completion in 1925, Twin Hills Golf and Country Club joined Dornick Hills, Muskogee Country Club, the Oaks, and Tulsa Country Club as the five premier courses in the state. Some who had played all five courses claimed Twin Hills was the best test of golf.

Conliff and Carter proved equally skillful as promoters and as competitors. They both were successful in the oil business, and each had a professional caliber golf game. But, talented as they were as competitors, their legacy to Oklahoma golf was in promoting the game. Through their efforts toward the development of Twin Hills, and later in bringing the PGA Winter Tour into the state, Conliff and Carter laid the groundwork that eventually landed the state's first major professional tournament—the 1935 PGA Championship.

While the Oklahoma Open continued annually as one of the top state opens in the nation, its run as an official PGA event lasted only two years, in 1923 and 1924. Conliff and Carter recognized the enthusiasm Oklahomans had for professional tournament golf and in 1926 secured financing to bring the PGA Winter Tour to Oklahoma. The first Oklahoma City Open, with a purse of $3,500, was held jointly at Lakeside Golf Club and the original Oklahoma City Golf and Country Club, in November of 1926.

"Bob Conliff was the ramrod of the thing," Lincoln Park pro Art Jackson recalled in 1960. "And he never did get the credit he deserved."[1] At that time, when virtually all professional golfers worked as club pros during the warm months, the PGA's Winter Tour was played in sunbelt states during the off-season. Jackson said the $3,500 purse was not hard to raise —each of Oklahoma City's four courses (Lakeside, Edgemere, Country Club, Lincoln Park) provided a share to supplement ticket sales. Conliff and Carter, with their contacts in the oil business, made up the rest.

Prior to stroke play, a seventy-two-player Pro-Am was held on Friday, November 26, 1926, at Oklahoma City Golf and Country Club with one pro and one amateur on each team. Pro Dave Trueffelli and his partner Neil Coburn, both of Wichita, Kansas, won the first Oklahoma City Open Pro-Am with a best ball score of 68. That was followed by two days of stroke play, thirty-six holes each day. Even in late November, during the some of the shortest days of the year, a field of fifty-four competitors played thirty-six holes at Lakeside (par 72) on Saturday and thirty-six at Oklahoma City Golf and Country Club (par 73) on Sunday.

Chicago's Al Espinosa, who three years later would lose a playoff to Bobby Jones in the U.S. Open, earned the $1,000 first prize with totals of 153 at Lakeside and 144 at Oklahoma City Golf and Country Club. Espinosa was the only player in the field to better 300 for the four rounds. Runner-up was Willard Hutchison, of Ponca City (303), while Ed Dudley of Oklahoma City finished third (306). Dudley later worked at Tulsa Country Club, before accepting an offer from Bobby Jones and Clifford Roberts to become head professional at Augusta National Golf Club.

Among amateurs in the 1926 Oklahoma City Open, Gus Mattson played best, tying for twenty-sixth at 329. Other prominent PGA players in the 1926 Oklahoma City Open field included "Lighthorse" Harry Cooper, playing out of Los Angeles, sixth at 311; Mehlhorn of Chicago, thirteenth at 316; Colonial Country Club architect John Bredemus of Dallas, seventeenth at 319; and Missouri's Horton Smith, twenty-fifth at 328.

The 1927 Oklahoma Open attracted an even stronger field, and the scoring reflected it. Among the newcomers were Gene Sarazen, Jock

Hutchison, and Tony Manero. That was one of only two appearances Sarazen ever made in Oklahoma. By then a winner of a U.S. Open and two PGA Championships (he would later win the Masters and British Open), the "Squire" found it tough sledding at both courses; Sarazen's total was sixteen over par.

Hutchison, winner of both the British Open and PGA Championship, became notorious for gouging out the faces of his irons to such a degree as to cause the USGA to implement groove standards. In the 1927 Oklahoma City Open, Hutchison had a 2-over 292 to finish sixth. Manero, who would be the 1936 U.S. Open champion, finished fourth at 289. The winner in 1927 was Cooper (283), who distanced himself by three strokes over the runner-up, defending champion Espinosa (286), and five clear of Smith.

A year before his victory in Oklahoma City, Cooper, an Englishman who had immigrated to Texas, picked up the nickname "Lighthorse" from legendary sportswriter Damon Runyan, who had seen Cooper and George Von Elm gallop around Los Angeles Country Club in two and a half hours. Cooper went on to win $3,500 at Los Angeles, then the richest first prize in golf.

After sixty-three holes in Oklahoma City, Cooper was stricken with a dreaded case of the "yips," an involuntary nervous twitch that worsens the closer a golfer gets to the hole. When a golfer is yipping, even a 12-inch putt can easily be missed. There being no known cure, Cooper opted to leave his putter in the bag and started using a 1-iron instead. It worked. According to reports, for the last nine holes he holed everything he looked at. Cooper scored 32 coming home, giving him a final round 68 and a winning total of 283, seven under par.

Cooper had a propensity for fast walking, quick putting, and second-place finishes. Some have suggested that his nervous on-course demeanor brought on bouts of impatience that cost him at the winner's circle. An excellent ball striker, Cooper has been labeled the best player in golf history not to win at least one of professional golf's four major championships. At the end of his competitive career, Cooper's runner-up total on the PGA circuit matched his victories—31. In 1999 he was still teaching golf in Westchester County, New York, well past his ninetieth birthday.

The first week in November of 1928 saw the election of Herbert Clark Hoover as the thirty-first president of the United States. In Oklahoma, it was the week of the third Oklahoma City Open and the first professional victory for Horton Smith, from nearby Joplin, Missouri.

"Horton Smith was a gentleman if there ever was one," recalled Jimmie Gauntt in a 1997 interview. "He was a beautiful dresser, clean looking, didn't smoke or drink, just a real nice guy to be around. We were having lunch one day at a club in Los Angeles. A girl came around and asked if we wanted dessert. Horton said, 'Brought my own, hon.' He had a piece of cookie with him, wrapped up in his napkin and that was his dessert."

In 1928, during the first two rounds on Saturday at Lakeside, Smith, at age twenty, played well enough, reaching the halfway point at a one-under-par 143. His nearest pursuer was the "Silver Scot," Tommy Armour, who had won the U.S. Open the year before. At one over par, Armour was breathing down Smith's neck. But on Sunday's final thirty-six at par-73 Oklahoma City Golf and Country Club, Smith showed a glimpse of the form he would later use to win two of the first three Masters. In the final round, Smith aced the second hole with a mashie-niblick (7-iron) from 119 yards; the ball landed with topspin and rolled 20 feet into the hole.

"It dribbled for the can and did a nosedive," the *Tulsa World* reported, "as the gallery of more than 1,000 sent up a mighty cheer. Horton just smiled."[2] Smith's four-round total of 288 was two under par and one stroke fewer than Tulsa pro Ed Dudley. Armour (292), Espinosa (294), and Mehlhorn (296) finished third, fourth, and fifth.

After dropping out of college to turn pro, Smith proved to himself and his peers that he would not be intimidated. The "Joplin Ghost" won thirteen times within the next two seasons, on the way to thirty career victories, which included the 1934 and 1936 Masters. Smith eventually competed on eight Ryder Cup teams and later became president of the Professional Golfers' Association.

By the fall of 1929, the Oklahoma City Open was entering its fourth year and had become something of a tradition on the PGA Winter Circuit. But unknown to players, fans, and organizers, circumstances far beyond their control would relegate the Oklahoma City Open to mothballs for twenty-seven years. The pros arrived in Oklahoma the fourth week of October. As they played practice rounds on Thursday, October 24, half a continent away the bottom fell out on Wall Street. In a stampede of sell orders, all trading records were broken with a turnover of 24 million shares between the New York Stock Exchange and the New York Curb Market. Businesses were estimated to have lost $40 billion. Black Thursday, or the Great Crash, as it came to be called, signaled the beginning of the Great Depression, which would last for much of the 1930s. Oklahoma would be one of the states hardest hit.

Nevertheless, the 1929 Oklahoma City Open was already set in motion. The tournament began on Saturday morning, with thirty-six holes scheduled for both Saturday and Sunday. Saturday was a fine fall day, but ominously, after three years of Indian summer weather for the Oklahoma City Open, the last Sunday of October turned raw. Sunday—the traditional payday for professional golfers—started with a slow drizzle, changing to a stinging rain out of the north. It rained so much that pools of water collected on the greens. Players not in contention retreated to the clubhouse. Only thirty of the original sixty-eight players bothered to finish.

"Play was over a new course, Nichols Hills," the *New York Times* reported, "and the soft turf, sodded only a few months ago, became a quagmire from the all day soaking. The driving rain and slippery footing created conditions that chilled to the bone, causing more than half the contestants to withdraw."[3]

Two of the players who toughed it out had a vested interest in seeing the tournament continue. As amateurs and tournament organizers, Conliff and Carter had no claim to any prize money, but they proved their golf games the equal of what most pros could do. Carter tied for twelfth. His morning round of 72 tied champion Craig Wood for the miserable final day's lowest score. Carter finished ahead of such notables as Dudley and Kansas City's Jug McSpaden. Conliff ended up twenty-first, just ten strokes behind Carter. Their totals were the lowest among twenty-one amateurs who entered the tournament.

Even though the Oklahoma City Open was not resurrected until three decades later, the 1929 tournament enabled the best professional golfers to see a Perry Maxwell–designed course. The new course was built by the membership at Oklahoma City Golf and Country Club, but it was temporarily called Nichols Hills Country Club to avoid confusion with the original Oklahoma City Golf and Country Club course. In 1930 some of the top amateur players in Oklahoma and Texas were introduced to Maxwell's Oklahoma artistry. In his instructional classic *Shape Your Swing the Modern Way*, Byron Nelson compiled a partial list of his career victories. The first tournament on that list was the 1930 Southwest Invitational Amateur, at Nichols Hills, not to be confused with the ongoing Southwestern Amateur, which dates to 1915.

The Southwest Invitational Amateur, which Nelson considered an important confidence boost toward a professional career, was the links version of the Oklahoma-Texas football game, a contest among the best amateur golfers from either side of the Red River. "Long-driving boys from Texas showed Oklahoma's best a thing or two about golf in the first qualifying round of the Southwest Tourney," read the lead paragraph in the *Daily Oklahoman*.[4]

Some ninety players teed it up in stroke play qualifying, with the low 32 advancing to match play. Besides Nelson, favorites included Oklahoma State Amateur winner G. A. Mattson, future University of Oklahoma NCAA champion Walter Emery, future Oklahoma Open champion Zell Eaton, and three-time Texas Amateur winner Gus Moreland of Fort Worth. In the qualifying portion of the tournament, Nelson and Moreland tied for low medalist with scores of 73. Following four rounds of match play that saw Moreland eliminated early, it came down to a thirty-six-hole final between the teenager Nelson and a wily forty-year-old veteran, Tommy Cochran of Wichita Falls, Texas.

Even after a strong 4 & 3 showing against Bud McKinney in the semifinals, Nelson, at age eighteen, was considered little more than an untested upstart. "The finalists never have met but each is itching to match his ability with the other's skill," wrote Bus Ham in the *Daily Oklahoman*. "Cochran, perhaps, is more eager for the titular fray than Nelson. Cochran was eliminated by a virtual unknown in the early rounds of the recent Glen Garden tourney at Fort Worth while Nelson went on to capture the cup. So Cochran is champing in his desire to get at Nelson Saturday. The wise-heads who have watched Cochran and Nelson stroke their ways into the title round have established Cochran as the lead horse. His greater tourney experience will beat Nelson, they predict."[5]

So much for wise-heads. The match, scheduled for thirty-six, ended at the thirtieth hole. Nelson, resplendent in a white dress shirt, tie, and plus fours, made short work of Cochran. The future Hall of Famer had a six-hole lead after eighteen, then coasted to a 7 & 6 victory.

"That was not my first amateur title, but it meant a lot," Nelson recalled during an interview at the 1997 Byron Nelson Classic. "I just won the Glen Garden Invitational [in Fort Worth] a few weeks earlier. The Southwest was important to my career, my confidence. There were some good players there. When I won it, I felt like I could play with anybody."

Even though Nelson was an unknown talent outside Fort Worth, and would not turn professional until 1932, his career was poised to take flight. At Oklahoma City he experimented with a new technology and swing motion that later revolutionized the game. "At first I had the typical old caddie swing," Nelson recalled, "low and around the shoulders, where the feet were kept pretty flat and we threw the clubface into the ball to get it square again. I was hooking something terrible. The hickory shafts I used then in my iron clubs had a lot of torque, or twist, in them. . . . So the swing was loose and flat—turn in a barrel we called it."[6]

In early summer of 1930, Nelson had acquired his first set of steel-shafted irons. Still, even with the stiffer shafts, he was prone to pulling the ball left. So Nelson went against conventional technique of the time and altered his motion to a more upright swing plane. "I decided I had to learn to take the club straight back," said Nelson. "When I got to the top of the backswing, I felt as if I would just let it fall, with my feet and legs helping to carry it straight back through the ball and keeping it on line toward the target. This would eliminate the hook that was troubling me."[7]

The results were dramatic, paying off at the Southwest Invitational. Sixty-seven years later, Nelson still had fond memories of winning in Oklahoma City. "I remember it very well," he said. "Bill Inglish recently sent me some old clippings and photos of the tournament. I've always had a warm place in my heart for Oklahoma City."

It took Nelson three full years after he turned pro in 1932 to win his first professional tournament, the New Jersey State Open, in August of 1935. But a month after New Jersey, he suffered a setback, failing to qualify for the 1935 PGA Championship at Oklahoma City's Twin Hills Golf and Country Club. "Failed," Nelson wrote in his diary, summarizing his

PGA prequalifying. Following that notation, Nelson scribbled the qualifying scores that told the story just as succinctly: "80-76."[8]

Even though Nelson did not qualify for the 1935 PGA, and neither did Ben Hogan and Sam Snead, who were still winless and in the formative stages of their careers, Oklahoma City's first major attracted most of the top professional players of the era. Among the early arrivals to Twin Hills the week of October 16–24, 1935, was the era's dominant professional player, Walter Charles Hagen of Rochester, New York. Hagen's career had reached its twilight by 1935. Already Hagen had captured thirty-nine of his forty career wins, including five PGAs, four British Opens, and two U.S. Opens.

Hagen's presence invited respect, as much among his fellow pros as with the fans. In Hagen's early years, when golf professionals were considered by most club members as little more than overpaid caddie-masters, he had ignored the "Members Only" signs at private clubhouses and traipsed in anyway, as if he belonged. His gregarious personality charmed them, his golfing skills dazzled them. He drank their whiskey and topped their stories with his own. He changed clothes in their lockerrooms, showered alongside, and taught them his secrets. Thanks to Hagen, golf pros thereafter, except for African Americans, were welcomed inside clubhouses. According to Lincoln Park pro U. C. Ferguson, "Hagen was the man."

On the thirty-six-hole PGA Championship qualifying day, thirty-five hundred Oklahomans descended on Twin Hills to see a lion in autumn. They were rewarded with a curtain call, a final stroke of panache, by a champion many considered the greatest match player—and personality—in golf history.

An often repeated story, perhaps apocryphal, had "Sir Walter" being chauffeured to the first tee, still tuxedoed, a cocktail in one hand and a lady at the other. Hagen would then proceed to top his first shot and foozle a few others, much to the delight of his opponent. However, sooner rather than later, he would find his form, sink a magnificent putt, and the methodical execution of his opponent would commence.

For Twin Hills qualifying, hordes of spectators came out to see "the man,"including some Oklahoma sports heroes. Baseball Hall of Famer Carl Hubbell, from nearby Meeker, was on hand. So, too, were legendary Oklahoma A & M (now Oklahoma State) wrestling coach Ed Gallagher, and OU All-Conference lineman Polly Wallace. Perry Maxwell, the course architect for Twin Hills, had driven over from Tulsa, where he was completing his design work at Southern Hills. Prior to 1935, all PGA qualifying took place in the weeks preceding the championship, at sites around the country. But beginning at Twin Hills in 1935, a new format was implemented. There would still be prequalifying, but in addition there would be a second qualifying stage, of thirty-six holes, at the site of the championship.

This meant that in 1935, the winner of the PGA Championship would have to complete prequalifying (36 holes), followed by two qualifying rounds at Twin Hills (36 holes in one day), followed by six days of matches (162 holes possible). Total holes for the seven days thus amounted to 198. By comparison, PGA Tour aspirants today play 108 holes in six days of the PGA Tour Qualifying School, considered the most rigorous test in golf.

Hagen arrived at the course early, clean-shaven, with his game face in place. His morning qualifying round of 67—four under par—set a Twin Hills competitive course record that stood for twenty years. Combined with his 72 in the afternoon, this earned Hagen medalist honors, at 139.

Unlike in modern match play championships, a low qualifying score in the 1935 PGA did not guarantee an opening match against a player with a high qualifying score. Pairings were purported to be purely random. The sixty-four names were supposed to be drawn from a hat two at a time, although for years there had been rumors of tampering. In the 1935 PGA Championship at Twin Hills, tournament officials announced their intention to conduct a fair and honest draw.

The qualifiers' names went into a hat, and as fate would have it, low qualifier Hagen would be matched against Wisconsin native Johnny Revolta, twenty years younger than Hagen and one of the top young players of the era. Revolta's qualifying score had been a respectable 144. If Hagen were to contend for a sixth PGA crown, advancing to the second round at Twin Hills would be clearing a major hurdle.

In the Hagen-Revolta match, Revolta turned the tables on the best scrambler in the game. Even though Hagen hit the most fairways and greens, Revolta showed the touch of a jeweler, saving par from everywhere. Revolta parlayed a hot putter to a three-up lead after seven holes, but Hagen got two strokes back on eight and nine. Leading one up at the turn, Revolta went two up at the twelfth, only to see Hagen win one back at No. 13. At the par-3 fourteenth, Hagen missed a four-footer that would have squared the match. Holes 15 and 16 were halved with pars. Revolta made bogey at the difficult eighteenth, where Hagen had a chance once more to square the match—but Hagen missed his putt for par, losing one up.

After a flawless performance in qualifying, Hagen's tough loss to Revolta closed the book on his brilliant record in golf's majors. Only one more time—in 1940 at Hershey Country Club—would Walter Hagen ever again qualify for the match play portion of the PGA Championship, a tournament he won five times.

For Revolta, riding a wave of good fortune and a surge of confidence, the match had a similarly dynamic but opposite effect. When it looked as if Revolta were headed for a fourth-round match against Gene

Sarazen, the first player to win all four of professional golf's major championships, Alvin Krueger did Revolta a third-round favor, defeating the Squire 2 & 1. Other favorites also fell. Among the early exits were Jimmy Demaret, Harry Cooper, Horton Smith, Vic Ghezzi, Ky Laffoon, long-hitting Jimmy Thompson, and defending champion Paul Runyan (3 & 2 to Al Zimmerman in the quarterfinals).

But Revolta would not coast. He defeated Zimmerman in the semifinals, which set him up for a final thirty-six-hole match with the "Silver Scot," World War I veteran Tommy Armour, runner-up at the 1929 Oklahoma City Open. Like Hagen, Armour—having previously won a U.S. Open, a British Open, and a PGA—was renowned on both sides of the Atlantic. At Twin Hills he had defeated Al Waltrous in the semifinals, setting the stage for the final match against Revolta.

Although Armour was the fan and oddsmaker favorite, it was Revolta who held all the trumps. In short game technique, Revolta was ahead of his time. He imparted extraordinary backspin on chip shots and his wide open putting stance, with the right foot forward and the left pulled back, caused purists to blanch—but not at Twin Hills, not at the 1935 PGA. In the final, Revolta's razor-sharp short game disposed of Armour in just thirty-two holes.

The outcome was even more lopsided than the 5 & 4 score would suggest. Revolta had fourteen one-putt greens and no three-putts. He used fifty putts altogether and Armour won only five of the thirty-two holes. Besides the touch he exhibited around the greens, Revolta did well elsewhere. Factoring the gusts of a biting north wind, Revolta blitzed the par 3s, with three deuces and five pars. At the 233-yard No. 7 in the morning round, Revolta hit the pin with a 4-wood, then made the putt for a two. At the short twenty-second (143 yards), his tee shot stopped two feet from the pin for his third par-3 birdie of the day.

"Johnny Revolta is a scrambler," reported the *Daily Oklahoman's* Vernon Snell. "Like all golfers, even though he is champion of America's great brigade of professionals, Revolta can miss a shot. He missed several against Armour on Wednesday, but once he flubbed a shot, he went right to work to get the stroke back and his scrambling batting average for the day was almost 1.000.

"It wouldn't have been so bad for Armour if those deadly approaches and one-putt greens happened only now and then. But the monotonous persistency of them kept Tommy gulping."[9]

At the awards ceremony, Armour praised his opponent and spoke of the sixteen-year difference in their ages. "It was the old story of a young man against a once young man," said Armour. "John showed that youth can take care of age most of the time. I'm not surprised that I was defeated today. I'm surprised I got this far. Because I shot terrible golf until today. I shot what I think was an excellent game against John, but he was too good for me." Then Armour tipped his hat to Oklahoma City and Twin Hills. "Oklahoma City is a great golf town," said Armour, "and I want to tell you I'll be here when they have another tournament."

Oklahoma's first major would be the Silver Scot's last appearance ever in the state. And it would be Oklahoma's last major championship until after World War II.

FOUR
Southern Hills

On the evening of June 13, 1996, as Tulsa businessman Larry Houchen was about to leave his Detroit hotel room to attend a Tigers–Baltimore Orioles baseball game, the telephone rang. Houchen and several other members of Tulsa's Southern Hills Country Club were in Michigan as guests of the United States Golf Association. It was Tuesday, two days before the start of the ninety-sixth U.S. Open at Oakland Hills Country Club in nearby Birmingham.

Each year during the week of the Open, the USGA invites representatives of various golf clubs around the country that have expressed interest in hosting a future U.S. Open to be official observers. By the time U.S. Open week came in 1996, venues for the Open had already been announced through the year 2000, and announcement of the site for 2001 was expected at any time. Southern Hills having hosted American golf's premier national championship in 1958 and 1977, most observers believed Southern Hills was somewhere in line for a third U.S. Open, perhaps as early as 2002, but more likely in 2003 after Merion (Pennsylvania) and Bethpage Black (New York) had had their turns.

Houchen picked up the phone. On the line was USGA Executive Director David Fay. Fay advised Houchen that he and the Oklahoma contingent should take a rain check on the ball game and attend a meeting with USGA officials instead. Fay said a press briefing would be held the following morning, announcing Southern Hills as host of the 2001 U.S. Open.

"We really had no idea it would happen," said Houchen, who had lobbied the USGA on behalf of Southern Hills since 1991. "We had kind of resigned ourselves that Bethpage State Park [a public course on Long Island] would get the Open in 2001 and we were hoping for 2002. But that's the way the USGA is. They don't let you know anything in advance."[1]

Instead, Bethpage was pushed to 2002 and Southern Hills would follow Pebble Beach (2000) in the U.S. Open rota. For five years, Southern Hills and Tulsa had courted the USGA for the Open and the estimated $3–$5 million windfall that comes with it. Still, most observers reasoned that since Southern Hills had hosted the PGA Championship in 1994 and the Tour Championship in 1995 and 1996, its chances to land the Open were better later than sooner. But the tradition of Oklahoma's most prestigious golf address, and its success at accommodating three top-shelf PGA events in consecutive years, impressed the USGA selectors.

"There are a handful of places, at most, that we know of today that we would like to visit on a regular basis, every 10 years or so," said F. Morgan "Buzz" Taylor Jr., chairman of the USGA Championship Committee. "There are others we would like to visit, and we have every intention of doing so if we are invited. Southern Hills is an exceptional setup with a proven history."[2]

As it turned out, the Southern Hills championship tree grew one branch more than planned. The 1994 PGA Championship had originally been awarded to Oklahoma, but not to Southern Hills. Oak Tree Golf Club in Edmond, designed by Pete Dye, had hosted the PGA Championship in 1988. So impressed had PGA of America officials been with the club's first major that they awarded Oak Tree the 1994 PGA Championship as well.

However in mid-1991, a worst case scenario hit Oak Tree and its quest for a second professional major. The club's parent corporation, Landmark Land Company, fell victim to government rules changes for banks. Because Landmark owned the golf club through an insolvent thrift (Oak Tree Savings Bank in New Orleans), club assets were seized by the Resolution Trust Corporation, freezing salaries and capital expenditures. As a result, Oak Tree Golf Club was forced to withdraw as host of the 1994 PGA Championship.

All was not lost for golf fans in Oklahoma, however. Southern Hills, out of the major championship loop since 1982, was offered the 1994 PGA. The Southern Hills membership readily accepted, keeping it all in the family and keeping the state of Oklahoma in professional golf's major tournament rotation.

"If we couldn't have it, I can't think of another course I'd rather have host it than Southern Hills," said Oak Tree pro Stan Ball.[3]

"Oh, absolutely," echoed Oak Tree's Hugh Edgmon, general chair for the 1988 event. "I think we all feel the same way about Southern Hills."[4]

By midsummer of 1994, word was out, to no one's surprise, that Southern Hills would be at its formidable best for the PGA. "Your sense of humor better be good," said Dave Stockton, winner of the 1970 PGA Championship at Southern Hills. "Nobody is going to beat up on that golf course. The person who has the best mental attitude will win."[5]

At the championship, South African Nick Price entrenched himself as the world's number one player. Price won the $310,000 first prize by six strokes over Corey Pavin. Most significant for its chances to host future majors, the sixty-year-old golf course designed by Perry Maxwell earned the respect of a new generation of players. "It's definitely in my top ten of courses in America," Price told the media. "I was telling my wife the other day I can't believe I had never played Southern Hills. It's such a shot-maker's course. Except for my 9-iron today, there wasn't one club in my bag that I didn't use every day."

Texan Ben Crenshaw, who partnered with Bill Coore to design a third nine holes for Southern Hills, tied for ninth at the PGA. Afterward, Crenshaw assessed the course with an architect's eye. "Perry Maxwell brought a Scottish influence to the region," said the two-time Masters champion. "He obviously had a gift for it—he made such a great impact on golf architecture. Southern Hills is a very stout driving challenge and the greens are gems. With their contours and undulations, they are works of art."

Even with new technologies in equipment, Southern Hills proved up to the onslaught of the game's best players. Only Price, in a league of his own at eleven under par, bettered Ray Floyd's Southern Hills championship record of seven under, set in the 1982 PGA. At the 1994 PGA only thirteen of the original field of 151 managed to break par for the seventy-two holes. Southern Hills drew praise from players, fans, and media.

"This is the best set-up I've ever seen," said sportswriter Donald Markus of the *Baltimore Sun*, who had covered ten U.S. Opens, seven Masters, three PGAs, and two British Opens. "And not just for a major, but for any tournament. The golf course, the spaciousness and amenities of the media center, combined with the proximity of the hotel accommodations, are second to none. Tulsa has done itself proud."

Tim Rosaforte, president of the Golf Writers Association of America, added: "Too bad they couldn't put this thing [the tennis building/press center] on wheels. The Southern Hills/Tulsa combo took a couple of steps beyond Inverness and Toledo. It was the best organized major I've ever been to."[6]

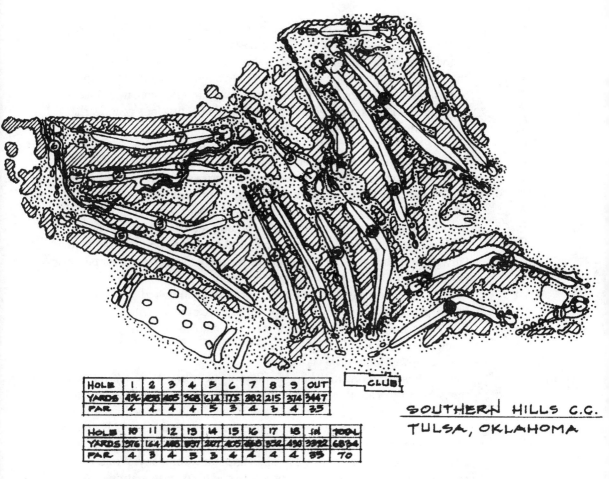

HOLE	1	2	3	4	5	6	7	8	9	OUT
YARDS	456	465	425	565	614	175	382	215	374	3447
PAR	4	4	4	4	5	3	4	3	4	35

HOLE	10	11	12	13	14	15	16	17	18	IN	TOTAL
YARDS	376	164	445	397	207	405	208	352	430	3322	6834
PAR	4	3	4	5	3	4	4	4	4	35	70

CLUB

SOUTHERN HILLS C.C.
TULSA, OKLAHOMA

Course Layout 1. Tulsa's Southern Hills Country Club, designed by Perry Maxwell. Drawing by Jep Wille, Austin, Texas.

The 1994 PGA also marked the last PGA Championship appearance of the game's best-known legend, Arnold Palmer. At Southern Hills Palmer was competing in his thirty-seventh and final PGA Championship. The PGA Championship was the only one of pro golf's four majors that Palmer would not win. Fittingly, the final time Palmer came close to winning the PGA had been at Southern Hills twenty-four years earlier, when he finished second to Stockton.

Even Oklahoma politicians volunteered for "Arnie's Army." Oklahoma governor David Walters declared Arnold Palmer Day in the state, and "the King" was awarded the PGA of America's Distinguished Service Award at a private dinner in Tulsa. Despite their hero shooting rounds of 79-74 and missing the cut by nine strokes, his army was out in full force, from the moment he hammered his opening tee shot on Thursday, 250 yards down the middle of the fairway, until he strode up the eighteenth fairway on Friday, evoking his heyday as he downed a 20-footer for par on his last hole of PGA Championship competition.

"People have been so great," Palmer said afterward in a drive-to-the-airport chat with Ben Wright of CBS. "If I can leave with the feeling that I have enhanced the game and people's enjoyment of the game, that would make me feel like I have accomplished something." He climbed into his private jet and was gone.

It is testimony to the doggedness of one Tulsan, W. K. Warren, and the generosity of another, Waite Phillips, that Southern Hills Country Club was built in the first place. In 1911, the young Phillips moved from Iowa to Bartlesville, Oklahoma, to join his older brothers, Frank and L. E., in the oil business. By the time Waite arrived in Oklahoma, Frank and L. E. had already founded what is now Phillips Petroleum Company. While Frank controlled the operations at Phillips, Waite had his own aspirations. Working as an independent, Waite leased thousands of acres of mineral rights across the state. In less than a decade, he sold most of his holdings to Barnsdall Oil Company for $25 million and the remainder to Frank for a hundred thousand shares of Phillips Petroleum, which made Waite Phillips a very wealthy man.

A miser he was not. At first Waite tried to spend his fortune as fast as he made it. In the mid–1920s, he used almost a million of it to build for his wife Genevieve a mansion in Tulsa patterned after a classic Florentine country estate. When Villa Philbrook was completed in 1927, the Phillipses gave the grandest party of the era, with a price tag of well over $20,000.[7] But soon, stung by critics who mocked the lavishness of their home, the couple became sensitive to their responsibility as a stewards of enormous wealth. It dawned on Phillips that "the only things we keep permanently are those we give away."[8]

Within a decade Waite and Genevieve donated Villa Philbrook to the citizens of Tulsa for a museum, which became the Philbrook Museum of Art. Today the gardens at Villa Philbrook are the most visited historical landscape in Oklahoma. By the time the Depression took hold in the 1930s, Waite Phillips had become chairman of Tulsa's First National Bank. With financial institutions failing left and right, Phillips used personal funds to buy up tracts of defaulted land. He was known around town as "Mr. Fifth National Bank." Perhaps the most desirable parcel he acquired was 770 acres in the scenic hills to the south of the city.

Phillips seemingly rode out the Depression unscathed, but other businessmen in the city were not as fortunate. One, Dr. S. G. Kennedy, whose son, James Kennedy, won four consecutive Oklahoma Amateur golf championships, owned the land in north Tulsa where the city's only private golf club, Tulsa Country Club, was located. Dr. Kennedy sent club members into a panic with an announcement that once the lease expired in 1936, the country club property would be put up for sale. Downtown

Tulsa Club members, who had a reciprocal arrangement with Tulsa Country Club, appointed W. K. Warren to negotiate a satisfactory sale price with Kennedy on their behalf. The then enormous sum of $285,000 was initially agreed upon, but at the last moment, the deal fell through.

Warren was at once frustrated and determined. Acting on a suggestion from Otis McClintock, Warren approached Waite Phillips on the day after Christmas in 1934 with an outlandish proposition: that Phillips not only donate 300 acres of his land in south Tulsa for a golf course but also underwrite the construction costs for the golf course, tennis courts, swimming pool, riding stables, polo field, skeet range, and clubhouse.

Even at Christmas, Waite Phillips's charitable spirit toward country club members had its limits. At first he branded the request "ridiculous." But he knew all too well how the Depression had ravaged the region's economy. After considering how many desperately needed jobs it would require to complete such a project, Phillips made a counteroffer: if Warren could secure $150,000 in pledges for construction costs, Phillips would donate the land. And there was one other caveat: a list of pledges had to be on Phillips's desk by January 15, 1935—in three weeks' time.

Warren and McClintock went to work. A dinner was held, attended by seventy-four, who pledged $1,000 each. After a whirlwind round of lunches and other fund-raisers, an additional sixty-six pledges were secured, many of the "pay later" variety. By January 14, Warren presented Phillips with 140 pledges, ten short of the goal, but enough to convince Phillips of the group's commitment.[9]

The first order of business was to hire an architect. The short list had only one name—Ardmore's Perry Maxwell. From 1923 until he was approached by the Tulsa group in 1935, Maxwell had flourished as a designer. First he added a second nine holes at Dornick Hills (1923), followed by eleven eighteen-hole courses in six states. Among them were two university courses—University of Michigan Golf Course (1931) and Veenker Memorial Golf Course at Iowa State (1934)—and five golf clubs in Oklahoma: Muskogee Country Club (1924), Hillcrest Country Club in Bartlesville (1926), Twin Hills Golf and Country Club in Oklahoma City (1926), Ponca City Country Club (1928), and Oklahoma City Golf and Country Club (1930).

When construction started at Southern Hills in 1935, Works Progress Administration (WPA) labor was available, and Maxwell's son Press said they sometimes had as many as five hundred men working at a time. "I was the top man on the totem pole," the younger Maxwell recalled in 1993. "I got 15 cents an hour for driving a team of mules. They were paying 10 cents an hour for labor then. It was the height of the Depression and every Monday morning men would be lined up for a mile down Peoria Street, shoulder to shoulder, wanting a job."[10]

Southern Hills opened for play in 1936. The cost of construction was $100,000; Maxwell's fee was $7,500. From the outset, club members believed that at par-70 and close to 7,000 yards in length, they had a special course. But nearly a decade would pass before Southern Hills matured into a course of championship caliber.

For six months during the war years, Ben Hogan attended Tulsa's Spartan School of Aeronautics and played at Southern Hills frequently. He had experience at other Maxwell courses in the state as well. Even before his stint in the air force, any time Hogan visited Oklahoma, he had made it a point to stop in Ardmore to practice or play at Dornick Hills. In 1933 Hogan finished third in the Oklahoma Open at the Maxwell-designed Hillcrest Country Club in Bartlesville.

Hogan had been so impressed with Southern Hills that he urged the USGA to hold a national championship there.[11] The USGA, its rotation of U.S. Open courses firmly ensconced at cooler venues back East, was skeptical about the greens at Southern Hills being satisfactory during U.S. Open week, which was always in the middle of June. So they hedged, instead awarding Southern Hills the U.S. Women's Amateur, scheduled for September of 1946.

As prelude to its first USGA championship, Southern Hills brought a PGA Tour event to Tulsa, the first professional tournament ever held at the club. Sam Snead, who would become American golf's winningest professional, captured the 1945 Tulsa Open at Southern Hills with a three-under-par total of 277. It did not hurt the status of Southern Hills in the eyes of the USGA that Byron Nelson, who was just coming off his all-time record streak of eleven victories in a row, could do no better than fourth place at the Tulsa Open, eight shots above par.

Incredible as Nelson's eleven-win streak was in 1945, Southern Hills was integral to an even longer streak, this one set by an amateur, arguably the greatest female athlete in history. On September 28, 1946, at Southern Hills, Mildred "Babe" Didrikson Zaharias won the final match of the U.S. Women's Amateur in record fashion, 11 & 9, over Clara Callender Sherman. It was the fourth of seventeen amateur wins in a row for Zaharias, which remains a record.

"I was pointing for that tournament, all right," wrote Zaharias, who later that summer won the British Women's Amateur. "You could say I'd been pointing for it more than 13 years, from the time I first took up golf."[12]

Babe—she picked up the nickname as a schoolgirl in her hometown of Beaumont, Texas—did not take up golf until she was twenty-one years old. At age twenty-six, Didrikson married pro wrestler George Zaharias. By the time her abbreviated life ended, she had won eighty-two tournaments, including thirty-one on the LPGA Tour.

Babe was born in Port Arthur, Texas, on June 26, 1911. In high school she starred in basketball and by the age of eighteen was playing for the Dallas Golden Cyclones, a women's amateur basketball team. Then she took up track. In 1930, she set national Amateur Athletic Union (AAU) records in the javelin and baseball throw.

In 1932 the national AAU Track and Field competition was held in conjunction with the Olympic Trials in Evanston, Illinois. Didrikson, competing as a one-woman track and field team, amassed 30 points. The second-place team was the twenty-two-member Illinois Women's Athletic Club, with 22 points. At the Olympic Trials, Babe finished first in the shot put, first in the javelin, first in the baseball throw, first in the high jump, first in the broad jump, first in the 80-meter hurdles, and fourth in the discus.

At the 1932 Olympics in Los Angeles, she was permitted by the rules to enter only three events. In winning two gold medals and one silver, Didrikson set Olympic and World records in both the javelin and 80-meter hurdles. It appeared she had tied for first in the high jump, but the International Olympic Committee awarded her the silver instead, ruling that she had gone over the bar head first. Babe was later voted the 1932 Associated Press female athlete of the year.

When Babe turned to golf in 1933, the USGA immediately revoked her amateur status, claiming she had played baseball one summer as a professional. In 1940, she applied to the USGA for reinstatement as an amateur golfer and, after sitting out an additional three years, was reinstated in 1943. But World War II halted most golf tournaments, and it was 1946 before Zaharias resumed her career as a full-time competitive golfer. She won three tournaments consecutively, then arrived in Tulsa for the 1946 U.S. Women's Amateur.

"Although I didn't know it, 1946 was going to be my one and only chance to take the National Women's Amateur Championship," Zaharias wrote in her autobiography. "Well my performance at Southern Hills was everything I could have hoped for. On the last day I was opposed by a girl I'd lost two close matches with in California right after my amateur status came back in 1943. This time it wasn't close. I was hot. She wasn't. My winning margin of 11 & 9 was the second biggest in the history of the tournament."[13]

In 1950, Zaharias helped found the Ladies Professional Golf Association. She went on to win three U.S. Women's Opens and in 1951 was inducted as a charter member into the LPGA Hall of Fame. Babe died in Galveston, Texas, on September 27, 1956, after a four-year struggle with colon cancer. It was the eve of the tenth anniversary of her victory at Southern Hills. Zaharias was forty-five.

For Southern Hills, the U.S. Women's Amateur of 1946 was only the beginning of its championship connection to the USGA. Over the next four decades, Southern Hills hosted six additional national championships: two U.S. Opens, one U.S. Senior Amateur, one U.S. Amateur, the first U.S. Women's Mid-Amateur, and the 1953 U.S. Junior Amateur, won by Rex Baxter Jr. of Amarillo, Texas. Eliminated at Southern Hills, in the fourth round of the 1953 U.S. Junior and in his first USGA competition ever, was fourteen-year-old Jack Nicklaus, from Columbus, Ohio.

No person had a greater role in bringing major golf championships to Southern Hills than the late John M. Winters Jr., a founding member at Southern Hills. Winters had respect in Oklahoma golf circles and beyond. A scratch player, he would later qualify for the 1961 U.S. Senior Amateur at Southern Hills, which was won by Dexter Daniels of Winter Haven, Florida. Besides being an excellent player, Winters was elected president of the USGA in 1962–63 and a member of the USGA Executive Committee from 1955–63. When the health of Masters founder Robert T. Jones Jr. deteriorated to the point that he was no longer able, Jones asked Winters to preside at the ceremony awarding the famed Green Jacket to the new Masters champion. Winters presided at the ceremony for five years, followed by former Arkansas football coach Frank Broyles, four-time Masters winner Arnold Palmer, and club chairmen Hord Hardin, Jack Stephens, and Hootie Johnson.[14]

In the spring of 1952 Winters arranged for the reigning U.S. Open champion to play Southern Hills. Hogan seemed every bit as impressed with the course in 1952 as he had been when he played it during WW II. "I was in the locker room listening to Hogan and John talk," recalled Robert W. Berry, a past president at Southern Hills. "There was a big crowd around them. Hogan just went on and on about the course. He said our course was damn marvelous. He said we should get a U.S. Open. It was through Hogan and John that it all got started."[15]

Six years later, Southern Hills had its first U.S. Open, and a high-strung shotmaker from the southeastern corner of the state became the second native Oklahoman to win a USGA National Open. Thomas Henry Bolt, of Irish descent, was born in Haworth on March 31, 1918. As a young man, he worked at a series of jobs in the Southwest, learning golf at Memorial Park Golf Course in Houston. He turned pro relatively late, in 1946, at age twenty-eight. At 6 feet, 2 inches, Bolt had a classic swing and a lantern jaw that made him one of the most stylish shotmakers in golf history. But it was his temperament, and especially his propensity for propelling shafted objects enormous distances, that earned him the nicknames "Terrible Tom" and "Ol' Thunder."

"You see, my reputation as a club thrower has gotten a little out of line," Bolt offered in a 1990 interview, "because all these pros have lost their temper at one time or another. It's just that I did it at some rather inopportune times. And I've got this Irish looking face that just makes me look like every time I miss a shot I've got to do something about it."

In 1958, during the swelter of an Oklahoma summer, Bolt kept his cool better than anybody else—well, most of the time—and earned himself a place in golf history. He credited his week at Southern Hills to two midcareer decisions. "The first," said Bolt, "was a suggestion from Hogan that I move my left thumb more on top of the shaft. Before then, I had always been a hooker of the ball. I really didn't know how to play. I just had to scramble around all the time and get it up and down." Bolt said the new thumb position made his swing path much squarer through the ball, all the better to play Southern Hills, with its narrow fairways and thick bermuda rough.

The other decision was a switch from teaching the game to playing. "I had just given up a job as a club pro out in California, and it was the best decision I ever made. I got the weight of the world off my shoulders. I discovered I just wasn't cut out to be a country club pro with five hundred bosses." In June of 1958, Ol' Thunder brought his new kinder, gentler personality to Southern Hills.

"I was playing pretty well when I got to Tulsa, and I was at peace with the world, and, more importantly, at peace with myself. I didn't have any enemies. And I had even been reading inspirational books, some Norman Vincent Peale stuff that had me feeling very positive. I could recite the Serenity Prayer by heart.

"Now you have to realize something. They say this game is 75 percent mental and that might ought to be 95 percent. When you're thinking well, everything else just seems to fall into place."

As was the custom in those days, all competitors played thirty-six holes on the last day of the Open. Bolt managed to shoot 69 during the morning round, despite a double bogey at No. 18. "I didn't let that or anything else bother me, though," Bolt recalled. "I felt so relaxed all week and knew that if I could just control my emotions, I would win the golf tournament. In fact, from the moment I birdied the very first hole, I knew I was going to win. That's how sure I was of myself."

Be that as it may, Bolt didn't quite make it through the week incident free. "Oh yeah, I did have one little-bitty flareup, but nothing major. The *Tulsa World* ran a headline that read, 'Bolt, Metz and Boros Tied in Open.' Then the story said, '59-year-old Dick Metz, 49-year-old Tommy Bolt, and 39-year-old Julius Boros are tied for the first round lead in the Open.'

"Well, when I saw that, I kind of got a little hot. When the writer, Tom Lobaugh, came out the next day, I cornered him and said, 'Hey, Tom, what do you mean quoting my age as 49 when I'm only 39?' And he said, 'Tommy, I'm sorry. That was a typo.' And I said, 'Typo my ——, that was a perfect four and a perfect nine!'"

Southern Hills was so demanding that nobody broke par for the seventy-two holes. Bolt's four-round total of three-over-par 283—good enough for the $8,000 first prize—put him four clear of South African Gary Player and six better than Boros. Hogan (294) finished tenth, Arnold Palmer (299) was twenty-third, and Jack Nicklaus (304) was forty-first. Among Oklahomans, amateur Charles Coe of Oklahoma City (295), Robert Goetz of Tulsa (296), amateur Jerry Pittman of Tulsa (297), and OSU golf coach Labron Harris (300) all made the cut. All pros who posted four-round totals of 299 or higher earned two hundred dollars.

A change in the official Rules of Golf came about in part from an incident during the week of the 1958 Open. According to contestant Jackson Bradley, who became a teaching professional in Austin, Texas, the fairways were excellent but the bentgrass greens were subject to stress in the searing heat. Every so often a siren would blow and all play would halt temporarily while the greens were syringed.

"During the second round," Bradley recalled in 1994, "as our group approached the par-4 thirteenth, I had been playing well and was one under par. But I hit my drive into the rough and came up short of the green. I then pitched on with my third and was about seven or eight feet right beneath the hole. Unfortunately, my ball had about half an ounce of mud caked on it."

In those days, players were not permitted to mark the ball on the green and clean it. Bradley was required to putt the ball with the glob of mud. "I putted it once and it jumped to the left," Bradley recalled. "Then I putted it again and it went way off to the right. Finally I got it up close enough to the hole, where, from about four inches I managed to putt it into the cup for a four-putt from seven feet."

Bradley was furious. "Talk about hot—my pulse must have been about 200," he said. "Then I noticed that standing just to the left of the green was Southern Hills president John Winters, who was on the USGA executive committee, along with USGA Executive Director Joe Dey, and some other officials. I was so angry that I took the ball, walked up to Mr. Winters, and placed the ball, mud and all, right in the palm of his hand. Then I asked him if he appreciated that fine example of golfing skill he just witnessed."

His concentration lost, Bradley said his game unraveled at the final four holes, causing him to miss the cut by one shot. By the next year, however, the USGA had changed the official Rules of Golf, allowing players to lift, clean, and replace the ball on the putting green. As a compromise, the PGA agreed to implement a USGA rule, reducing the maximum number of clubs a player may carry from sixteen to fourteen for all competitions.

At the 1965 U.S. Amateur at Southern Hills, another rules dilemma played a role in the outcome. For the first time in the history of the U.S. Amateur, which began in 1895, the Amateur of 1965 was held at stroke play instead of match play. The field included some of the most prominent names in the annals of amateur golf: William C. Campbell, A. Downing Gray, Charles Coe, Billy Patton, William Hyndman III, William Hyndman IV, Michael Bonallack, Dale Morey, Harvie Ward, and Ed Tutweiler. James Vickers—OU's 1952 NCAA champion—eventually placed fifth. Other players with Oklahoma ties to make the cut were Jim Jamieson, Dave Eichelberger, Roger Brown, and Bob Dickson.

Besides Coe, Oklahoma's best chance rested with Dickson, a cagey tactician from Muskogee, who became an All-American at Oklahoma State. Dickson posted a confident 71 the first day but was blindsided the next day.

"A contestant from Fort Worth had a black bag like mine," Dickson recalled in 1997. "And our bags were next to each other in club storage. He had a name tag—a band—on his wedge. Warming up before the second round, I looked at but didn't physically count my clubs. But I did look. And everything looked fine."

On the second hole of the round, Dickson reached in the bag for his sand wedge. "And here was this club that I'd never seen before in my life— with a name band on the shaft. I'm sure what happened was that in the bag room it was lying in the rack—it was an extra club for him too. So I'm sure the club attendant saw it and thought, 'Oh, this guy forgot his club,' and put it in my bag. It was an inadvertent accident."

"I WAS SO ANGRY THAT I TOOK THE BALL, WALKED UP TO MR. WINTERS, AND PLACED THE BALL, MUD AND ALL, RIGHT IN THE PALM OF HIS HAND. THEN I ASKED HIM IF HE APPRECIATED THAT FINE EXAMPLE OF GOLFING SKILL HE JUST WITNESSED."

Accident or not, it was a four-stroke penalty for Dickson, two strokes for each hole where he carried the extra club. Fifty-two holes later, Dickson ended up losing to Bob Murphy by one stroke. Still, he refused to blame the loss on the penalty. "I overcame the penalty," said Dickson. "With two holes left in the tournament I was leading by one. But I made bogeys at 17 and 18. That's what cost me a chance to win outright or get into a playoff."

Dickson said the oversight taught him a lesson. "What it taught me, and I knew it beforehand, [was that] had I counted my clubs on the first tee, it wouldn't have happened. Now of course, and for the past thirty-two years, I count my clubs religiously, so that doesn't happen anymore."

Afterward, the new champion, Bob Murphy, who later earned close to $10 million on the regular and senior PGA Tours, was philosophical: "I wouldn't like the life of a pro golfer. After college, I just want a nice job as a football coach."[16] Murphy never coached football, but he did return to Southern Hills for the PGA Championship in 1970 and tied with Arnold Palmer for second place.

The eventual champion in 1970, Dave Stockton, switched caddies early in the week, ending up with Tulsan Jed Day, a near-scratch player and a member of Southern Hills.

"Getting Jed was the biggest break I could have possibly gotten that week," said Stockton. "Before Jed came into the picture, I had a caddie who had no idea what he was doing. He was putting the bag in a bunker, putting the bag on the green. I later found out he was the son of a guy who owned a neighborhood bar the caddie master frequented. I had never fired a caddie in my life, but I had to fire him. The next thing I know, I've got a guy who's a 1 or a 2 (handicap). I go from the worst I could have had to the best. Jed was great that week."[17]

So strong was the sentiment for Palmer that according to Day, Stockton felt some in Arnie's Army wore combat boots. "Dave knew how popular Palmer was and that most of the cheering was a natural reaction," Day said later, after he had become a banker in Tulsa. "But there were some things Dave didn't appreciate, like people cheering when he hit his ball into the lake."[18] Stockton's one-under-par total of 279 was two better than Murphy's and Palmer's. Jack Nicklaus and five others tied for fourth at 282.

The U.S. Open came to Southern Hills for a second time in 1977, and on that occasion there was a more intense heat than Tulsa's typical ninety-degree afternoons in June. Midway through the final round, someone phoned in a death threat against leader Hubert Green. Green has declined to talk about the incident, but Sandy Tatum, the USGA official walking with Green's group, remembered it vividly.

"It was on the 10th hole when the chief of security got a hold of me and said they'd received a call from a woman," Tatum recalled. "The woman said there was a plan by three men to shoot Hubert when he came to the 15th green. The thing that made it of some substance was that Southern Hills had a construction fence around it, and the fence was heavily hedged. The only place on the golf course where there was a hill to see down on the green was behind the 15th hole."[19]

As FBI agents peered through ABC-TV cameras, scanning the crowd, Tatum felt obligated to inform Green, even though the head of security said he believed the threat was a hoax. Between the thirteenth green and fourteenth tee, Tatum told Green of the threat. He was leading by two at the time.

"Hubert had those extraordinarily penetrating eyes," recalled Tatum. "He looks and says, 'You don't suppose it was somebody I was taking out?'"[20]

Tatum asked Green if he wanted a delay while security checked things out. But Green said to play on. After snap-hooking his tee shot into the rough at No. 15, Green's approach somehow found the putting surface. His fellow competitor Andy Bean and both caddies had been told of the threat. Tatum said once the players marked their balls, Bean and both caddies moved smartly away. Nobody was left on the green but Tatum and

Hubert. Green took an amazingly long time over his first putt before lagging it close and two-putting for par.

Green finished with a birdie, par, and bogey, good enough for a two-under-par 278 total, a one-stroke margin over Tennessean Lou Graham.

In the pressroom afterward, Graham, playing ahead of Green, was asked what he thought when he learned about the threat. "I thought they meant it was for me," Graham said. "At the presentation ceremony I thought about asking Hubert to stand on the other side of the green just in case."[21] Television viewers were not told about the incident, and nothing out of the ordinary happened. The origin remains a mystery.

In August of 1982, Raymond Floyd stormed Southern Hills with an opening 63, leading the PGA Championship wire-to-wire, for a three-stroke victory over Lanny Wadkins. Five years later, Southern Hills hosted the first U.S. Women's Mid-Amateur Championship, a tournament for amateurs aged twenty-five and older. It produced an all-California final, Cindy Scholefield of Malibu defeating Pat Cornett of Corte Madera, 7 & 6.

Into the 1990s Southern Hills remained a worthy test. As recently as October of 1995, at the Tour Championship, won by Billy Mayfair, nobody broke par for the seventy-two holes. "A lot of people can learn from Southern Hills that you don't need high rough to make a golf course play hard," said Corey Pavin, winner of the 1995 U.S. Open. "The course played hard, but fair. It's just a very difficult golf course. But it doesn't matter what we shoot as long as it's fair."[22]

And yet when the rains fall and the course gets soft, Southern Hills is vulnerable to the talents of the best players in the world. At the 1996 Tour Championship, Tom Lehman took advantage of the conditions and erased fifty years' worth of Southern Hills championship records, posting a twenty-under-par total of 260.

There were also record galleries that week, as Tiger Woods qualified for his first Tour Championship. Tiger, whose father Earl had to be rushed to St. Francis Hospital with chest pains, had a poor week, finishing twenty-second out of thirty players, with a score of 288. The elder Woods remained hospitalized for several days after the Tour Championship was completed.

Despite all that had happened, Tiger could still share a laugh. "Hey Tiger," said Tulsa attorney Charlie Prather, while the young phenom was signing autographs, "thanks for missing that 30-footer last year at the NCAAs, so OSU could win."

At the 1995 NCAA Championship in Columbus, Ohio, Woods, then a Stanford freshman, had left a 30-foot putt an inch short, on line to drop in the middle of the cup. Had it fallen, it would have clinched the team title in regulation for Stanford. Instead, a playoff ensued, which Oklahoma State won.

Woods looked up and smiled. "Oh come on—you still remember that?"

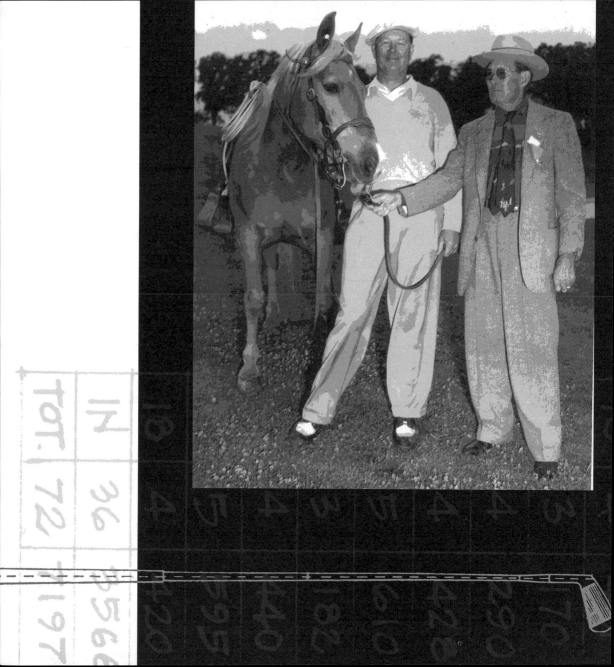

FIVE
Burneyville

Of all the venues in the United States ever to host a professional golf tournament, few would seem less likely than tiny Burneyville, Oklahoma, tucked away in the cotton and ranch country of the Red River Valley, about halfway between Oklahoma City and Dallas.

Even at the beginning of the twenty-first century, almost fifty years after PGA and LPGA stars brought the dateline "Burneyville" to sports pages around the country, so modest is the south-central Oklahoma hamlet at a bend on the Red River that state highway maps do not even assign it a population. The nearest major airport is 150 miles away.

This tract of Love County, just south of the Old Indian Trail between Marietta and Spanish Fort, was settled in 1844 by the Burney family, prominent citizens of the Chickasaw tribe, who emigrated to Oklahoma from Mississippi. A post office was opened on May 5, 1879, and the name Burneyville was chosen to honor one of the first settlers from Mississippi, Wesley B. Burney, and his son, David C. Burney.

Even during its "boom" years between 1910 and 1915, Burneyville topped out at a population of eighty-five. There were two doctors, a grocery, hotel, church, blacksmith, drugstore, cotton buyer, and two general merchandise stores. Ninety years later, all that remained of Burneyville were a post office, a couple of dozen homes, a Baptist church, and a cemetery. An L-shaped country lane dips down off State Highway 32 to take locals and the curious there.

But back along the main highway, heading a little farther west, two indications of more of humanity come into view: an expansive, one-story structure, proudly flying the American and Oklahoma flags, with block letters across the front of the building proclaiming "Turner Schools," and a nearby fountain standing sentinel beside a flagstone-gated entrance bearing the name "Falconhead."

The guarded gate leads into what turns out to be a scenic 4,000-acre resort and retirement community of four hundred homes, complete with private club, lodge, inn, five lakes, chapel, fire department, 4,200-foot airstrip, and historic eighteen-hole golf course.

Neither Falconhead nor the Turner School would exist today were it not for public school teacher-turned-oilman Waco Turner, who, like Burneyville's founding father, came with his family from Mississippi to a farm near Burneyville. Waco Franklin Turner was born in Mississippi on February 15, 1891. His family arrived in Indian Territory in 1897 and they settled in Love County, southwest of Ardmore. Turner's father taught school to Chickasaw children.

According to an article by Bill Hamilton, former managing editor of the *Daily Ardmoreite*, "Turner worked his way through Southeastern State College at Durant by washing dishes for tuition. He found himself more interested in geology than any other subject and began buying oil leases."[1] In May of 1921, having taken a job teaching at nearby Overbrook, Turner married Opie James, a teacher at Burneyville who had come to southern Oklahoma from Honey Grove, Texas. Waco and Opie lived at the Turner homestead near Burneyville.

Soon after their marriage, Waco took an interest in prospecting for oil. In order to raise capital for wildcat well drilling, he temporarily relocated to Texas, investing his savings from a previous oil strike and even some of his wife's money in a cotton brokerage business. When the cotton market collapsed, the Turners went broke.

By the early 1930s, Waco's interest in geology surpassed even his love for teaching. He hustled work as a lease hound for Gulf States Oil, earning commissions while trying to acquire drilling rights on behalf of the company. But jobbing for somebody else was just a means to get into the game. As soon as Turner cached enough for his next grubstake, he was back to punching holes.

At first Turner engaged in a high-wire act called "poor boy drilling," not unlike a golfer playing thousand-dollar Nassaus with one hundred dollars in the bank. Poor boy drillers, whose solvency teetered one trip to the bank ahead of their creditors, were masterminds at the art of check flotation. And few were better at it than Waco Turner. Many a time Turner would write a worthless check after the banks closed on Friday, rig up and drill like a madman on Saturday, then spend Sunday trying peddle enough interest in the well to cover the check on Monday.

Some of the time it worked, but as often as not, dry holes did him in. Turner had drained most of his savings a second time before he finally caught a break. Sometime in 1931, Ardmoreite "Dad" Joiner, a seventy-year-old hickory nut of a failed prospector whom Turner had befriended, called Turner from a lease in East Texas and told him to beat it down there in a hurry. This time Dad guaranteed it. He had a gusher. Waco made a beeline for East Texas and upon arrival bought all the oil leases he could get his hands on. By the time Turner returned to Oklahoma, he was a millionaire several times over.

Rival geologists claimed the college-educated Turner was not much of a scientist, but even they could not dispute that he had a nose for oil. When the time came to spud in, Turner made all the decisions himself.

His routine was to walk around the lease a while, pick the spot, then slam down his boot heel and say, "Put her here."[2] Often enough, whether by science or not, Turner's oil instincts were right on the money. Waco and Opie had struck it rich.

For the next two decades the Turners made more money than they could ever spend. Estimates of the Turner fortune varied from "they don't know what they're worth" to $1 million a day to "$4,000 an hour, 24 hours a day."[3] Much of their income was reinvested in their business, drilling for oil, but there was more than a little left over for entertainment. Burneyville freelance writer Barbara Sessions wrote: "The Turners spent a fortune, estimated at $40–$50 million, doing just what they pleased. And what pleased them most was sports, especially professional golf."[4]

With wealth and time to enjoy it, both Waco and Opie delved into sports, particularly baseball and golf. They joined the prestigious Dornick Hills Country Club in Ardmore, the course designed by Perry Maxwell. Waco bought the Ardmore Cardinals baseball team in the Sooner State League and Opie devised an incentive plan for the players: paying out $5 for a double or stolen base, $7.50 for a triple, and $10 for a home run or win by a pitcher. The bonuses were a concept the Turners would later bring to golf.

FOR THE NEXT TWO DECADES THE TURNERS MADE MORE MONEY THAN THEY COULD EVER SPEND. ESTIMATES OF THE TURNER FORTUNE VARIED FROM "THEY DON'T KNOW WHAT THEY'RE WORTH" TO $1 MILLION A DAY TO "$4,000 AN HOUR, 24 HOURS A DAY."

In June of 1951, the Turners attended the Inverness Four-Ball Invitational at Toledo, Ohio. On the way home the idea for an Ardmore Open was born.

The first steps for attracting the PGA circuit to Ardmore (it was not yet called the PGA Tour) were to hire a prominent golf professional and refurbish the Dornick Hills Country Club course. Supporting the effort out of his own pocket, Turner brought in a

highly respected and competitive Arkansas pro—E. J. "Dutch"Harrison—
who had already won eleven professional tournaments. Turner's first as-
signments for Harrison were to build a new pro shop and oversee improvements to the golf course.

Turner brought in tool pushers and roughnecks, who were earning upwards of forty dollars a day, from his oil rigs to do the work. They cut
weeds, trimmed trees, dug ditches for drainage, and poured concrete for
parking. When word went out in June of 1952 that a wealthy Oklahoma
couple was about to sponsor one of the richest tournaments in professional golf history, their names were immediately linked with that of the
philanthropic Chicagoan George S. May as the most generous in golf.

The Turners lived up to the hype. The week of the tournament,
they announced that the purse had been raised from $10,000 to $15,000,
making it the third richest golf tournament in the world."We don't want
anybody to go away hungry or empty handed," proclaimed Waco. Borrowing from Opie's idea of paying baseball players bonus money for extra
base hits, the Turners did the same for golf. Not surprisingly, the Ardmore
Open entrants renamed birdies and eagles "Wacos" and "Opies." Wacos
paid $15, chip-ins $25, Opies $250, and holes-in-one were $2,500. The
bonus money, paid out in cash after each round, was brought to the eighteenth green, under armed guard, in a potato sack.

The 150-player event, held the week before the 1952 U.S. Open,
was the eleventh professional tournament (other than the Oklahoma
Open) held in Oklahoma since 1922. Unfortunately the field was missing
many of the game's top names, since the tournament coincided with the
annual Sam Snead Golf Festival at White Sulphur Springs, West Virginia.

It was a scheduling conflict destined to plague every men's tournament the Turners ever hosted. Byron Nelson, Ben Hogan, Cary Middlecoff, Bobby Locke, and Jimmy Demaret had all committed to Snead's
event and could not play at Ardmore in 1952. Even so, there were several

prominent PGA players entered: U.S. Open champions Dick Mayer (1957), Lawson Little (1940), and Lloyd Mangrum (1946); future U.S. Open champions Julius Boros, who would earn that title the following week, and Tommy Bolt of Haworth, Oklahoma; future British Open winner Roberto De Vicenzo of Argentina; Texas Golf Hall of Famer Shelley Mayfield; multiple Canadian PGA winner Ted Kroll; 1947 U.S. PGA champ Jim Ferrier, future holder of that title Jerry Barber, and reigning Oklahoma PGA section champion Dick Metz from Maple City, Kansas; future Masters winner Doug Ford; 1956 Oklahoma City Open champion Fred Hawkins; Fred Haas; Bob Toski; Toney Penna; Al Besselink; Earl Stewart Jr.; Smiley Quick; Porky Oliver; Joe Kirkwood; Marty Furgol; and host pro Harrison. Jackie Burke Jr. of Houston, the PGA's leading money winner in 1952, played two practice rounds at Dornick before a knee injury forced his withdrawal.

Oklahoma was also well represented. Tulsans Robert H. "Skee" Riegel (1947 U.S. Amateur champion), Bob Inman, John Garrison, Bill McPartland, Art Ashton, and John Higgins were entered, as were Floyd Farley, Jimmie Gauntt, Ed Hamilton, and Bud Ecton of Oklahoma City. Besides Harrison, other Ardmore pros included Eddie Miller and Filmore Vaughn. Enid's Dan Langford, Bennie Adams of Altus, Loddie Kempa (1948 National Lefthanded Champion) and Oklahoma State golf coach Labron Harris of Stillwater, Ky Laffoon of Miami, Bo Wininger of Guthrie, University of Oklahoma golf coach Ted Gwin, and Andy Anderson of Norman rounded out the contingent of home state pros.

Heading the list of Oklahoma amateurs in the field for the 1952 Ardmore Open were Charles Coe, the 1949 U.S. Amateur champion; future U.S. Open champion Orville Moody of Chickasha (1953 state high school champion at Capitol Hill); and reigning NCAA champion Jim Vickers of OU.

Other Oklahoma amateur entrants were: E. J. Rogers, Lou Masters, Sig Harpman, Chris Gers, Glen Fowler, Jack Ritter, Johnny Johnson, Jim Payne, Charles Lane, Loy Masters, and E. G. Rainey, all of Oklahoma

City; Bill Smith, Hank Edwards, Bill Parker, Bill Duvall, Leonard Young, J. C. Hamilton, Howard Warren, and 1933 University of Oklahoma NCAA champion Walter Emery, all of Tulsa; Neil Smith, Everidge Gosley, Bart Jenkins, Ed Miller, Joe Karlick, Harry Wood, H. M. Hughes, Jeff Villnes, Everett Watkins, and Paul Dickinson of Ardmore; OSU varsity player George Bigham and Tod Tischer of Stillwater; Warren Gibson of Pauls Valley; and Bill Jones of Miami.

From the outset, the Ardmore Open, and later the Waco Turner Open, were anything but ordinary PGA events. For starters, on the night before the first round, Turner flew in 250 choice steaks from Chicago, which were served to players and guests at nearby Lake Murray Lodge.

In addition to the announced purse of $15,000 and the bonus pool, Opie added $3,000 to the $2,400 winner's share, thereby increasing the purse to $18,000. As further incentive for host pro Dutch Harrison, if Harrison happened to win, the Turners agreed to pay him a bonus of $3,000, making the potential first prize for Harrison $9,400. But Harrison finished where he began the final round—two strokes behind winner Dave Douglas of Newark, Delaware.

Including expenses, the Turners laid out almost $100,000 for their first pro tournament. Galleries reportedly averaged five thousand a day, with tickets sold for $3.50. Most of the players expressed elation with their lucrative week in Ardmore. However, already there were signs of dissatisfaction that would ultimately terminate the Turners' relationship with Dornick Hills Country Club, spurring them to move the tournament and to change it from an open competition to an invitational one.

Although Dornick Hills is not a particularly long golf course (6,483 yards), Douglas was the only player in the field to break par for seventy-two holes. Some pros were overmatched by the tight fairways and Maxwell greens. Still boiling from a rules rhubarb earlier in the week, Jim Ferrier, the temperamental Australian, withdrew before Sunday's final round.

Porky Oliver, who started the movement to rename birdies and eagles Wacos and Opies, hit a ball out of bounds on the thirteenth hole of the third round and tore up his scorecard.

The infamous Dornick Hills cliff hole, the 533-yard sixteenth, lived up to its billing as "Old Stone Face." Bill Jelliffee, a low-ball-hitting Denver pro who said he had been playing golf for fifty years, could not negotiate the ascent. After watching numerous attempts carom off the craggy out-croppings of Old Stone Face, Jelliffee finally got one airborne and posted a nineteen on the hole. Nevertheless, perhaps in a gesture to appease the golf gods, Jelliffee turned in a scorecard, complete with a 97, good enough for last place among the 75 who made the cut.

The amateurs were more incensed with the PGA than they were with the golf course. Before each round, they were required to pay a three-dollar fee that went into the PGA's promotion fund. The pros also had to pay the fee but, unlike their unpaid fellow competitors, could more than win it back by making a birdie. Some of the amateurs said they did not know about the assessment beforehand, and including the practice rounds, those who qualified were required to subsidize the PGA with an eighteen-dollar greens fee.

If 1952 had been a get-acquainted party, the next two years were blowouts, although the uproar from a premature news leak almost sabo-taged the event in 1953. When more than one media outlet is involved in coverage of a PGA or LPGA event, it is customary for announcements involving the tournament to be made available to all media at once. Hence with seven newspapers, two wire services, one magazine, four radio sta-tions, and one newsreel covering the 1953 Ardmore Open, it was some-thing of a public relations disaster when the *Daily Oklahoman*'s Wally Wal-lis broke a story late in the week, ostensibly with a tournament official as the source, that Turner had set up an endowment fund to perpetuate the tournament for the ensuing twenty-four years, "Whether I live or die."[5]

It was computed that Turner would need an endowment of $650,000 to generate enough prize money to sustain the tournament. The *Oklahoman* ran a clarification three days later saying that the announcement had been premature:"The Turners are prepared to make the endowment, but two important hurdles remain to be cleared. A contract with the Professional Golfers Association and another with the directors at Dornick Hills."[6] The PGA hurdle was later overcome, but the one with the directors proved insurmountable.

In 1953, the Turners raised the Ardmore Open jackpot to $21,300, placing it behind the Tam O'Shanter World's Championship as the second richest tournament in professional golf. First prize went up from $5,400 to $6,400. In honor of Jelliffee's 19 from the year before, Turner had a plan to pay a hundred dollars to the player taking the most strokes at Old Stone Face. But that idea was nixed by the PGA, pointing out that someone out of the running might intentionally run up a high score.

Like Turner's idol Bobby Jones, who founded the Masters Tournament, Turner wanted amateurs always to be part of his tournaments. A qualifier was held in which one hundred amateurs went after fifteen spots. Special invitations, called exemptions, went out to other low-handicap amateurs and celebrities. The 1934 U.S. Amateur runner-up David "Spec" Goldman of Dallas and Oklahomans Coe, Vickers, and former state amateur champion Ken Rogers each received an exemption into the 1953 Ardmore Open.

Snead's tournament in West Virginia still conflicted with the Ardmore Open, but virtually every PGA pro who played at Ardmore in 1952 returned the following year, in addition to newcomers Cary Middlecoff (1949 U.S. Open winner) and Art Wall Jr., who would win the 1959 Masters. Also competing for the first time was Oklahoma City pro Duffy Martin, who, with his family four decades later, would add new dimension to the landscape of Oklahoma golf.

Winner of the 1953 Ardmore Open was Dallas pro Earl Stewart Jr., a playing and teaching legend, who won three times on the PGA Tour despite playing only three full years. In winning the 1963 Dallas Open at Oak Cliff Country Club, Stewart made golf history as the last club pro to win a PGA Tour event on his home course. He later coached a national championship women's team at Southern Methodist University and proposed the idea for the first PGA Tour school.

As the 1953 tournament wrapped up, Wallis wrote in his column: "Here there is growing evidence that the Turner turkey-trot is nearing the end of the honeymoon. The story of the Ardmore Open's 24-year endowment was spilled at Thursday night's pro party. Only by accident did a majority of the reporters find out about it the following morning. Old-time members of Dornick Hills are not pleased, either. They have nothing against the tournament or its players, but they feel that they have been circumvented. They feel that they built Dornick Hills and they feel that they should be counted in on more of its doings. Turner is now club president. Endowed now for the next 24 years, the tournament has an interesting future ahead."[7]

Despite the media hubbub and snubs from golf's biggest names, by 1954 more pros began to take notice of the Turners' largesse: $27,000 in 1952 and $47,000 in 1953. By 1954, entries came in like birds to a feeder. Suddenly, there were 191 qualifiers plus fifty exempt, for a record 241 entrants. Ten top amateurs received sponsor invitations from Waco himself. Sixty more amateurs went after another eleven spots. The final field was set at 145 pros and twenty-one amateurs.

Even fitness guru Frank Stranahan, two-time winner of the British Amateur, accepted an invitation to play, as did legend Byron Nelson, by then semi-retired on his ranch in Roanoke, Texas. "Waco contacted me more than once about playing up there," Nelson said in 1997. "Even though it was pretty big money for those days, and he offered extra money for birdies and eagles and such, I wasn't really interested. But he told me if I would come up and play, he would give me a fine horse." Nelson said he did not play well (78-71-75-74, tying for fifty-first) but that Turner delivered on his promise, unexpectedly including saddle and bridle.

"When the tournament was over, the sheriff of Ardmore rode up to the eighteenth green on a beautiful palomino mare and I climbed up on her. But I could tell right away we probably weren't going to get along— she was wall-eyed and turned out to be the meanest, toughest horse you ever saw in your life. They delivered it to my ranch down in Roanoke. I tried to ride her a couple of times, even in a plowed field. But it was no use. I finally gave her to a friend of mine in the oil business who had a ranch south of Fort Worth.

"I said, 'You got some good cowboys down there?' He said he did. 'Well give 'em this horse.' A month later he told me, 'You were right, they couldn't handle her either.' She probably ended up as dog food."

Most of the headlines at Dornick Hills in 1954 belonged to sweet-swinging Julius Boros, who had won the U.S. Open two years earlier. Boros, nicknamed "Moose," led all the way, earning the $7,200 first prize and a one-shot victory over Jerry Barber. Bo Wininger—Guthrie resident, Oklahoma A&M star, and head pro at Oklahoma City Golf and Country Club— was a model of consistency, finishing two strokes back in third place, with rounds of 70-71-70-70.

The 1954 Ardmore Open was the last PGA event in Oklahoma for two years and the last Turner-sponsored men's tournament until 1961 (for an account of the LPGA's Opie Turner Open, see chapter 7). Unable to resolve his differences with the board of directors at Dornick Hills, Turner took his seemingly inexhaustible bankroll and found a new playground: he would build his own golf course at his Burneyville ranch in Love County and host his tournament there. As his course architect, Turner hired Robert Charles Dunning.

Dunning, a native of Kansas City, Kansas, had taken a B.A. degree at Emporia State College in 1921 but opted to become a professional golfer. In those days, there was precious little money to be made competing, so Dunning learned the club pro business, apprenticing under Art Hall in Kansas, then took a position as pro and greenskeeper at McAlester Country Club in Oklahoma. He subsequently attended the Massachusetts Turfgrass School and spent World War II with the U.S. Army Corps of Engineers, developing bermudagrass runways in Texas. When Dunning opened an office in Tulsa, Turner learned of the Kansan's expertise at building golf greens on terrain consisting almost entirely of sand.

Turner's money and Dunning's expertise were a perfect match for the sandy, salty soils of the Red River basin. It took almost four years to construct the lodge and golf course. In 1961, Turner once again sponsored a PGA tournament, this one the same week as the Tournament of Champions in Las Vegas. Its official name was the Waco Turner Open, but Turner like to call it the "Poor Boy Open," in tribute to the year's nonwinners (who did not qualify for the Tournament of Champions) and his own lean times as an oil prospector. Notable traditions from Dornick Hills—bonus money and parties—were carried forward to Burneyville.

Turner treated the pros to vaudeville acts, yacht rides (there were seven lakes on his Oklahoma spread), fresh seafood in bowls of carved ice, sides of beef, whole turkeys, and fresh milk (white gold) poured from miniature oil derricks. "Waco and Opie would sit up on the ledge of the main scoreboard," wrote golf historian Al Barkow, "like bleacher kids, their feet dangling over the edge as they watched the golf and reveled in their open-handedness."[8]

The first Poor Boy Open, held in May of 1961, brought together all the nonwinners on the PGA Tour from the previous twelve months plus a good number of Oklahoma pros and a few surprise entries. For starters there was forty-nine-year-old Nelson; he had vowed seven years earlier that he would never play for Turner again, but somewhat amused by Turner's eccentricities and Burneyville being less than 200 miles from his ranch in Texas, Nelson agreed to play, fifteen years after his official retirement. He made the cut (73-73-75-76), finishing tied for forty-seventh.

World class players at Burneyville in 1961 included four-time British Open champion Peter Thomson of Australia and his fellow countryman Kel Nagle, who had won the 1960 British Open. (In those days the British Open was not considered an official PGA event, hence winning it carried no invitation to the Tournament of Champions.) Australian Bruce Crampton also played at Burneyville, as did 1955 U.S. Open champion Jack Fleck; future Masters winners Gay Brewer and Tommy Aaron; NFL quarterback John Brodie; Chi Chi Rodriguez; future PGA champion Don January; and a brilliant pro and future British Open champion from San Leandro, California, named Tony Lema, whose abbreviated life would be linked to Oklahoma forever.

The lineup of Oklahoma pros in the 124-player field was impressive enough: from Oklahoma City came Joe Walser, Don Sechrest, Bud Ecton, Chris Gers, Bernie Pell, Buster Cupit, Chuck Tiede, Duffy Martin, baseballer/golfer Lou Kretlow (who pitched for the Chicago White Sox), and Ab Justice; pros from other cities were Jack Higgins of Broken Arrow, Bo Wininger of Guthrie, Woody Kerr of Chickasha, Bill Shelton of Duncan, John Langford of Enid, Jim Shelton of McAlester; and Tulsa pros playing were Johnny Palmer, Johnny Harmon, Jerry Pittman, Art Hall, and Bob Goetz.

Butch Baird, a rookie fresh out of Lamar University in Beaumont, Texas, claimed the first Turner Open at the par-73, 7,600-yard layout. First prize was $2,800 out of a $20,000 purse, not including the $18,200 in bonus money for birdies and eagles. By comparison, the Tournament of Champions had a purse of $52,000.

Louisiana State alumnus Johnny Pott, who would play on three

Ryder Cup teams and win five times on the PGA Tour, triumphed at the second Turner Open in 1962.

Once again, Turner made certain that the state's best amateurs had a chance to tee it up with pros. One of the youngest nonprofessional entrants was three-time Oklahoma state amateur champion Glen Fowler of Oklahoma City. Ada's Terry Wilcox, an Oklahoma State standout, also had a spot, as did Labron Harris Jr. of Stillwater and OSU; later that summer Harris would capture the U.S. Amateur championship. Ardmore High School star Bruce Wilkinson was paired with Jimmy Powell and Bobby Verwey, while Wilkinson's teammate Lynn Watkins went off with Bert Yancey and Frank Higgins. Wilkinson not only made the cut (78-73-76-72) but finished as low amateur, beating all but thirty pros in the 109-player field.

However, the big story at Burneyville that year was a brilliant young player from Columbus, Ohio, who had turned pro less than a year before and had earned less than $15,000 in his career. But his amateur record was outstanding: two U.S. Amateur titles and one NCAA Championship. The headline of the *Daily Ardmoreite* on May 3, 1962, proclaimed: "Pros Open Fire Today in Turner Tournament: Nicklaus the Man to Beat."

Oklahomans had seen Jack Nicklaus as an amateur twice before, in the 1953 U.S. Junior at Southern Hills and the 1958 U.S. Open at the same club. Nicklaus had not won on either occasion—he came in forty-first at the U.S. Open, and he lost 5 & 4 in the National Junior quarterfinals, to Robert G. Ruffin of Winston-Salem, North Carolina. During that first week of May in 1962, Nicklaus made it no secret that he would rather have been at the Tournament of Champions. The week before, he lost a playoff at the Houston Open. Already, the twenty-three-year-old Nicklaus had finished in the money at all thirteen of his previous tour events, including a tie for fifteenth at the Masters.

At Burneyville, Nicklaus took third place (71-73-70-71) jointly with Buster Cupit and Tommy Aaron. Five weeks later Nicklaus would capture the U.S. Open at Oakmont, his first victory as a professional and third of twenty majors. The man who would come to be called the "Golden Bear," and later would be voted by his peers the greatest golfer of the twentieth century, had played in his last Poor Boy Open.

"Waco called it the Poor Boy Open, but he took good care of us," recalled Gay Brewer, who would win the tournament in 1963. "The course was a nice layout but it was never in very good condition. Waco could be helpful to a fault. One day Frank Wharton, a pro from Akron, Ohio, came in and said, 'Waco, you have a vice back there? I want to bend my putter.' Waco said, 'No problem, Frank. Just set it there in the corner and I'll get right to it.'"

With all the bonus money he offered, Turner did not worry unduly that his course was still maturing. It was said that the fairways were as hard as runways and some of the greens had sprouted wild onions. He constructed a deer park and planted gardens and orchards abutting the fairways. He grew pumpkins, watermelons, pears, peaches, radishes, cucumbers, and beets that were canned in the kitchen of the lodge and served in the dining room. "The thing I remember most about the course was hitting my ball into the rough and having it land behind a watermelon," recalled Susie Maxwell Berning.[9]

One year Turner furnished an old Cadillac to chauffeur players between the nines. "But you better not make him mad," a veteran pro recalled. "One year he'd greet you with a fistful of cash, the next year with a shotgun." Reports of Turner's split personality may have been exaggerated. Still, when he was doling out enormous sums of cash, he came to expect loyalty in return. If a player complained about poor course conditions, Turner did not invite him back.

The final tournament Waco Turner sponsored turned out to be the most historic. By the spring of 1964, the summer after the assassination of President John F. Kennedy, civil rights unrest had permeated the world of sports, golf included. In the years leading up to 1962, the PGA devised a system to discourage black participation in professional golf tournaments. "Invitational" tournaments sprang up to avoid having Monday qualifying rounds, whereby blacks could play their way in. Occasionally blacks like Bill Spiller, Charlie Sifford, and a few others found a sympathetic tournament sponsor and managed to be tolerated—*invited* is too strong a word—at a handful of PGA events.

California was the exception. Most of its tournaments were "opens." In 1957, though he was not a member of the PGA Tour, Sifford became the first black to win an official PGA event, the Long Beach Open. But as of May 1964, no African-American *member* of the PGA Tour had ever won an official, PGA-sanctioned event. That was about to change in—of all places—Burneyville, Oklahoma.

Pete Brown of Jackson, Mississippi, entered the 1964 Waco Turner Open as two-time champion of the Negro National Open (1961–62), winner of the 1962 Michigan State Open, and five-time winner of the Lone Star Open. Already, he had made eight cuts on the year, his best finish being a tie for twenty-third at the 1964 Azalea Open.

"BUT YOU BETTER NOT MAKE HIM MAD. ONE YEAR HE'D GREET YOU WITH A FISTFUL OF CASH, THE NEXT YEAR WITH A SHOTGUN."

That Brown developed a golf game to contend with the Palmers, Players, Caspers, and Nicklauses on the PGA circuit was a minor miracle. In the segregated South of the 1950s, there were few golf courses where blacks could play, none in Mississippi. Brown became a caddie instead, looping for fifty-five cents a round. Once a week, an hour or two after midnight on Sunday, Brown and a couple of friends would steal away to New Orleans, where blacks were permitted to play a nine-hole course for three dollars on Monday.

"We were always a little nervous back then," Brown recalled. "Four young black guys going through those Southern towns at night, you could find yourself in trouble for nothing. And you sure didn't want to run out of gas."[10]

find yourself in trouble for nothing. And you sure didn't want to run out of gas."[10]

As a beginner, Brown traveled light. "I had a 5-iron and a 2-iron and used to go out in the fields at Jackson and hit golf balls," he recalled. "I was only 15 years old but learned to chip, putt, drive and everything else with those two clubs."[11]

Incredibly, at Houston's all-black 1954 Lone Star Open, Brown entered as a professional, even though it would be the first time he ever played an entire eighteen-hole round of golf. Still a teenager and using borrowed clubs, Brown shot a 79. The next year, at age nineteen, he won the Lone Star Open.

Soon afterward, just as Brown's golf game was beginning to take flight, he was visiting a friend in Detroit when he was diagnosed with polio. He spent the next year in a Detroit hospital. Brown recovered but the disease affected him for the remainder of his career. "My weight went down from 172 pounds to just over 100," recalled Brown. "I couldn't move, couldn't see, couldn't swallow. The doctors said if I lived, I'd be in a wheelchair.[12]

"But I was very lucky in one respect. I didn't come out of it in too bad a shape. None of my muscles were twisted and I didn't have a limp."[13]

Nine years later, during his second season as a member of the PGA, Brown entered the 1964 Waco Turner Open. First prize for the winner was $2,700. A qualifying tournament narrowed the field to 150, including twenty Oklahoma pros and amateurs: Jim Shelton of McAlester; Wewoka-born Dale Douglass; past, present, and future OSU varsity players Don Sechrest, Labron Harris Jr., Dave Eichelberger, George Hixon, Jim Hardy, and Duke Evans and their coach Labron Harris Sr.; Hugh Edgmon

"WE WERE ALWAYS A LITTLE NERVOUS BACK THEN. FOUR YOUNG BLACK GUYS GOING THROUGH THOSE SOUTHERN TOWNS AT NIGHT, YOU COULD FIND YOURSELF IN TROUBLE FOR NOTHING. AND YOU SURE DIDN'T WANT TO RUN OUT OF GAS."

of Seminole; Chris Gers of Burneyville; Richard Burney of Ardmore; Cotton Dunn, Bobby Richardson, and Bill Shelton of Duncan; Glen Fowler and Jack Martin of Oklahoma City; Jerry Pittman of Tulsa; Paul Hanks of Broken Arrow; and Elmer Shelton of Enid.

The biggest PGA names in the field were future Masters champions Raymond Floyd, George Archer, Tommy Aaron, and Charles Coody. Rounding out a surprisingly strong field were Texans Terry Dill, Miller Barber, and Don Massengale; Pete Fleming of Hot Springs, Arkansas; Gardner Dickinson; former Dornick Hills pro Dutch Harrison; Australian Bruce Crampton; Sifford; Dan Sikes; Bert Yancey; R. H. Sikes; Tom Shaw; Rod Funseth; Buster Cupit; Marty Furgol; and Bobby Verwey of Johannesburg, South Africa.

The course was shortened to 7,040 yards and played to par 72 instead of 73. Brown opened 71-71-68 and was a stroke behind Dudley Wysong entering the final round. On Sunday, Brown sank a nervous four-footer at the seventy-second hole for a one-shot victory over Dan Sikes. Brown was still shaking as he signed the scorecard.

As the first black member of the PGA to win a Tour event, he knew the victory would have repercussions. Though black winners on the PGA were still eleven years away from being invited to the Masters, the win at Burneyville automatically made Brown eligible the very next week for the Colonial National Invitation Tournament in Fort Worth, one of the tour's most prestigious—and exclusive—events.

After accepting the $2,700 winner's check from Turner, Brown immediately telephoned his wife Margaret and four young children in Los Angeles. "She didn't believe me when I told her I won," Brown said later. "She just said, 'Oh, sure you did. Quit lying.'"[14]

At the victory ceremony, when Turner informed Brown that he would be invited to Colonial, another tournament at which no black had ever participated, Brown naturally had reservations. But Turner told him not to worry. "Waco showed me a couple pistols," Brown recalled. "He said, 'If they give you any trouble, I'll escort you around.'"[15]

Brown traveled from Burneyville straight to Fort Worth, where at first he encountered a chilly reception. "I was really afraid and didn't want to play there," he said. "And early on there were hecklers in the crowd. When I'd get ready to putt, they'd yell, 'Miss it, nigger!'

"Well I never retaliated, but Bob Goalby [1967 Masters winner], who played with me, went after some of them. He told me, 'You play. I'll take care of these people.' Then an interesting thing happened. The young kids began to follow me and by the end of the week, I was a crowd favorite.[16]

"I can't remember where I finished at Colonial [he tied for 12th], but I played well. Before the week was over I had every player talking to me. Even [Ben] Hogan. He never talked much. People came up and said, 'What did he say?'"[17]

Brown won a second and final PGA Tour title at the 1970 Andy Williams–San Diego Open, but no invitation to the Masters was forthcoming. It would be five years before Augusta National invited Lee Elder, thereby breaking the color barrier at the Masters.

Brown's best year on Tour was in 1969, when he earned $56,069 for thirty-fifth on the money list. He finished among the top sixty money earners for three seasons on the PGA Tour, but the polio from fifteen years earlier began to take its toll. After three years on the Senior PGA Tour, Brown accepted a position as head professional at a driving range in Los Angeles and later at Madden Golf Course in Dayton, Ohio, in 1981. The course flourished under Brown, and he organized the Pete Brown Open in Dayton, which annually draws 150 pros and amateurs.

As for Waco Turner, his Poor Boy Open was canceled after 1964, two years after Opie's death. "Dissatisfaction over increasing demands of players," explained the *Daily Oklahoman*, "and threats from the PGA tournament committee to degrade the tournament to 'unofficial' status led to the cancellation. Turner's letter to the PGA said it was his feeling that a conclusion of the event would make the situation easier for all."[18]

Long before this, the Turners' contributions to golf had earned them sufficient appreciation from Oklahoma City pro U. C. Ferguson for him to have nominated them for the USGA's prestigious Bob Jones Award in 1954. As Ferguson explained on the nomination: "Webster says sportsmanship is skill in, devotion to, or understanding of sports of various kinds, especially conduct becoming to a sportsman involving honest rivalry, courteous relations and graceful acceptance of results. That's Mr. and Mrs. Turner to a tee."[19]

Waco Turner died in 1971. Two years before his death, Turner sold most of his Love County holdings, golf course included, to the Leonard Company. In 1970, the resort was purchased by the Diamondhead Corporation of Bay City, Mississippi. Besides acquiring an additional 1,800 acres of adjacent property, Diamondhead brought in noted architect Robert Trent Jones to redesign the golf course. By 1984 the resort encompassed 4,000 acres and was sold by Diamondhead to Falconhead Development Corporation, which renamed the course Falconhead.

The Falconhead Development Corporation gradually turned over daily operations and ownership of the facilities to the Falconhead Property Owners Association, which elected its own board and operates the golf course, water system, garbage collection, streets, security, country club building, campground, airstrip, playgrounds, and other common facilities. Year-round residents occupy some three hundred private homes, townhouses, and condominiums. Most of the remaining three thousand lots are not yet built upon. The fire department is on site, and ambulance service is provided from the county seat, Marietta, eleven miles to the east. The Falconhead Resort Course, which is open to the public, plays 6,376 yards from the back tees.

Tiger Woods and gallery at
hole No. 1 in the opening
round of the 1996 PGA Tour
Championship at Southern
Hills.

Photo: Tony Hansen.
Courtesy *South Central Golf.*

Arnold Palmer, who won twice in Oklahoma, signs autographs at his final PGA Championship appearance, in August of 1994 at Southern Hills.

Courtesy *South Central Golf.*

Dale Fleming McNamara, seven-time winner of the Oklahoma Women's Amateur, coached the University of Tulsa's women's team to two NCAA and two AIAW National Championship team titles.

Courtesy University of Tulsa.

A Maxwell original: with its classic lines and subtle bunkering, the par-4 fifteenth hole greets golfers at Dornick Hills Country Club, Ardmore.

Courtesy Jep Wille, Golf Course Architect.

New kid on Tour: rookie pro Tiger Woods and caddie Fluff Cowan, during a practice round before the 1996 Tour Championship at Southern Hills Country Club in Tulsa. Photo: Tony Hansen.

Courtesy *South Central Golf.*

FAR LEFT: The late Labron Harris Sr. and
Mike Holder, the only two coaches in the
fifty-four-year history of OSU golf programs,
won eight NCAA titles between them
and twenty-four conference titles each
(through 2000).

Courtesy Oklahoma State University.

In the spring of 2000, Oklahoma State
All-American Charles Howell won the Big 12
and NCAA individual titles while leading the
Cowboys to team titles at both the Big 12 and
NCAA Championships.

Courtesy Oklahoma State University.

Oklahoma State's Jo Jo Robertson, a two-time winner of
the U.S. Women's Amateur Public Links Championship,
played on the 1998 U.S. Curtis Cup team.
Courtesy Oklahoma State University.

In 1996, Atlanta-based architect Bob Cupp combined two of Perry Maxwell's original holes to create the 575-yard, par-5 ninth hole at the Jimmie Austin–University of Oklahoma Golf Course, Norman.

Mike Klemme/Golfoto.

FAR LEFT: Two-time University of Oklahoma All-American Hunter Haas was the 1998 Big 12 Conference champion, 1999 Porter Cup champion, 1999 U.S. Public Links champion, and a member of the 1999 U.S. Walker Cup team.

Courtesy University of Oklahoma.

Oklahoma State All-American Edward Loar, a member of the 1999 U.S. Walker Cup team and 2000 NCAA Championship team, under the watchful eye of Cowboy coach Mike Holder.

Courtesy Oklahoma State University.

Oklahoma State coach Mike Holder with Ping golf club inventor Karsten Solheim and wife Louise Solheim, major benefactors of OSU's Karsten Creek Golf Course.

The 436-yard sixteenth hole at Karsten Creek Golf Club, designed by Tom Fazio, on the banks of Lake Louise, Stillwater.

Courtesy Jep Wille, Golf Course Architect.

The "hangin' tree" at the par-5 sixteenth hole, Oak Tree Golf Club, Edmond.
Mike Klemme/Golfoto.

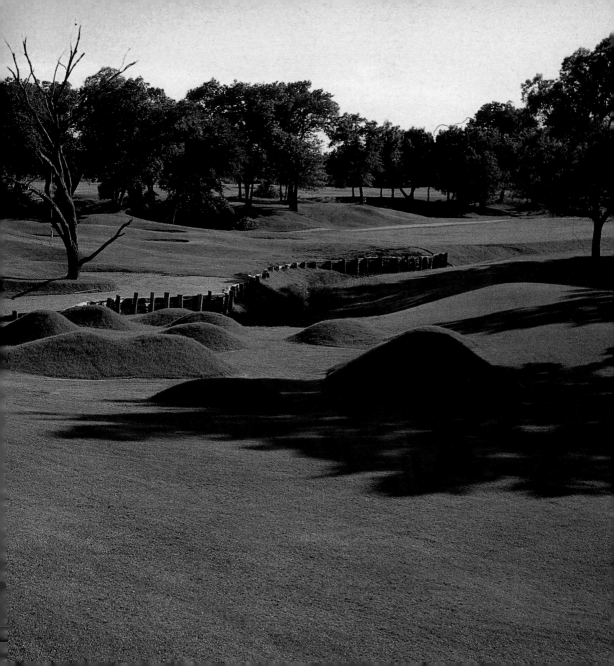

Tiger Woods at James E. Stewart Golf Course in Oklahoma City in May 2000 with sixteen-year-old Treas Nelson of Lawton Eisenhower High School, the first African-American state golf medalist in Oklahoma high school history.

Courtesy Terry Dungee.

SIX
Quail Creek

"Give me 280," said Jimmie Gauntt, "and I'll just sit up on the porch and let the boys shoot at it."[1]

It was the second week of September, 1956. The porch mentioned by Gauntt, who would win the fourth of his five Oklahoma Opens a month later, was at Oklahoma City's Twin Hills Golf and Country Club. The 280 meant a four-round total of eight under par at Twin Hills, where Gauntt was head professional.

Gauntt knew about such things. Once, in a medal play tournament at Twin Hills, he made nine fours and nine threes. Half a century later, the course record was still 63.

In late July of 1956, nobody in Oklahoma City had any inkling that the city would be hosting the nation's top professionals six weeks later. But a canceled PGA event in another city led a PGA official to contact some Oklahoma Citians known to have an interest in golf. In response, U. C. Ferguson, Allie Reynolds, Jim Norick, Sig Harpman, Johnnie Johnson, and Maurice Woods, among others, took it upon themselves to promote a $15,000 event at Twin Hills.

Within a matter of days they secured 111 sponsors willing to put up $100 each. Normally, for a $15,000 purse, the PGA required 150 sponsors pledging $100 each. But this was short notice; the plan was to solicit the remainder of the pledges in the weeks before the tournament. The 1956 Oklahoma City Open would mark the first PGA-sponsored event in the state of Oklahoma since the Ardmore Open in 1954; the first in Oklahoma City since the 1937 Oklahoma Four Ball; and the first at Twin Hills since the 1935 PGA Championship.

The weekend before the tournament, Gauntt hedged on his prediction. Keeping in mind that several of the top American players were entered (Billy Casper, Don January, Bob Rosburg, Gardner Dickinson, Dick Mayer, Jay Hebert, Frank Stranahan, Fred Haas, Bob Toski, and Bo Wininger of Guthrie), Gauntt said he could not guarantee that 280 would win at the 6,673-yard, par-72 course, only that it would earn a sizable check.

The first order of business was an eighteen-hole qualifier, at Twin Hills, for nonexempt amateurs. Exempt amateurs included Harpman, two-time National Amateur winner Charlie Coe of Oklahoma City; 1936 Walker Cupper Walter Emery of Duncan; past state open and amateur champion Emmett Rogers; former state amateur champs Ab Justice of Oklahoma City and Harold Corbett of Tulsa; Twin Hills club champion Hank Edwards; Glen Fowler; J. C. Hamilton; and Gerald Hefley. Thirty-nine nonexempt amateurs tried to qualify for twenty-five spots into the 135-player field. It required a score of 82 or better to make it.

Oklahoma amateurs who successfully qualified for the 1956 Oklahoma City Open were Harlow Gers Jr., Ed Hamilton, H. T. Greenhaw, Jack Martin, Bo Faulkenberry, Kenny Vaughn, Keith Johnson, Bud Hoch, Jim Hoch, and Dick Dillingham of Oklahoma City; Bobby Goetz, R. P. Wilson, Tommy Beck, and Bill McPartland of Tulsa; Jim Moeller and Bevo Olivo of Holdenville; Jack Moore and Robert Babcock of Duncan; Everett Watkins of Ardmore; Jim Brooks of Cushing; Harold DeLong of Shawnee; and Bobby Vickers of Norman.

In addition to Gauntt, Ferguson, Wininger, and Woods, Oklahoma pros who entered were E. H. Marshall, Loddie Kempa, Chris Gers, Zell Eaton, Ralph Robinson, Paul Robinson, Joe Walser Jr., Duffy Martin, Bud Ecton, Jim Shelton, Fred Schindler, and Don Addington of Oklahoma City; Bill Wotherspoon, Bill Parker, Ted Gwin, Jack Shields, Ben Dickson, Douglas Smith, Dick Waters, Jack Higgins, Johnny Palmer, and George Whitehead of Tulsa; John Langford and Dan Langford of Enid; R. C. Stanley and Woodrow Kerr of Lawton; Labron Harris Sr. of Stillwater; Johnnie Stapp of Miami; Dwight Travis of Bartlesville; Bill DeMoss of Blackwell; Fillmore Vaughn of Ardmore; Dick Hicks of Midwest City; and Bill Shelton of Duncan.

Former World Championship winner Bob Toski of Holyoke, Massachusetts, grabbed the first-day lead with a 68, with Billy Casper one stroke behind. At the halfway point, Texan Billy Maxwell (70-68) stood in first with host pro Gauntt a stroke back. After three, Gardner Dickinson (71-69-67) was one up on Maxwell. When Sunday's final round teed off, nine players were within six strokes of the lead. At the turn it was a three-way tie for first: Gauntt, Dickinson, and an obscure Illinois pro, playing out of El Paso, Texas—Fred Hawkins.

Hawkins, born in Antioch, Illinois, had been a professional since 1947. His only win had come at the 1950 Cavalier Open. But after the final nine holes at Oklahoma City, Hawkins had recorded victory number two. He had four birdies on the inward nine, including back-to-back 40-footers at the seventieth and seventy-first. His 279 total beat Dickinson by two, Gauntt and fellow Oklahoma Citian Bud Ecton by four. As it turned out, Gauntt's prediction of 280 would have been good enough after all.

Former OSU and New York Yankees flamethrower Allie Reynolds

presented Hawkins with the first place check of $2,400. Hawkins never won again, but he took enough momentum from Oklahoma City to qualify for the 1957 U.S. Ryder Cup team. He was immediately labeled the U.S. team's weakest player. However, Hawkins proved his critics wrong, in a losing cause at Lindrick Golf Club in Yorkshire, England. Hawkins was the only American to win a singles match—defeating Peter Allis 2 & 1. Great Britain trounced the Americans, $7^1/_2$ to $4^1/_2$.

The PGA tour had no cancelations for 1957 or 1958, so it was not until 1959 that Oklahoma City had an opportunity to host another professional tournament. The city welcomed the opportunity. Promotion for the 1959 Oklahoma City Open was a three-way collaboration by Golf Incorporated, Twin Hills, and oilman Waco Turner.

Turner, ever the innovator, had been out of the golf loop since the 1954 Ardmore Open. He was anxious to renew ties with the PGA, so for the 1959 Oklahoma City Open, he bankrolled a novel idea for PGA tournaments—the Pro-Junior. Prior to the 1959 Oklahoma City Open, all PGA events were funded in part by amateur sponsors, who played in the midweek Pro-Ams. Turner's idea was for a Pro-Junior instructional round, followed by a clinic. It proved to be quite popular. In addition to Turner, 239 individual sponsors donated $100 apiece to fund the Pro-Junior.

During the eight-year run of the Pro-Junior, hundreds of Oklahoma kids got a firsthand look at the pro game. Some of the professionals' skills apparently made an impact. Besides Bob Dickson, who went on to win the U.S. and British Amateurs in the same year, a few of the other junior participants who made names for themselves in golf were Labron Harris Jr., Danny Edwards, Mike Holder, and Mark Hayes. After paying the professionals, all proceeds from the Pro-Junior went toward the Golf Incorporated college scholarship fund.

It was no surprise that legends Ben Hogan and Sam Snead chose to bypass the $25,000 Oklahoma City Open, a new event on the PGA circuit. But 1946 U.S. Open champion Lloyd Mangrum—winner of fifty PGA events in his career—entered, as did the reigning U.S. Open champion Tommy Bolt and past champions Dick Mayer and Ed Furgol.

Also entered was a twenty-nine-year-old Pennsylvanian whose father, a former millworker named Deacon Palmer, was superintendent-pro at the nine-hole Latrobe Country Club, thirty miles east of Pittsburgh. By 1959, Oklahomans had seen Arnold Palmer play in their state twice before—in the previous summer's U.S. Open at Southern Hills, where he finished tied for twenty-third, and at the 1953 U.S. Amateur at Oklahoma City Golf and Country Club. Palmer did not win that year either (Gene Littler did), losing one up in the quarterfinals to Don Albert of Alliance, Ohio.

Said future U.S. Congressman Jack Westland of Everett, Washington, after a third-round loss (3 & 2) to Palmer in the 1953 Amateur: "You know, I believe I have just been beaten by a young man destined for golf greatness. Arnold Palmer is a fierce fellow.

"He doesn't know the meaning of fear. The putts he doesn't make he knocks four or five feet past the hole and when he drives he swings so hard he almost falls down. He'll try any kind of shot regardless of the danger, and he gets away with it. Mark my words, you'll hear a lot about Arnold Palmer before very long."[2] Indeed, soon after joining the PGA in 1955, Palmer caught fire, winning eleven times in four years. At the 1958 Masters, he distinguished himself as a major champion—winning the first of four Green Jackets.

In the opening round at Twin Hills in 1959, Palmer gave no hint of what was to follow: 73 strokes, tied for thirty-fifth. But the next day he missed no fairway and few putts. Palmer rang up two eagles and four birdies for a 64, passing all but two players.

The third round was vintage Arnie—an army of eighteen thousand spectators trailed him around the 6,500-yard course as he made up six shots on Tommy Jacobs with a wild 67 that began and ended with bogeys. Palmer's seven birdies were putts of 10, 16, 15, 14, 2, 12, and 3 feet. At day's end he was two in the lead. Sunday was a washout. Five thousand came out on Monday to see the final round. Paired with Jacobs and Bob Goalby, Palmer carved out a 69 that paid $3,500 for first.

Low amateur was Oklahoma Citian Glen Fowler, already a two-time State Amateur champion. Fowler's rounds of 68-70-72-71 were good enough for seventh place.

By the time Palmer and arrived for the 1960 tournament, the Oklahoma City Open had newfound respect. No longer was it considered a "replacement tournament." The Professional Golfers' Association, impressed with local support and promotion in Oklahoma City, moved the event to the favored schedule slot the week before the U.S. Open, which guaranteed a quality field. And it did not hurt that Palmer, the most celebrated player in golf, was the defending champion. Not only had Palmer won six times since the 1959 Oklahoma City Open, in April of 1960 he had captured his second Masters.

The 1960 Oklahoma City Open, held June 9–13 at Twin Hills, had a starting field of 147, which included past or future major championship winners Palmer, Tommy Bolt, Doug Ford, Jackie Burke, Julius Boros, Lionel Hebert, Art Wall, Gene Littler, Bob Goalby, Dave Marr, Gay Brewer, Al Geiberger, Bobby Nichols, Mangrum, and amateur great Charlie Coe.

The first-round leaderboard had an Oklahoma flavor: Tulsa pro Bobby Goetz and Ernie Vossler, originally from Fort Worth, shared the lead at 66. Vossler, a proven winner on the PGA circuit, had captured titles at the 1958 Kansas City Open, the 1959 Tijuana Open, and the 1960 Panama Open. A year later he would be named the first head professional at Oklahoma City's Quail Creek Golf and Country Club. In the late 1970s, he and

Oklahoma pro Joe Walser, also in the field at the 1960 Oklahoma City Open, teamed to build the Oak Tree Golf Club in Edmond.

Goetz and Vossler were not alone atop the leaderboard. Palmer (68) was also in the running. The next day he added a 66 for a lead over Littler (71-64), Goetz (136), and Wininger (137). Vossler dropped five back, at 139. With Palmer slipping to 75 in the third round, Littler closed the deal with 70-68. Art Wall finished second at 274.

For Palmer the third-round 75 proved too much to overcome. Nevertheless, he shot 67 in the final round, good enough for third place. More important, he may have discovered something in his golf swing that Monday in Oklahoma City.

Six mornings later, at Cherry Hills Country Club in Denver, Colorado, Palmer shot a rather ordinary 72 (by Palmer's standards), in the third round of the U.S. Open, to go with previous efforts of 72-71. With scoring unusually low for a U.S. Open, Palmer's name had not been seen on the leaderboard the entire week. However, that afternoon, Palmer birdied six of the first seven holes, passing thirteen players, including Ben Hogan and Jack Nicklaus. The final-round 65 earned Palmer his only U.S. Open title.

In June of 1961, Palmer was scheduled to return to Oklahoma City as the reigning U.S. Open champion. The Oklahoma City golf community seemed more enthused than ever about hosting the nation's top professionals. Once again they had secured the prestigious date the week before the U.S. Open.

However, on the weekend before the tournament, Golf Incorporated officials in Oklahoma City were contacted by the PGA's Ed Carter with a last-minute request. Carter was asking for the release of the top six players who had signed commitments to play in Oklahoma City, Palmer included. There was a Pro-Am in Ann Arbor, Michigan, where first prize was a new Cadillac and where the PGA was courting corporate sponsorship.

Upon receipt of the letter, Sig Harpman Jr., tournament chairman for 1961, thought he had a better idea and wrote back, suggesting that the PGA simply send the six stars to Oklahoma City and release everybody else. Harpman reasoned that the Oklahoma City Open would have better galleries with a half dozen name players than with all the others put together. At that point the combination of politics and bruised egos further damaged matters, and the result was cancelation of the 1961 tournament. In a twist of irony, Australian Bruce Crampton had traveled to Oklahoma City a few days early, to get in a few practice rounds at Twin Hills. When the tournament was canceled Crampton caught a flight to Michigan, secured a spot in the Pro-Am, and won the Cadillac.

After the falling out in 1961, some predicted that the PGA would not return to Oklahoma City. But a year later the tournament was back, only this time at a different golf course—the newly constructed Quail Creek Golf and Country Club in the northwest part of the city.

"I was quite proud of the original routing at Quail Creek, which was a project of the Johnson family," said course architect Floyd Farley, who retired to Sedona, Arizona. "It was a position player's course. And to my knowledge it was one of the first courses built in Oklahoma in conjunction with a residential development." As its first professional Quail Creek hired Texan Ernie Vossler, who had most recently worked at Midland (Texas) Country Club. A five-time winner on Tour, Vossler had the respect of the PGA players, which helped draw a strong field to Oklahoma City.

None of professional golf's Big Three—Jack Nicklaus, Arnold Palmer, and Gary Player—submitted entries for 1962. Reportedly they were tied up with "television commitments." But 105 other players entered, including Tommy Bolt, Terry Wilcox of Ada (making his first start as a professional), Don January, Ken Venturi, Labron Harris Sr., Bobby Nichols, Charlie Coe, and colorful Doug Sanders, called "the peacock of the fairways."

Sanders, a native of Cedartown, Georgia, joined the tour in 1956. His golf swing was said to be so short and quick that he could tee off in a phone booth. Decades later Sanders explained his whipsaw technique as "increased wrist-cock on the *downswing*. The course in Georgia where I started wouldn't allow us caddies to play, but we used to sneak on and play a hole that had honeysuckle on one side and a creek on the other. I swung that way so I wouldn't lose any balls."

Sanders was not a player gifted with enormous power, but his game featured an impressive array of shots. He was known as a fantastic wind player, his specialty the "quail high" wedge. With his color-coordinated outfits and patent leather shoes to match, some said he looked more like a clown, or a house painter, than a professional golfer. Tommy Bolt once described Sanders as a "jukebox in spikes." But Sanders made no apology for his wardrobe or his golf. His record stood its own: in 1956 Sanders had become the only amateur in history to win the Canadian Open. And in the previous Oklahoma City Open, Sanders had tied Jimmie Gauntt's course record of 63.

Sanders loved to wager on the golf course, and one of his favorite gambling games was called Oklahoma Whip-Out, in which all bets were settled in cash at the end of each hole. Sanders wrote: "Golfers who grew up playing in Oklahoma, like TV and motion picture star James Garner, are accustomed to abiding by those terms. Besides eliminating the possibility of disagreements occurring later on, it keeps a lot of bills and coins changing hands, a psychological stimulant. Most important, you find out which of your opponents 'forgot to bring cash' that day."[3]

In 1962 Sanders arrived in Oklahoma City on the heels of victory at the St. Paul Open. However, after a practice round at Quail Creek, he promptly announced his withdrawal from the Pro-Junior Clinic, due to a pulled muscle in his groin. Today if a player withdraws from a Pro-Am, he must also withdraw from the tournament. Not so in 1962. "Sanders Hurt, May Miss $35,000 Tourney," headlined the *Daily Oklahoman*. "He is undergoing treatment by a local physician and it will not be known until Thursday whether the strained muscle has responded to medication, heat and therapy."[4]

Sanders healed in time for the first round, but others should have stayed in bed. During the second round, Dow Finsterwald became so frustrated that he four-putted from close range on one green, three-putted at another. After the round, he withdrew. Ken Venturi made a hole-in-one of sorts. A wayward Venturi tee shot bounced into fellow competitor Bud Ecton's trouser pocket as Ecton stood in an adjacent fairway. Venturi took a free drop and went on to birdie the hole. At one hole, Gay Brewer hooked a long iron shot that was headed out of bounds but richocheted off the leg of a spectator. He, too, made birdie. Oklahoma City airman Ralph Morrow opened with 81, but made the cut with a second-round 72.

Going into the final round, Sanders was six behind leader Don Massengale and promptly opened with bogey at the first hole. Then he steadily started making up ground, with help from Massengale, who four-putted the third hole and sputtered in with a 77. At the seventy-second hole, a par 5, Sanders played a second-shot 2-wood to 22 feet and drained the eagle for a 67, good enough for his second tour victory in as many weeks. Johnny Pott (282), two back, finished runner-up, with OSU sophomore George Hixon (293) taking low amateur honors.

As a new course, Quail Creek was still rough around the edges. But the PGA was impressed enough to sign a five-year contract that would assure pro golf's return to Oklahoma City at least through 1967.

The tournaments held in the two weeks prior to the 1963 Oklahoma City Open were the Waco Turner Open at Burneyville, won by Gay

Brewer, and the Colonial Invitational, won by Julius Boros. Both Brewer and Boros had committed to play in Oklahoma City, but most of the media attention was directed at two young players—Raymond Floyd and Bob Charles. A third-year pro from Christchurch, New Zealand, Charles had three weeks earlier won the Houston Open, making him the first left-hander to win a PGA event. Two months after Oklahoma City, he would win his only major—the British Open at Royal Lytham.

Floyd, a twenty-year-old from Fayetteville, North Carolina, was described as "a chunky 200-pounder who looks more like a high school football player than anything else."[5] Earlier in the year Floyd had won the St. Petersburg Open, becoming the youngest victor on tour since twenty-year-old Gene Sarazen had won the Southern Open in 1922.

"I guess I was numb all over by the time that last round at St. Petersburg was over," explained Floyd. "Until then, I'd just been playing to make the cut and I'd done that just once. When I made it at St. Petersburg I decided to try and win the tournament. It was a brand new approach for me and I guess I was too stupid too choke up."[6] Though he did not win the 1963 Oklahoma City Open, Floyd demonstrated that he was "too stupid to choke up" another twenty-two times on the regular PGA Tour, including at the 1982 PGA Championship in Tulsa.

As it turned out, the 1963 Oklahoma City Open, with its purse of $35,000, attracted a sizable contingent of international players. A record number of professionals (145) entered, from twenty-six states and four continents. Kel Nagle, the 1960 British Open champion, came in from Sydney, Australia; Harold Henning from Johannesburg, South Africa; Canada and Great Britain were also represented.

After the third round, Don Fairfield, a little-known pro from Illinois who had not won a tournament in more than three years, held a one-shot lead. But he had plenty of company. Seven players were tied for second, one shot back. Thirty others were within five strokes of the lead.

If ever a player set himself up to be jinxed, it was Fairfield, before the final round of the 1963 Oklahoma City Open. Lounging as the third-round leader in the clubhouse, Fairfield did not even go to the putting green, preferring instead to watch the leaderboard with reporters, filling their notebooks with such Fairfield pearls as "What do you know, I'm the leader," "It sure feels good being at the top," and for good measure, "My putts are falling—that's all. That's the secret of this game, you know. No three-putts and you're in good shape."[7]

So how badly did Fairfield jinx himself?

After predicting that a score of 280 would win, Fairfied went out and shot 69 the last day, hitting sixteen greens in regulation and scoring 280, right on the money. Tied with Julius Boros, Fairfield needed a birdie at the par-5 eighteenth to win. Aided by the north winds of a cool front, Fairfield drilled his drive, leaving a 5-iron approach, which stopped on the back edge of the green. The first putt, a downhiller, he left four feet short. "I guess I choked on that first putt," he explained later, "so I made up my mind to get the next one to the hole. I sure did. It really rattled the cup when it went in."[8]

By 1964 the Oklahoma City Open had both a Pro-Junior clinic and a Pro-Am, to raise money for the Golf Incorporated Scholarship Fund. The Pro-Am, which might have been called a Pro-Celebrity, included native Oklahoman actor James Garner, comedian Don Adams, and pro footballers Yale Lary, Max McGhee, King Hill, Buddy Dial, Johnny Burrell, and Ray Renfro. Also in the field were one-time coaching rivals Bud Wilkinson, the retired University of Oklahoma coach, and University of Texas coach Darrell Royal, a native of Hollis, Oklahoma.

Told that Quail Creek keeps golfers honest down the middle, Royal replied, "Well then count me out. Everybody knows that a guy with an eight handicap sprays 'em everywhere." When asked if Wilkinson's retirement would hurt the OU-Texas rivalry, Royal shook his head. "Those 75,000 folks will keep on showing up at Dallas no matter who coaches the teams. And I suspect there'll always be a little interest in the outcome."[9]

After two days of monsoon conditions, the first round finally got under way on Saturday, with six 68s tied for the lead: host pro Ernie Vossler, Cotton Dunn of Duncan, Jay Hebert, Mike Souchak, Pete Fleming of Hot Springs, Arkansas, and Terry Dill of Muleshoe, Texas. They played the second round Saturday afternoon, with the cut falling at 148. Among those who survived the cut was fifty-four-year-old Dutch Harrison, the former pro at Dornick Hills and an eighteen-time winner on the PGA Tour. George Bayer and Lionel Hebert were tied for the lead at 138.

But the player to beat was only three shots off the lead. In 1959, the only previous time that the Oklahoma City Open had finished on a Monday, Arnold Palmer had staged one of his patented comebacks. As in 1959, Sunday's play was rained out, moving the final round to Monday. Trailing by three, Palmer shot 69 during the morning, followed by a 67 after lunch, for a 277 total. At the sixtieth hole (No. 6), he drove 367 yards onto the green and two-putted for birdie. At the par-4, 469-yard seventy-first, with a creek on the right and out-of-bounds stakes to the left, Palmer struck with an 8-iron to 18 inches for birdie. He managed to make but two bogeys during the thirty-six holes on Monday and hit thirty-four greens, good enough for a two-stroke margin over runner-up Hebert. Don Sechrest, course architect for Stillwater Country Club, was low Oklahoman, with a 290 total. Charlie Coe (294) was low amateur, followed by Jim Vickers of Wichita, the 1952 NCAA medalist for OU.

At 6:30 P.M., Palmer strode into the media room with a trophy and the winner's check for $5,800. "I came up here to give everybody all the information they want," said Palmer. "Then I've got to run." Piloting his own airplane, Palmer was due at a dinner party in Dallas at 7:00. The next morning he would play an exhibition match there with Bob Charles, Byron Nelson, and the talented young Californian Tony Lema, who also played in the Oklahoma City Open. Two months later Lema would win the British Open at St. Andrews.

Lema's final-round score at the 1964 Oklahoma City Open was 66. He tied for eighth.

For the 1965 Oklahoma City Open, a last-minute flood of entries necessitated a qualifying tournament across town, at Twin Hills. For the first time, the Oklahoma City Open would be broadcast on network television, which boosted the purse from $40,000 to $65,000. To showcase Oklahoma City's western heritage, all the caddies were given cowboy hats.

Defending champion Palmer hit town late on Tuesday, from Wichita, aboard a new Cessna he was about to purchase. Former Oklahoma City football star Jim Wade was the pilot. On Wednesday a Pro-Junior tournament was scheduled, once again featuring some youngsters destined to make names for themselves in Oklahoma golf: Doug Tewell of Stillwater, Mike Holder of Ardmore, and Ted Goin of Seminole. However, the Pro-Junior was rained out.

Picking up where he had left off the year before, Palmer shot 68 the next day to win the Pro-Am. But he ballooned to 75 in the first round of the tournament.

For two rounds the story was all about Bo. Francis Gerald "Bo" Wininger, born in Chico, California, had lived in Oklahoma since boyhood. Listed on pairings sheets as 5-8 and 185 pounds, Wininger was the Tour's Lee Trevino before Trevino. When Trevino hit the tour in 1966, intentionally or not, he looked like Bo, dressed like Bo, walked like Bo, wore his hat like Bo, and even told stories like Bo.

But Wininger, a big-game hunter nicknamed "Bwana" by his fellow pros, was an original. Unlike Trevino, Wininger did not win any major championships, although he won five regular PGA events. But Trevino did not hunt. Bo's storytelling was equal to Trevino's, except that instead of being limited to golf, Bo's stories were set in exotic locales all over the world, from the Arctic to the casinos of Nevada and the jungles of Africa.

Bo was passionate about hunting. In 1962 he bagged a 600-pound forest hog in the Congo. Another time he skipped the Oklahoma City Open to hunt Cape buffalo in East Africa. A favorite Wininger story was about hunting polar bears in the Aleutian Islands, just a few miles from Siberia, when his group met up with a party of Russians. "A blizzard hit and nobody could hunt for two days," said Wininger. "We drank so much coffee with the Russkies we were about to float. And believe me, at forty below zero, all men are created equal."

Wininger was proud of his golf and had the goods to show for it— he won five times on tour. Once he saw his old college coach, OSU's La-bron Harris, and asked about the Muskogee phenom Bob Dickson. "He's awfully good," said Harris. "In fact, he may be the best amateur I ever coached." Wininger did not miss a beat. "Has he ever won four straight conference championships?" asked Wininger, who had. "We may have a war here, coach."

At Quail Creek in 1965, Bo nearly whiffed his opening tee shot, then rebounded for a 69. "Bad lie," explained Bo. The next day he followed with a 70, good enough for a one-stroke lead. "This just proves I can still beat you flat-bellies," he announced to everyone within earshot. "Always could."[10]

Veteran Dave Marr, the 1965 PGA Champion, stood a stroke back of Wininger at 140. But the stagecoach Wininger was riding to the victory circle turned into a pumpkin on Saturday. He bogeyed the last three holes and fell into a tie for sixth, three shots behind Phil Rodgers (72-71-69), the 1958 NCAA Champion from Houston. "My boss is a little mad at me, so I needed this," explained Rodgers, who had a bandage on his nose, still recuperating from a car accident in San Diego the week before. "He told me I'd been playing so bad he was having a hard time selling my clubs."[11]

But Rodgers faded on Sunday, leaving the door open for Jack Rule, a veteran from Waterloo, Iowa. Perhaps there were professional reasons why Jack Nicklaus waited until 1966 to make his debut at the Oklahoma City Open. Or perhaps he got word that "the Ruler," would be in the field. In 1956 at Williamstown, Massachusetts, Nicklaus had had his best chance to win the U.S. Junior but had been upset by Rule in the semifinals. Later that year, at the seventy-two-hole U.S. Jaycee Junior, Rule tied Nicklaus in regulation, then defeated him the next day in a playoff, 69 to 71.

When Rule overcame an early triple bogey on Sunday at Quail Creek to shoot 70, he had his second and final win on the PGA Tour. A year later, Rule returned to Oklahoma, putting croquet style, soon to disappear from the tour.

Noticeably absent from the 1965 Oklahoma City Open was "Champagne" Tony Lema, the stylish player from the San Francisco Bay area. Having grown up in wine country, the son of a laborer, Lema forever endeared himself to sportswriters (and earned a nickname) when he ordered a case of Moët and Chandon delivered to the pressroom following his victory at the 1962 Orange County Open. Bubbly for the scribes became a tradition with Lema any time he finished first. The international press had a taste of his hospitality at St. Andrews, in 1964, when he held off Nicklaus to win the British Open. The champagne flowed and the nickname stuck.

Lema had added incentive for a return visit in 1966—Oklahoma City was his wife's hometown. Lema and Betty Cline were married in 1965. Her mother and stepfather, Mr. and Mrs. A. D. Baxter, lived in Oklahoma City and were huge fans of their son-in-law. To open the 1966 tournament, Lema fired a solid 69.

Even without the hard-charging Arnold Palmer in the field, Palmer having withdrawn because of illness, Lema was a long way from victory. The other two members of golf's big three—Jack Nicklaus and Gary Player—were making their first appearances in Oklahoma City. And Lema had not won in almost two years.

"The quickest way to get Champagne Tony Lema to pop his cork," wrote Doug Todd in the *Daily Oklahoman*, "is to ask the 32-year old professional why he hasn't won a golf tournament in nine months."[12] Lema responded, "I think it's very unfair to say it's been so many months since somebody has won a tournament. If I don't ever win another one, I'm ahead of the game. I've already won far more than I ever thought I would." Then he added: "I hope we have occasion to use some of that champagne pretty darn quick. I've forgotten what the stuff tastes like."

Normally it takes a little good luck to win a golf tournament. And rarely is good luck disguised as a two-stroke penalty. But it worked out that way for Lema. At the fifteenth hole of the second round, Lema drove his ball into an area marked "ground under repair," illegally took a drop at a spot farther from the hole than "within a club length of the nearest point of relief," hit the ensuing shot to within five feet of the hole, and sank the putt for an apparent birdie.

However, after the round, playing partner Ernie Vossler, head pro at Quail Creek, alerted Lema that he had taken an improper drop. Lema agreed, added two strokes to his card, and signed for a 68 instead of 66. Afterward, Lema publicly thanked Vossler for calling attention to the mistake. "I would have been disqualified for signing an incorrect scorecard," Lema said. "It's better to be here in second place than on my way to the next tournament."[13]

Lema's 69-68 start left him four shots off the lead (Johnny Pott, 133), but six ahead of Nicklaus (73-70) and nine ahead of Player (76-70). "Distance means zero on a course like this," groused Nicklaus. "You can't go for the par 5s. You have to use layup shots." On Saturday fourteen players shot in the 60s, none better than Nicklaus's twenty-putt 65. But Tom Weiskopf, Jack's former Ohio State teammate, had 68, his third round in the 60s, to take the lead at 205.

Asked how he was adjusting to life as a professional, the twenty-three-year-old Weiskopf explained, "It's better than college." Like Nicklaus, Weiskopf had attended Ohio State. "I used to literally jump out of windows to get out of class. A women's P.E. bus would pick me up at the corner and take me to the golf course. You know, it was funny—I never got caught. I failed the course, but I never got caught."

Entering the final round, Lema was alone in second at 206, with Nicklaus at 208. Five-time British Open champion Peter Thomson (71-75-65), suffering from what he described as "a bit of nasal catarrh caused by pollen," used eleven putts to shoot 29 on the front. For the first three rounds, the winds of Oklahoma were eerily calm, which suited Lema fine. "If the wind does not blow tomorrow," said Lema, as he left the pressroom on Saturday night, "I'm never coming back. I want to remember Oklahoma just the way it was today."[14]

On Sunday the players had ideal playing conditions, and Lema had the shots to match. "How sweet it is!" he proclaimed, escorting Betty into the pressroom after a final round 65. The champagne flowed and so did Tony. "It gives it some added lustre to win here in my wife's hometown," he said, adding in his best Oklahoma drawl, "in front of all mah kinfolk."[15]

Not only had Lema bettered Palmer and Littler's tournament record by two shots—his six-stroke victory margin over Weiskopf was the biggest on tour all year. Nicklaus finished third. Lema was playing the best golf of his career. He did not make a single bogey in seventy-two holes; his only bauble was the double bogey on Friday. Lema's scores of 69-68-69-65 extended his string of subpar rounds to fourteen.

Lema departed Oklahoma City that night to be on Pit Row the next morning, Memorial Day, at the Indianapolis 500. Vossler had arranged a private plane to take him north. But before he exited the pressroom, Lema had one final remark for the media: "As high as I'm going to be flyin' in a little while, I don't think I'll need an airplane."

Less than two months later, Tony and Betty Lema were dead. On Sunday, July 24, 1966, after the final round of the PGA Championship, the Lemas caught a flight in Akron, Ohio, for a trip to Chicago. Their lives ended in the burning wreckage of a chartered light plane at a suburban Chicago golf course. The 1966 Oklahoma City Open was the last tournament Tony Lema would ever win.

"A group of players had all committed to stay over at Firestone and play the next day in a Pro-Am," recalled Gay Brewer in 1997. "But at the last minute Tony got a better deal to go to Chicago, so he changed his mind. The next morning we all go over to the clubhouse for breakfast and it came over television that Tony Lema had been killed. And he should have been sitting right there with us, having breakfast."

Four years later, in the 1970 British Open at St. Andrews, Doug Sanders, the 1962 Oklahoma City Open champion, arrived at the seventy-second hole leading Jack Nicklaus by one. Suddenly a man in the gallery ran up to Sanders, handed him a white tee, and said, "Tony Lema used this tee when he won the 1964 Open. Would you use it in his honor?" Not wanting to offend the man, and figuring the tee would not make much difference anyway, Sanders agreed. However, he three-putted the hole, fell into a playoff with Nicklaus, and lost the next day, 73-72. Ever since, there have been British golf professionals who will not use a white tee.[16]

The final Oklahoma City Open, held in May of 1967, was won by Miller Barber, nicknamed the "Mysterious Mr. X." Besides his ever-present sunglasses and frequent ingestion of allergy medication, X was a balding but worldly bachelor, who swung a golf club like a man opening an umbrella. To keep expenses down, Barber made his way between Tour stops by driving the cars of players who would rather fly. That is what he was supposed to have done after the 1962 Seattle Open, where he won $10,000 for a hole in one.

"Miller was supposed to drive Jim Ferree's car to Bakersfield," recalled the late Dave Marr. "But he never showed up. He finally surfaced a week later at the next tournament. To this day he won't tell us where he was. All we know is he had a car, $10,000, and a case of Canadian Club that Jimmy Demaret had bought for his dad. When Miller caught up with us there was only one bottle left. That's how Miller got the name the Mysterious Mr. X."[17]

Barber, born in Shreveport, Louisiana, in 1931, learned the game in nearby Texarkana, where he caddied for Byron Nelson and worked at Bryce's Cafeteria. In 1950, Barber enrolled at Texas A&M but later transferred to Arkansas to play on the golf team. Since there were no golf scholarships in those days, he was listed on the Razorback football roster and even tried out for halfback, where one of his teammates was Pat Summerall, who would become an NFL star and network commentator. "Miller got wiped out on one play and came back to the huddle, peering through an earhole in his helmet," Summerall recalled. "He said, 'I gotta find me another game.'"[18]

For the first eight years after turning pro in 1959, Barber managed only one win, at the 1964 Cajun Classic. He had a history of blown opportunities.

At the 1963 Oklahoma City Open, Barber was tied for the lead going into the last hole, with a 15-footer for birdie. He whispered to Dow Finsterwald, "I'm going to lag it."

"What?" said Finsterwald, stunned. "You go for it."

Barber ran the first putt well by the hole and three-putted to finish fourth. When Arnold Palmer heard about it back at the hotel, he congratulated Barber for his courage. Palmer's words took the sting off blowing the tournament, but from that time forward, any time he had a putt to win, Barber kept his thoughts to himself.[19]

At the 1967 Oklahoma City Open, Mr. X sneaked up on the field and birdied the seventy-second hole to tie Gary Player. After two pars in the playoff, he birdied the third and got the victory. Winning at Oklahoma City was like a jumpstart for Mr. X. He went on to win at least one tournament in each of the next eight years.

The last regular PGA Tour event held in Oklahoma City was the 1968 PGA National Team Championship, at Twin Hills and Quail Creek, bringing together 125 two-player teams and featuring players from three eras. Veterans Tommy Bolt and Sam Snead showed up. So did the three dominant players of the 1960s: Nicklaus, Palmer, and Casper. The newly crowned U.S. Open champion Lee Trevino played, as did Chickasha's Orville Moody, who would be the next U.S. Open champion, and Hale Irwin, who would in due course win three U.S. Opens. Oklahoma-born U.S. Amateur champions Bob Dickson and Labron Harris Jr. teamed together.

Palmer and Nicklaus—the defending champions and obviously the team to beat—opened with a 64. But round two, at Quail Creek, derailed their chances. They shot even par—two bogeys and two birdies. The Hill brothers, Mike and Dave, led after each of the first two rounds (62-65), but they deflated in the third, at Quail Creek, with a birdie-free 73. That allowed Irwin–Dale Douglass (68-65-65) and Rives McBee–Monty Kaser (67-64-67) to share the top spot going into the final round.

Enter Kentuckian Bobby Nichols and George Archer, the California cowboy, who were lurking two strokes back (65-66-69). Nichols, the 1964 PGA Champion, said later that Quail Creek owed him one. In the

1965 Oklahoma City Open, Nichols had opened up a three-shot lead but made quadruple bogey at the seventy-first hole. On the last day of the National Team Championship, Nichols and Archer extracted some measure of revenge. While others found trouble, Nichols and Archer shot a 65, earning a three-shot victory.

After 1968, the regular PGA Tour did not return to Oklahoma City. At least nine other cities would outbid Oklahoma City the next year for the prized schedule slot the week after Colonial. The Atlanta Open got the late May slot in 1969. But the pros did return to Quail Creek five times as members of the Senior PGA Tour. In 1987 Chi Chi Rodriguez captured the Silver Pages Classic. At the Southwestern Bell Classic, from 1988 to 1990, the winners were Gary Player, Bobby Nichols, and Jimmy Powell.

And then there was the tragedy at Oklahoma City's Murrah Federal Building, in April of 1995, which shocked the nation to its soul. The bombing killed 169 persons, the worst act of domestic terrorism in U.S. history. Included among the 169 dead were fifteen children, in two separate day-care facilities. It was two months before the last surviving child came home from the hospital. Four months after the bombing, the Senior pros returned to Quail Creek for a tournament to help raise funds to rebuild a child-care center.

Dave Stockton, winner of the 1970 PGA at Southern Hills, and Quail Creek professional Larry Fryer enlisted pros to play in the tournament. The Heartland Pro-Am, held on August 29, 1995, drew twenty-eight professionals and 112 amateurs, more than half of whom were from out of state. Six thousand spectators turned out to watch. Amateurs paid a minimum of $1,500 to play; most contributed more. The teams captained by Palmer and Trevino raised another $50,000.

The celebrity participants included singers Vince Gill and Toby Keith, Oklahoma City Mayor Ron Norick, and U.S. Senator Don Nickles.

ESPN's Jim Kelly emceed the auction and post-play awards. Organizers of the Burnet Senior Classic in Coon Rapids, Minnesota, secured sponsors' donations of auction goods. American Airlines helped defray travel costs and Southwestern Bell bought tee times. More than four hundred people volunteered for three hundred marshal spots. The auction included auto-graphed baseballs donated by Binger native and Hall of Famer Johnny Bench, firehats belonging to rescuers at the bombing, Ryder Cup posters, and other items. All told, the event raised $400,000, which was presented to Jim Everest of the YMCA Heartland Child Development Center.

The PGA tour pros who participated were Jim Albus, Isao Aoki, George Archer, Miller Barber, Homero Blancas, Charles Coody, Bruce Devlin, Bob Dickson, Dale Douglass, Al Geiberger, Larry Gilbert, Simon Hobday, Tony Jacklin, Don January, Robert Landers, Larry Laoretti, Rives McBee, Bob Murphy, Bobby Nichols, Mike McCullough, Arnold Palmer, Jimmy Powell, Art Proctor, Dave Stockton, Rocky Thompson, Lee Trevino, Bob Tway, and Scott Verplank.

SEVEN
Women

"Where's the Babe?" was the question posed in the lead paragraph of a *Daily Oklahoman* article in June of 1949. One year before the founding of the Ladies Professional Golf Association, and three years after Babe Didrikson Zaharias won the U.S. Women's Amateur at Southern Hills in Tulsa, the Women's Western Open brought together the top competitors in women's professional golf—a match play championship and one of the three major golf championships for women.

The Women's Western, which also invited amateur players, was the first women's major, begun in 1930. It rotated on an annual basis among member clubs of the Women's Western Golf Association, based in Golf, Illinois. The other two major championships for women were the U.S. Women's Open, first played in 1946, and the Titleholders Championship, which dated to 1937 and was held next door to the Masters, at Augusta Country Club.

In June of 1949, the Women's Western had come to Oklahoma City Golf and Country Club for the first time. It was also the first open golf championship for women ever held in Oklahoma. Didrikson Zaharias, who had recently turned pro for the second time (in 1935, because of Didrikson's baseball and basketball earnings, the U.S. Golf Association had rescinded her amateur status for eleven years), had been married to pro wrestler George Zaharias for twelve years.

Ten months after baseball legend George Herman Ruth's death in August of 1948, the nickname "Babe" lost none of its lustre when it referred to Didrikson Zaharias. Her personality was every bit as engaging as Ruth's, and her records spoke for themselves. As noted (see chapter 4), Didrikson had won a record seventeen amateur golf tournaments in a row and already owned Olympic records in the javelin and 80-meter hurdles. She had been named the Associated Press Woman Athlete of the Year six times.

And what a gallery draw Didrikson Zaharias had been for the women's pro game—a fact not lost on executives at Oklahoma City local affiliate WKY-TV. Four years before a professional men's tournament was first televised (the 1953 Tam O'Shanter in Chicago), WKY televised the 1949 Women's Western for three hours on each of the first three days. It was estimated that the matches were available to some three thousand households in range of the midday signal. The station did not televise the semifinals but aired the final match on Saturday. Even WKY Radio got in the act. For the final, WKY had roving reporters using walkie-talkies to broadcast the action to listeners on both AM and FM.

One Oklahoma City department store had been selling tickets for months, promising Oklahomans a chance to witness the golf skills of world's greatest female athlete at a course designed by Perry Maxwell. Even Maxwell was interested. He interrupted work on a project at Bayou de Siard Country Club in Monroe, Louisiana, to return to Oklahoma and see women's pro golf make its first visit to one of his courses.

Oklahoma City Golf and Country Club head professional Harrell

Butler, apparently having played in his share of Pro-Ams, wrote a humor column for the *Oklahoman*, advising members of the gallery on how to best follow the action with their five-dollar tickets (good for the week), keeping in mind some simple rules. "Do not wander aimlessly about the course," cautioned Butler. "It is dangerous in the fairways. Keep out of the sand traps and never walk across the putting greens."[1]

Didrikson Zaharias showed up on Sunday afternoon and immediately hit the course for a practice round, teaming with Marilynn Smith (the newly crowned National Intercollegiate Women's champion from Wichita), against pro Betty Bush of Hammond, Indiana, and reigning U.S. Amateur champion Grace Lenczyk of Newington, Connecticut. They played to a tie.

The next day, with WKY cameras rolling (and no qualifying exemptions for anybody), 104 players, including forty-two Oklahomans, tried to qualify for thirty-two spots into the title flight. Three Oklahoma amateurs made it: Margaret Williford of Ponca City, Patti Blanton of Enid, and Mrs. Earl Rumbaugh of Oklahoma City. Besides Smith, who turned professional the week of the tournament, the best-known qualifiers were amateurs Lenczyk, Betsy Rawls, Beverly Hanson, Polly Riley, and pros Didrikson Zaharias, Peggy Kirk, Louise Suggs, Bettye Mims White, and Oklahoman Betty Jameson. Lenczyk was qualifying medalist with a 66.

If there were doubters, the matches proved that the women could play. The Babe boomed some mammoth tee balls to polish off Lenczyk, 2 & 1, in the round of sixteen. At the dogleg right, par-4 second hole, Didrikson Zaharias took dead aim at the green and hammered one 317 yards to within eight feet of the pin. She dropped the putt for an eagle.

The next day Zaharias met up with Fort Worth amateur Polly Riley, who already had the Babe's number. A year earlier in the finals of the Texas Open, Riley had inflicted the worst defeat in Babe's illustrious twenty-year career, winning 10 & 9. What did Riley do for an encore? In an Oklahoma City quarterfinal match witnessed by fifteen hundred people, she defeated the Babe again, 3 & 1. "I was pretty terrible, wasn't I?" was about all the Babe could say.[2]

The semifinals matched Suggs against Patty Berg, Riley against Jameson. Suggs and Jameson advanced to face each other the final. Elizabeth May Jameson, a founder and charter LPGA Hall of Famer, was born in Norman, Oklahoma, on May 9, 1919. As a tournament golfer, she exhibited a soft politeness and deliberate manner but no lack of self-confidence. Jameson played at her own distinct pace, which some described as methodical. But they said the same thing about Ben Hogan. Like Hogan, Jameson was rarely intimidated by fellow competitors.

Once, when Jameson was in her sixties, she was informed that a chapter about her would be included in a book alongside chapters about Hogan, Byron Nelson, Lloyd Mangrum, Jimmy Demaret, Babe Didrikson Zaharias, Lee Trevino, and Kathy Whitworth. "So you're in good company," the author assured her. "Well," said Jameson, "so are *they*."[3]

Jameson took up golf in 1930, at age eleven. Two years later she won the Texas Public Links Championship. Even though her competitive professional career spanned just eleven years, Jameson established a brilliant amateur record between 1932 and 1945. "I think Betty had one of the best golf swings I've ever seen," Hall of Famer Berg said in 1999. "She was a great player with a great record, who did very much to help the LPGA get where it is today."[4]

Jameson's legacy to golf was unique. Until the LPGA Hall of Fame revised its membership criteria in 1999, Jameson, portrayed in the *1999 LPGA Media Guide* as "the first golf glamour girl," was the only Hall of Fame member with less than thirty professional victories. She had

thirty. thirteen.

In 1967, perhaps with an eye toward the turnstile mentality of the College Football and Pro Football halls of fame (their combined membership now approaches a thousand), the LPGA set stringent guidelines to ensure that entry into the LPGA Hall of Fame would be one of the most difficult achievements in sports: "A player must have been a member, in good standing, of the LPGA for 10 consecutive years and have won at least 30 official events, including two major championships, or 35 official events with one major championship, or 40 official events exclusive of major championships."[5]

So how was Jameson, with thirteen professional victories, voted into the LPGA Hall of Fame? A cofounder of the LPGA, Jameson was elected to the Hall as a charter member in 1951, before specific entry criteria were established, based in large measure on her brilliant amateur record and victories in the majors. In addition to the 1932 Texas Public Links, Jameson won the 1934 Southern Amateur, four Texas Women's Amateurs, two Women's Trans-Nationals, two Women's Western Amateurs, two Women's Western Opens, two U.S. Women's Amateurs, and the 1947 U.S. Women's Open at Starmount Forest Country Club in Greensboro, North Carolina. The U.S. Open, U.S. Amateur, and Women's Western are considered major championships, giving Jameson five career majors.

If she had not turned professional in 1945, Jameson's amateur record might have rivaled that of Bobby Jones. Giving up her amateur status was a decision she later regretted. "That was the wrong time to turn pro," Jameson said. "I could have had a much more exciting finish to my career. I couldn't play in the British [Amateur], a tournament I really wanted to win, and I couldn't play against Babe anymore. I had such a hot, glorious, wonderful time as an amateur. Those were the sweetest days of my life."[6] It was after Jameson turned professional that Didrikson Zaharias won seventeen consecutive amateur tournaments.

At the time of her eightieth birthday, Jameson lived in Boynton Beach, Florida, spending her days painting and reading poetry. In the finals of the 1949 Women's Western Open at Oklahoma City Golf and Country Club, Jameson never had command of the match nor control of her golf swing, losing to Suggs, 5 & 4.

Five years would pass before women's professional golf returned to Oklahoma, this time for the 1954 Ardmore Women's Open. Held at Dornick Hills Country Club, it was underwritten by Waco and Opie Turner. Like her husband, Opie Turner enjoyed being generous. The $5,000 purse, plus bonuses of $7,200, made the 1954 Ardmore Women's Open the second richest women's golf event ever held. (The George S. May–sponsored 1954 Women's World Championship at Tam O'Shanter Country Club in Chicago paid out $12,000.)

Whereas only six professionals entered the 1949 Women's Western in Oklahoma City, by 1954 the LPGA Tour had been in existence for four years. Instead of just a handful of pros competing against amateurs in a match play contest, the 1954 Ardmore Women's Open featured twenty pros for a seventy-two-hole stroke play competition. Even Babe Zaharias returned, though in rehabilitation from cancer surgery that in less than two years would claim her life.

Zaharias struggled to an opening-round 82, but her companion, fellow Texan Betty Dodd, shot a one-under-par 73 and was the only player in red numbers. Patty Berg led after two rounds, Jacqueline Pung after three. Berg held on for the victory, inspiring in the *Oklahoman* some prose worthy of sportswriting legend Grantland Rice: "Patty Berg, who puts the pressure on like a mustard plaster and keeps it there until something gives, won the first annual Ardmore Women's Open with a magnificent rally."[7] Berg won $1,100 plus bonuses of $687. As her husband had done a few months earlier for Byron Nelson, Opie presented Babe Zaharias with her own palomino horse, as a gift to the most remarkable female athlete of the twentieth century.

Afterward, in a gesture of appreciation to the Turners, Zaharias and Dodd jammed on the No. 9 green. "Miss Dodd played the git-fiddle, sang, and acted as master of ceremonies," reported the *Oklahoman*, "while Babe played the mouth-organ. Before the act was over, Betsy Rawls, a Phi Beta Kappa from the University of Texas, was singing cowboy songs with a lonesome note, and petite Ann Breault, of Chicago, a former nightclub entertainer, was telling jokes. It was a show that Mr. and Mrs. Turner entertained with zest and the entire crowd was still on the grounds at nightfall."[8]

As it turned out, the 1954 Ardmore Women's Open was the last professional tour event held at Dornick Hills. A year later the LPGA returned to Oklahoma but this time to Oklahoma City's Lincoln Park Golf Course, for a fifty-four-hole affair called the Oklahoma Golfiesta.

In addition to fifteen of the top LPGA Tour players and international player Fay Crocker of Montevideo, Uruguay, the starting field boasted seven amateurs, including three-time Oklahoma amateur title holder Margaret Williford of Ponca City; Lincoln Park champion Lucille Dunson; long-hitting Linda Melton of Oklahoma City; junior players Jill Kreager and Susan Casey of Tulsa; and fourteen-year-old Beth Stone of Muskogee. Invited but unable to attend were Babe Didrikson Zaharias (hospitalized with cancer); national junior champion Wiffi Smith of LaCanada, California; reigning Oklahoma girls' and women's champion Betsy Cullen of Tulsa; and na-

"MISS DODD PLAYED THE GIT-FIDDLE, SANG, AND ACTED AS MASTER OF CEREMONIES WHILE BABE PLAYED THE MOUTH-ORGAN. BEFORE THE ACT WAS OVER, BETSY RAWLS . . . WAS SINGING COWBOY SONGS WITH A LONESOME NOTE, AND PETITE ANN BREAULT, . . . A FORMER NIGHTCLUB ENTER-TAINER, WAS TELLING JOKES. IT WAS A SHOW THAT MR. AND MRS. TURNER ENTERTAINED WITH ZEST AND THE ENTIRE CROWD WAS STILL ON THE GROUNDS AT NIGHTFALL."

tional junior quarterfinalist Judy Bell of Wichita, Kansas, who would one day become president of the United States Golf Association.

Despite a final round 80, Louise Suggs rode out a brutal duststorm and captured her second trophy from Oklahoma in six years, by three strokes, holding off Alice Bauer (whose caddie was Oklahoma City amateur Jack Ritter), and Hawaiian Jacqueline Pung. At the conclusion of the 1955 Golfiesta, LPGA officials indicated they would like to return to Oklahoma City in 1956.

As it turned out, a resourceful community leader in southwestern Oklahoma convinced the LPGA to come to Lawton instead. In 1956, Lawton Municipal Golf Course probably did not seem to be an obvious candidate as a potential LPGA tournament site. On land adjacent to the municipal airport, the golf course had been designed and built in 1955 almost single-handedly by a Texas transplant named Jack Greer, whose previous claim to architectural fame was the bowling alley on the outskirts of Lawton.

"He had a small physique, but was always busy, and tough as they come," recalled Lawton Municipal assistant pro Leon "Spanky" Moody, who won the 1954 Oklahoma state high school championship at El Reno and whose first cousin Orville, from Chickasha, would become a U.S. Open champion (see chapter 10). Leon's father, Dale Moody, had built the greens at Quail Creek (Oklahoma City) and rebuilt the ones at Southern Hills (Tulsa). He also assisted Greer in the construction at Lawton Municipal.

"Even today, I'd put these greens up against any in the state," Leon said in December of 1998. "And they've never been replaced." Moody said good drainage was the key. He explained that when Greer originally agreed to build the golf course, the land was strewn with granite and sandstone boulders left over from the ice age. Instead of hauling them off,

Greer and Dale Moody scalloped out greensites, then filled them with the boulders. Covered with fill dirt and sand, the boulders created an excellent seed bed. "The bentgrass on these greens has roots longer than your arm," Moody said. "Without the boulders the sand would have compressed, collecting water, eventually rotting the roots."

In the same city as the Perry Maxwell–designed Lawton Country Club, and with the Fort Sill course nearby, Greer needed someone to proclaim the municipal course satisfactory for professional golf. To do the honors, he called on a friend from Fort Worth. In the spring of 1956, three years after winning the last of his nine majors, Ben Hogan played an exhibition over the 7,112-yard Lawton Municipal Course, shooting 72. Greer and Hogan had known each other for years and Hogan said afterward he was delighted to help out an old friend.

The fifty-four-hole Lawton Open, in late October, would close out the 1956 LPGA season. It was the twenty-seventh tournament of the year and twenty-three pros were entered. Among the amateurs in the field were future University of Tulsa women's coach Dale Fleming; Dottie McNamara of Fort Sill; Joan Godlove and Irene Runyan of Lawton; Lucille Dunson of Oklahoma City; Beth Stone of Muskogee; and Jewel Morris of Tulsa.

Playing from the men's tees (6,977 yards), at men's par (72), and using Lawton city champion Jim Shaw as her caddie, Betty Dodd put together rounds of 74-73-67, to beat runner-up Patty Berg by five shots. Her two-under-par total of 214 was good enough for the $880 first prize and was Dodd's first win as a professional.

"No doubt city champ Shaw deserved a lot of credit," wrote Tom Wright in the *Lawton Constitution*. "Besides clubbing Dodd expertly, Shaw lined up putts and Dodd rammed home two long birdies on the front nine. Remember that Shaw caddied for Hogan when he carded 72. Hogan didn't consult Jim while lining his putts. With all due respect to the master, his putter was much more contrary than Betty's."[9]

Then Wright told of the champion's ties to Lawton: "Dodd took up golf at Fort Sill, while her father, Colonel Francis T. Dodd, was stationed at the artillery center. Betty's first lessons came under pro Bob Mayer. A couple years back, we watched Billy Maxwell literally burn up the Fort Sill course with four great rounds in the 60s. And a few months ago we watched the incomparable Ben Hogan breeze around the Municipal layout in a routine 72—despite high winds and a spattering of rain.

"But neither of them hit any better golf shots than Dodd. You just don't leave much room for error when you require only 67 shots to play 18 holes."

Dodd's 67 broke Ab Justice's course record by one stroke. The win came almost a month to the day after the death of her companion, Babe Didrikson Zaharias.

Three and a half years after the longest win streak in college football history began, and six months before it would end, Minnesota pro Patricia Jane Berg showed up for the second Lawton Open—in April of 1957—with a few childhood memories of the streak's architect. Between October 10, 1953, and November 16, 1957, the Bud Wilkinson–coached University of Oklahoma Sooners won forty-seven football games in a row.

"Even as kids, it was obvious Bud was going to be a great leader," recalled Berg from their days as youngsters in Minneapolis. Berg played alongside Wilkinson, on her brother Herman's back-lot football team, nicknamed the "50th Street Tigers."[10] Berg said the Tigers were so tough that they had one play—called 22-Split—in which they all took off in any direction they wanted. "But we never lost a game," Berg reminded. "Only teeth."[11]

In the 1957 Lawton Open, Marlene Hagge overcame a two-stroke penalty the final round, when her caddie stepped on her ball, to defeat

Betsy Rawls by three shots. The purse, underwritten by Lawton area merchants, was $5,000, of which Hagge earned $880.

By 1958, tournament founder Greer was due for a break with the weather. The first two Lawton Opens had been deluged. The joke in Comanche County was: "Jack Greer doesn't need any gadgets to produce rain. All he has to do is put $5,000 on the line for a golf tournament."[12]

For two years, all profits from the tournament were funneled back into the Lawton Business Club's fund for cerebral palsy victims. So it was poetic justice that in May of 1958, during what turned out to be the Lawton Open's final year, the weather turned chamber-of-commerce perfect. Beverly Hanson, who would win two major championships during her LPGA career, set the Lawton Open tournament record (212), beating Marlene Hagge by three strokes.

"ALL THE 105-POUND CREED DID WAS TOUR THE LONG AND TREACHEROUS LAYOUT IN 74 BLOWS TO TURN THE FACES OF THE 29 VISITING PROFESSIONALS A BRIGHT RED."

Women's pro golf had run its course in Lawton after three years, but a name already familiar to Oklahomans was ready to pick up where Greer left off. By late summer of 1958, Waco and Opie Turner had built their dream course in Burneyville and had contracted with the LPGA for a tournament at their Love County property. The LPGA Tour rolled into Burneyville the last week in August of 1958.

For the Turners, who insisted on inviting amateurs to participate in their tournaments, it was fitting that a nonprofessional, Clifford Ann Creed, from Opelousas, Louisiana, grabbed the first-day headlines. "All the 105-pound Creed did was tour the long and treacherous layout in 74 blows," reported Vernon Snell, "to turn the faces of the 29 visiting professionals a bright red."[13]

However, Creed used up all her red numbers the first day. She shot 83 in round two and thereafter the tournament evolved into a shoot-out between the veteran Louise Suggs and twenty-three-year-old Califor-nian Mickey Wright, who would rewrite all the LPGA records. Playing the course at 6,631 yards, to a par of 78, Wright toured the last two rounds in 71-71, to win by five shots over Suggs. On Saturday, Wright had eleven birdies for eighteen holes. It was Wright's sixth victory as a professional. Amazingly, she would win seventy-six more times before her retirement in 1969. After Sunday's round, she said it was the first time she had ever played eighteen holes without a bogey.

The LPGA's second and final year at Burneyville was the 1959 Opie Turner Open. Six amateurs were in the field: Patty David and Jeannie Thompson of Tulsa; sisters Jean and Joan Ashley of Chanute, Kansas; Vir-ginia Edwards; and a state high school champion from Oklahoma City's Northeast High School—Sue Maxwell—who during the next fifteen years would become one of the great champions in the history of American golf.

Once again, Louise Suggs, already twice a winner in Oklahoma, fin-ished runner-up at Burneyville, this time to a South Carolina native destined for eight major titles as well as the LPGA Hall of Fame—Elizabeth Earle Rawls. The Opie was Betsy Rawls's tenth triumph as a pro and worth $3,737. Opie Turner had paid out $6,515 in unofficial bonuses, plus the $7,500 purse, making hers the top-dollar tournament on the 1959 LPGA Tour.

After a two-year hiatus, women's pro golf returned to Oklahoma in May of 1962, at Muskogee Country Club, another Maxwell course, which within a decade would play host to the U.S. Women's Open (see chapter 10). From the outset, the city of Muskogee and Muskogee Country Club had the feel of a site well suited to host a national championship one day. Opened in 1924, the course was awesome, cut in among the hardwoods north of downtown. There were rolling hills, undulating greens, and con-venient viewing areas for spectators. The course wound its way back to the clubhouse four times in eighteen holes.

Ninety Muskogee business owners put up a minimum of a hundred dollars apiece to underwrite the 1962 Muskogee Civitan Open. Any profits were earmarked for improvements to park and recreation facilities in Muskogee. The LPGA determined that the women would play it from the men's championship tees: 6,665 yards, par 70.

In 1962 interest was heightened locally by the entry of hometown favorite Beth Stone. Stone, the 1960 Oklahoma Women's Amateur champion, returned to Muskogee on the heels of a solid rookie season: twenty-third on the LPGA money list and a scoring average of 78.76. So far in 1962, she had made the cut at every tournament she had entered. It would be Stone's first time to play as a professional in her hometown.

Oklahoma amateurs in the first Muskogee Civitan Open field included Nelrose Gabriel, Lila Hall, Jeannie Thompson, Gwen Brownlee, Roberta Dierken, Shirley McCoy, Denah Gills, Mary Perrin, Margaret Williford, Jill Herndon, Jackie Riggs, Dinah Dills, Coralee Savage, Dottie Biddick, and Gertrude Marshall. At Tuesday's Pro-Am, Marlene Hagge set the course record for women from the men's tees: 68. But once the tournament began, Hagge drifted back in the pack.

As it turned out, the Muskogee Civitan Open was the final victory ever for the great Patty Berg. The first president of the LPGA, Berg arrived at Muskogee as a golf legend. She had already won fifty-seven official LPGA events in her twenty-two-year professional career, eighty-one events if you counted professional and amateur wins combined. Berg's fifteen major professional championship victories set a women's record that still stands, second only among all golfers to Jack Nicklaus's eighteen.

By May of 1962, Berg had turned forty-four, and it had been two years since her last victory. Perhaps sensing the end of an era, the *Oklahoman*'s Wallis interviewed Berg after the third round, while she practiced one pitch shot after another.

WW: Why did you turn professional?

PB: Golf was my hobby. There was a great field opening up for exhibitions and I felt that a tour for women was sure to come. Golf has no age limit. It is not restricted to one sex. It is a physical fitness program and a health tonic. Nothing else opens so many doors to new and important friendships. That and because golf was one game which a woman could be the player and not the spectator.

WW: What's the real secret of good golf?

PB: There's a big difference between the will to win and the wish to win. Players have to master the game until there isn't a flaw left. If one flaw is left, it will come out when the pressure is highest. And faith is important. If you've eliminated the flaws, have the courage to have faith in yourself.[14]

The next day Berg's short game practice paid off. After a poor tee shot at the par-4 fourteenth, and a worse second, she played her 3-iron to the back fringe. From there Berg holed out for par. She went on to shoot 73, for a 290 total and a two-stroke victory over Ruth Jessen and Shirley Englehorn. The 1962 Muskogee Civitan Open was Berg's fifty-eighth and final win on the LPGA Tour.

The following May, at the second Muskogee Open, Mickey Wright did her best Jack Nicklaus imitation and overpowered the field by eight strokes. "This is one of the best rounds I've ever played," Wright said after her final-round 72. For Wright, it was the fourth of thirteen Tour victories in 1963, setting an LPGA record.

At Muskogee, the LPGA enforced its pace of play guidelines: three players—Muskogee's own Beth Stone, Judy Kimball, and eventual runner-up Marilynn Smith—were penalized two strokes, during the third round, for slow play. "We did what we thought we had to do," said tournament committee member Marlene Hagge. "Nobody is going to agree 100 percent."[15]

A year later Susie Maxwell, the reigning Oklahoma Amateur champion, chose the 1964 Muskogee Open for her professional debut. She did not disappoint anyone. Maxwell was joined at Muskogee by another newcomer on the Tour, African-American tennis star Althea Gibson, who broke color barriers in both tennis and golf. Earlier that spring Gibson, winner of Wimbledon and the U.S. Tennis Open in both 1956 and 1958, became the first African-American member of the LPGA Tour.

A prodigious driver of the golf ball, Gibson struggled around the greens. Her week at Muskogee (79-80-81) epitomized her seven years on tour. She never played golf to the brilliance of her tennis. Gibson's best finish ever was a playoff loss to Mary Mills, at the 1970 Len Immke Buick Open in Columbus, Ohio.

Muskogee's Stone also returned in 1964 and was tied for the lead after an opening-round 73. Stone, a week shy of her twenty-fourth birthday, eventually tied for eighth. A week earlier, in an effort to improve her concentration, she had allowed herself to be hypnotized prior to the St. Louis Open. She then had her best showing as a professional, winning $755, followed by the top-ten finish at Muskogee.

Amateurs who qualified for the 1964 Muskogee Civitan Open included former state champions Dale McNamara and Linda Morse; Susan Basolo, Nelrose Gabriel, Jackie Riggs, Martha D'Amico, Suzzi Friels, Kathy Sheets, Suzanne Willis, Dottie McNamara, Jay Sheppard, and Mickey Ryser. In a encore performance of her action the year before, the spotlight shone once again on Mickey Wright, the greatest LPGA player in history.

Even though the tournament was shortened from seventy-two to fifty-four holes, Wright actually played better than in 1963. Instead of an eight-stroke margin of victory, she won by nine. It was Wright's fifty-third victory as a professional and the first of eleven times she won in 1964. Wright's post-tournament comments lauded the play of Maxwell, who finished in sixth place, thirteen strokes behind Wright. Wright compared Maxwell's professional debut to her own in 1955, when she tied for fourth.

Susie Maxwell and Perry Maxwell were not related, but there were similarities. Perry Maxwell's courses seemed ideal for major championship golf, and so did Susie Maxwell's golf game. Born in Pasadena, California, on July 22, 1941, Susie Maxwell first came to Oklahoma as a teenager in the 1950s. At the age of fifteen, while a student at Oklahoma City's Northeast High School, Maxwell took up golf. Within a few months, she won the first of three Oklahoma State High School championships, followed by three consecutive Oklahoma City Women's Amateurs. For her golf teacher she found a perfect match. "I fell in love with her, as everybody else did," recalled U. C. Ferguson, Maxwell's teaching pro at Lincoln Park. "She practiced all day long. She practiced her short game an awful lot. She earned her success."[16]

An often-told story is that one day Susie was riding her horse around the perimeter of Lincoln Park when she wandered near one of the greens. When Ferguson heard about it, he made an offer to Susie: if she would keep her horse off the course, U. C. would teach her to play golf. "Fergie definitely was the instigator of my career," Maxwell Berning told John Rohde of the *Daily Oklahoman*. "He was simple with the golf swing. He taught us how to swing the golf club, not hit the golf ball. That was his secret."[17]

In 1960, Maxwell attended Oklahoma City University on a Golf Incorporated Scholarship, where she played on the men's golf team. "Both my brother Roger and I received scholarships," Maxwell Berning recalled in a 2000 interview. "He attended Oklahoma State and I attended Oklahoma City University. At OCU I played on the men's golf team. Our coach —make that our cheerleader—was Abe Lemons, whom they borrowed from the basketball department. One of my first college tournaments was at Kansas University, where Abe entered me into the tournament as 'S. Maxwell.' The KU coach wanted to know what 'S' stood for. Abe said 'Sam' would do and that was my nickname all through college."

At the 1965 Muskogee Open, on the day after the Kathy Whitworth–led team of W. S. Dandridge, Calvin Moore, and Tom Gafford won the Pro-Am, Maxwell, the still winless 1964 LPGA Rookie of the Year playing out of Southern Hills, fired an opening round 71, followed by a 72. Entering the final round of the fifty-four-hole event, Maxwell was deadlocked with Kathy Cornelius, while Wright, the best player on the Tour, was two strokes behind.

With a gallery of fifteen hundred looking on, Maxwell seized the moment. By the ninth hole she had made three birdies and opened up a four-shot lead. Maxwell won by five for her first victory on the LPGA Tour. One month later, on June 13, she struck again, this time at what prior to 1960 had been designated a major championship, the Women's Western Open, at Beverly Country Club in Chicago. She shot four under for the championship and earned her second victory as a professional.

Maxwell went winless in 1966 but won twice more in 1967. In June of 1968, Susie Maxwell married Dale Berning. For a wedding gift, Dale bought her a classic 1912 Maxwell Roadster.

Going into the 1968 U.S. Women's Open, at Moselem Springs Golf Club in Fleetwood, Pennsylvania, LPGA Tour members were still smarting from the year before. In 1967 at Hot Springs, Virginia, a nineteen-year-old amateur from France, Catherine Lacoste, had shocked the best female professionals in American golf, winning the U.S. Women's Open by two shots. As it turned out, Lacoste's closest pursuers were two Oklahomans: Maxwell and Beth Stone.

At Moselem Springs, Maxwell Berning opened with a 69 and followed it with rounds of 73-76-71, for a plus-five total of 289 and a wire-to-wire victory. At that time, her final-round 71 set the record for the lowest final-round U.S. Women's Open score ever posted by the champion. Mickey Wright, who closed with a 68, finished second, three shots back. Lacoste tied for thirteenth.

"Susie has marvelous concentration," Wright said after the final round. "She is a good trouble player and can get the ball down from anywhere, if she has a swing." Asked what she would do with the $5,000 winner's check, Maxwell Berning remembered her new roadster. "My husband likes to collect antiques," she replied. "I'm going to buy him a trailer to pull the car."[18]

By the time the 1972 U.S. Women's Open came around, Maxwell Berning had added two more LPGA victories to her resumé, and she and Dale had begun a family. They had traveled some twenty thousand miles in the previous twelve months, in a mobile home.

Daughter Robin was nineteen months old when the first round teed off, on June 29, at Winged Foot Golf Club in Mamaroneck, New York. Maxwell Berning opened with a fat 79, which put her in thirtieth place, seven strokes behind leader Shirley Englehorn. Champions do not always win, but they seldom panic. In the second round, her mastery of the greens yielded a 73, the best score of the day.

"I know the greens here and she was taking advantage of what I know," said her caddie, Russ Barton, whose number Susie drew out of a fishbowl. "I guess two heads are better than one." Added Maxwell Berning: "These greens are tricky. Russ knows them like a book."[19] However, the third round was a setback. She made triple-bogey eight at the twelfth and ballooned to a 76. Going into the final round Maxwell Berning was four behind Mississippi pro Pam Barnett.

Then she resorted to a strategy that had worked nicely seven years earlier at the Muskogee Civitan Open: in a tight match, make birdies. Maxwell Berning posted 34 going out, the lowest front nine of the day. At the turn, she was one stroke out of the lead, with Barnett in her crosshairs.

Then Maxwell Berning bogied hole No. 10 and No. 15 and nearly blew the tournament. But at Winged Foot East's famed 200-yard, par-3 seventeenth, with the tournament on the line, Susie Maxwell Berning reached for the golf club that hung for many years afterward on a wall in U. C. Ferguson's home—a cherry-colored Macgregor Tommy Armour driver, model 845.

"To get home," Susie explained, when asked later why she used the driver at the par-3 hole. "I let it go."[20] Not only did the shot find the putting surface—she sank the 20-foot putt for a birdie two.

A half hour later, Barnett faced the same shot. Nursing a one-stroke lead, she selected her 4-wood, which was not enough club. She came up well short of the green and failed to save par. The result was Barnett's sixth bogey of the round. Sitting on the clubhouse terrace, Maxwell Berning had taken the lead.

Under a blistering sun, Barnett needed birdie three at the last to tie. She made four. Maxwell Berning's 299 total was a stroke better than the score Barnett shared with two Texans—Judy Rankin of Midland and Kathy Ahern of Denton. Maxwell Berning had claimed her second U.S. Open title in five years. During the championship her tee-to-green play was razor sharp. She hit 65 of 72 greens in regulation figures. Decades later she rememberred the tee shot at Winged Foot's seventeenth hole as the greatest shot of her career.

"In the winter of 1967, Fergie gave me the driver I used to hit that shot—it was his personal driver," Maxwell Berning recalled. "He said with no hesitation that he knew I could use it and that it would fit me. As always, he was right. For the three Opens and every victory for the rest of my career, that golf club never left my bag." Maxwell Berning's opening 79 remains the highest first-round score ever posted by the winner of a major men's or women's stroke-play championship.

One year later, Maxwell Berning defended her title at the Country Club of Rochester in Rochester, New York. July 22, 1973, was her thirty-second birthday and the final round of the twenty-eighth U.S. Women's Open. This time, the contest was not even close. Riding a wave of confidence befitting a two-time Open champion, Maxwell Berning not only putted in an unorthodox fashion, with her right toeline positioned against her left instep—she used an old putter that Dale had bought three months earlier, for five dollars, in an Oklahoma City pawn shop.

She did not miss a fairway during the final round and managed to save par six of seven times from greenside bunkers. Her 290 total, two over par, bettered runners-up Gloria Ehret of Dallas and Shelley Hamlin of Fresno, California, by five shots. Amateur Anne Quast Sander, of Seattle, was solo fourth. When Susie came off the eighteenth green, Dale was carrying Robin, now aged three, and some roses to greet his wife. The U.S. Women's Open Championship Cup was hers for the third time, with the winner's share of $6,000 from the $40,000 purse—indeed a happy birthday.

"My trap play saved me today," said Maxwell Berning, who had used a 1935 Wilson R-90 sand wedge, also a gift from U. C. Ferguson. As she had done with the Tommy Armour driver, she later returned the sand wedge to her teacher, who until he passed away in September 1999 proudly showed it to anyone who asked.

Maker of masterpieces:
Ardmore banker
turned architect
Perry Duke Maxwell
in his element (circa 1935).
Courtesy *South Central Golf.*

LEFT: Betty Jameson, a native of Norman, Oklahoma, and a charter member of the LPGA Hall of Fame, warms up before the third round of her victory in the 1947 U.S. Women's Open at Greensboro, North Carolina.

AP/Wide World Photos.

ABOVE: Tulsan Robert H. "Skee" Riegel, winner of the 1947 U.S. Amateur at Pebble Beach, tees off at hole No. 9 in his quarterfinal match with Bob Rosburg.

AP/Wide World Photos.

ABOVE: Oklahoma City oilman Charles Coe, with wife Elizabeth (wearing necklace), accepts the Havemeyer Trophy from USGA president Fielding Wallace for Coe's 1949 U.S. Amateur victory in Rochester, New York. At left are finalist Rufus King and his wife.

AP/Wide World Photos.

RIGHT: Class by himself: Gentleman Charles Coe, the 1949 U.S. Amateur Champion, with the trophy he would hold again nine years later, at the Olympic Club in San Francisco.

AP/Wide World Photos

LEFT: With this third-round birdie putt, Tommy Bolt began a torrid streak of six 3s in seven holes, securing the lead for good at the 1958 U.S. Open.
AP/Wide World Photos.

RIGHT: Serenity at Southern Hills: Tommy Bolt sinks this par putt at the final hole to win the 1958 U.S. Open by four strokes over Gary Player.
AP/Wide World Photos.

ABOVE: Future LPGA Hall of Famer JoAnne Gunderson (Carner) holds the traveling trophy and admires the Cox Trophy after capturing the 1960 U.S. Women's Amateur at Tulsa Country Club. With her are USGA vice president John Winters of Tulsa and runner-up Jean Ashley.

AP/Wide World Photos.

RIGHT: Body language: JoAnne Gunderson (Carner), the "Great Gundy," tries to lean one in at the 1960 U.S. Women's Amateur, hosted by Tulsa Country Club.

AP/Wide World Photos.

ABOVE: McAlester native Bob Dickson poses with the Havemeyer Trophy for winning the
1967 U.S. Amateur in Colorado Springs.
AP/Wide World Photos.

RIGHT: A high-stepping Robert B. "Bob" Dickson: with his 1967 victory at the Broadmoor in
Colorado Springs, Oklahoma State All-American Dickson became the fourth player—and
the last since 1935—to win both the U.S. and British Amateurs in the same year.
AP/Wide World Photos.

Oklahoma City's Susie Maxwell Berning cards
a second-round 73 at Moselem Springs Golf
Club in Fleetwood, Pennsylvania, in 1968, two
days prior to winning the first of three U.S.
Women's Opens.
AP/Wide World Photos.

In U.S. Open heat, Susie Maxwell Berning
stayed cool as this Pennsylvania stream, one
day before winning the first of three U.S.
Women's Opens.
AP/Wide World Photos.

FAR RIGHT: In 1972 Susie Maxwell Berning won
the U.S. Women's Open Championship Cup
for a second time, at Winged Foot in
Mamaroneck, New York.
AP/Wide World Photos.

LEFT: Final round touch: Chickasha's Orville James Moody with the mallethead putter and cross-handed grip that won him the 1969 U.S. Open.
AP/Wide World Photos.

ABOVE: Oklahoma State All-American Danny Edwards, with silver platter he received as low amateur in the 1973 British Open at Royal Troon.
Courtesy Oklahoma State University.

FAR LEFT: Champion Jan Stephenson tees off at the seventy-second hole, 1983 U.S. Women's Open at Cedar Ridge Country Club in Tulsa.

AP/Wide World Photos.

BELOW: Jan Stephenson poses with U.S. Women's Open Championship Cup at Cedar Ridge in 1983; runner-up Patty Sheehan (in white cap) would pose with the cup in 1992 and 1994.

AP/Wide World Photos.

ABOVE: Satisfied smile: Australian Jan Stephenson upon winning the 1983 U.S. Women's Open in Tulsa.

AP/Wide World Photos.

Andy Dillard of Tyler, Texas, a three-time All American at OSU, checks out his ball at Pebble Beach after the fifth of six consecutive birdies to begin the 1992 U.S. Open, setting a USGA record.

AP/Wide World Photos.

Yes! The softspoken Gil Morgan permits himself a
jubilant moment over a birdie during his opening-round
66 in the 1992 U.S. Open at Pebble Beach.
AP/Wide World Photos.

EIGHT
Modern

By the time Perry Maxwell died in Tulsa, on November 17, 1952, he left for the enjoyment of Oklahoma golfers an assortment of fourteen traditionally designed courses in twelve cities, from Enid and Lawton in the west to Bartlesville and Muskogee in the eastern half of the state. In addition, Maxwell set a standard for the next generation of course architects in Oklahoma.

Beginning in the early 1930s, Maxwell's son, James Press Maxwell, apprenticed on numerous projects of his father's, operating mule teams and Fresno scrapers at Southern Hills and Augusta National. After returning from the army air corps during World War II, Press Maxwell joined his father's firm. With the elder Maxwell's health failing, four of the final five Maxwell courses in Oklahoma were collaborations between father and son: Oakwood Country Club in Enid (1947); the first nine holes at Lawton Country Club (1948); University of Oklahoma Golf Course in Norman (1950); and Lake Hefner North Course (1951). In 1954 Press also designed the first nine holes at Meadowbrook Country Club in Tulsa.

The younger Maxwell continued his father's business, designing forty-one courses in nine states. Other than the Oklahoma courses, his best-known courses are San Antonio's Pecan Valley (site of the 1968 PGA Championship and 2001 U.S. Amateur Public Links) and resort courses at Snowmass and Vail, Colorado. He retired to raise Appaloosas on a ranch near Morrison, Colorado, and died in December of 1999.

As early as the 1930s, while the Maxwells were building Southern Hills, a young pro from Kansas City, Missouri, became a student in the Maxwell method. Floyd Farley came south to Oklahoma City and took a position as professional at Twin Hills Golf and Country Club, a classic Maxwell creation that would host Oklahoma's first major—the 1935 PGA Championship.

By 1932 Farley had built his own course in Oklahoma City, the Woodlawn Country Club, which he operated for the next fifteen years. The Woodlawn site at Thirty-sixth and Santa Fe eventually gave way to development and the headquarters for a grocery chain. But during its time, Woodlawn was the site of many tournaments, especially high school matches and junior tournaments. "Floyd wanted you to play it in three hours, maybe 3:15, and we did," said Sig Harpman, accomplished amateur player and longtime member of the Oklahoma City Golf Commission. "It was a golf course with no rough, a few grass bunkers, real good fairways and greens. It was a good place to learn."[1]

Farley was quite talented as a player. Besides two victories in the Oklahoma PGA Section Championship (1936 and 1942), he won the 1937 Oklahoma Match Play Open. When Woodlawn closed after World War II, Farley turned to golf course architecture full-time, showcasing his abilities at a series of projects in El Reno (El Reno Golf and Country Club), Wewoka (later called Dr. Gil Morgan Golf Club), Norman (the first nine at Westwood Park), Alva (Alva Golf and Country Club), Altus (Altus Golf Club), and

Duncan (the second nine at Duncan Golf and Country Club). Beginning with the 1954 opening of Oklahoma City's eighteen-hole Walnut Hills Country Club, Farley designed a variety of new courses around the state.

"When I first got into the business there was no formal training for it," Farley said in a 1998 interview. "You built one and if it was any good, somebody'd tell you to build another one." At first, most of Farley's designs were nine-hole courses: Brookside, McAlester Country Club, Midwest City, and nine-hole additions at Lawton Country Club and Lew Wentz in Ponca City. In 1957 and 1958, Farley completed eighteen-hole projects at Mohawk Park in Tulsa and Sand Springs Golf Club. As the popularity of Farley's courses became evident, the Oklahoma legislature authorized funding for him to design state park courses at Kingston (Lake Texoma); Hulbert (Sequoyah); Watonga (Roman Nose); Checotah (Fountainhead); and Fort Cobb.

By 1960 Farley was involved with two projects, a hundred miles apart, that would define his architectural style and legacy to Oklahoma golf: LaFortune Park Municipal Course in Tulsa and Quail Creek Country Club in Oklahoma City. Both courses featured the clean lines and avenues for recovery that became Farley trademarks.

"I don't like vertical lines on a golf course," Farley said. "If you've got something there, like steep fairway bunkers or railroad ties, that precludes the possibility of a player going forward to recover, I'm not for it. I think hitting a variety of shots should always be part of the game."

At LaFortune Park, Farley incorporated elements characteristic of urban parkland courses. The first and tenth tees and ninth and eighteenth greens were positioned near the clubhouse. With its adjacent par-3 course, enormous bentgrass putting greens, and deep driving range, city-operated LaFortune evolved into a preferred site for staging USGA qualifiers, city championships, and collegiate tournaments.

Simultaneous with the construction of LaFortune, the Quail Creek Development Company commissioned Farley to build a championship course in northwest Oklahoma City. It was one of the first courses in Oklahoma constructed in conjunction with a real estate development. "I think it's a darn good golf course," said Farley, "but over the years greens committees have made changes to it—like reversing the nines—that I don't necessarily agree with. However, it belongs to them and they can do with it what they want. I've just always believed it ill-advised to have a first hole that faces directly into the morning sun."

Four public eighteen-hole Farley courses opened in Oklahoma in the early 1960s: the Oilfield Recreation Association Golf Club in Healdton; Broadmoore Golf Course in Moore; Adams Park Municipal in Bartlesville; and Lake Hefner South in Oklahoma City. Before retiring to Sedona, Arizona, in the mid–1970s, Farley completed several additional nine-hole projects (Atoka; first nine at Kingfisher; Shattuck; Hook and Slice in Oklahoma City; and the first nine at Beavers Bend State Park). He signed off in Oklahoma with a flourish of big courses: the remodeling of thirty-six holes at Lincoln Park; John Conrad Regional in Midwest City; Kickingbird in Edmond; Earlywine South in Oklahoma City; and a trio of courses in Guthrie with Duffy Martin.

Edmond's Kickingbird, which opened in 1971, hosted the Oklahoma Open from 1979 through 1985. Earlywine, in southwestern Oklahoma City, is known for its excellent greens and outstanding finishing holes. According to Farley, the three courses he did west of Guthrie with Duffy Martin (Cedar Valley Augusta, Cedar Valley International, and the Cimarron National Course), could well represent the future of public golf.

"Duffy was always an excellent player and he's even better as a course owner and builder," Farley said in 1998. "At a time when developers were hesitant to go beyond city limits, Duffy went out in the country thirty-two miles and he's doing pretty good. Players enjoy the courses and he's keeping the greens fees down, which is what we need more of all over. The greater Oklahoma City area could still support six or eight more courses just like Duffy's."

As of 1998 Martin had three eighteen-hole courses opened for play west of Guthrie, with forty people employed, and a par-3 course under construction. One of Martin's trade secrets was to do everything in-house, whenever possible. "What I build for one million will cost your regular cats $4 million," said Martin, a former lumberjack, ironworker, cab driver, and golf pro. "Money is like ice. You let a lot of people handle it and it's gone."[2]

After a good deal of searching, Martin discovered that some of the best land for golf was right under his nose. "We looked all over for a place that had the right feel," Martin recalled. "I went to New Orleans. I went to Texas. I went every place and right here in Guthrie, in the Cimarron Basin, Mother Nature put a beautiful, natural place for a truly great golf course."[3]

Even though he constructed the courses himself, Martin sought out the services of a professional course architect—Farley—and turf experts Roy Calvert and Gene O'Bryant. Martin consulted with Farley at each of the eighteen-hole courses—Cimarron National, Cedar Valley International, and Cedar Valley Augusta.

Once the courses opened, part of the Martin success story was to keep play moving. His policies reflected golf's Scottish origins; in Scot-

> "WE LOOKED ALL OVER FOR A PLACE THAT HAD THE RIGHT FEEL. I WENT TO NEW ORLEANS. I WENT TO TEXAS. I WENT EVERY PLACE AND RIGHT HERE IN GUTHRIE, IN THE CIMARRON BASIN, MOTHER NATURE PUT A BEAUTIFUL, NATURAL PLACE FOR A TRULY GREAT GOLF COURSE."

land people still believed in a three-hour round. "I think of golf a little different from some of the guys who are in the business," Martin said. "I don't want any rough on my golf courses. I want everything mowed. I don't want people to hunt balls. If they lose a ball in the water, they can drop another one and go ahead on. Keep play moving. Life is too short to hunt balls. Last I checked they're making golf balls 24 hours a day."[4]

An architectural contemporary of Farley's, who grew up in Kansas City, Kansas, was Robert Charles Dunning. Dunning graduated from the University of Kansas in 1921 and took a job as head professional and greenskeeper at Oklahoma's McAlester Country Club. While at McAlester Dunning worked on several course remodeling jobs.

In addition to Dunning's work for Waco Turner at Burneyville, he also designed nine-hole courses at Pauls Valley (1951), Elk City (1953), Woodward (1954), and—his final Oklahoma project—Hobart (1965). The best example of Dunning's style may be the scenic Sunset Hills Golf Course in the Panhandle town of Guymon. With bluegrass fairways and tumbling bentgrass greens, Sunset Hills has adequate amounts of two resources richly appreciated in the windswept reaches of what once was called "No Man's Land": water and trees.

Since 1971, Sunset Hills has hosted the Jim Hitch Memorial Junior Tournament, in memory of a young man and passionate golfer who died while he was a senior at Guymon High School. Jim Hitch, aged seventeen at the time of his death, was the youngest son of Ladd and Lala Moores Hitch, a prominent Oklahoma ranching family. Jim played golf until sunset on March 3, 1970, but died during the night of fulminating viremia, a rare and often fatal disorder.[5] In 1998, Stewart Dodson, a sophomore at nearby Perryton (Texas) High School, shot a 62 at the Jim Hitch Memorial, setting the competitive course record for Sunset Hills.

A year after Dunning's work at Hobart Country Club, Donald R. Sechrest of St. Joseph, Missouri, was the architect of record for the new Stillwater Country Club. Sechrest's background in golf came by way of competition. While a student at Oklahoma State, he had played for coach Labron Harris Sr. on three consecutive Missouri Valley Conference championship teams (1953–55). After graduating in 1956, Sechrest tried his luck on the PGA tour, while assisting Harris at Stillwater's Lakeside Memorial and with the OSU golf team.

In 1966, Sechrest designed and supervised the construction of the Stillwater Country Club and served for a short time as its golf professional. The Men's NCAA Division I golf championship came to Oklahoma for the first time in June of 1973, to Stillwater Country Club.

Going into the 1973 NCAA Championship, Ben Crenshaw of the University of Texas had dominated college golf as only four players had previously: winning back-to-back NCAA individual titles. At Stillwater Country Club, Crenshaw extended the streak. The future two-time Masters winner made NCAA history in Stillwater, becoming the first player ever to win NCAA medalist for three straight years. However, the Longhorns' bid for three consecutive team titles was derailed by the University of Florida. Sechrest's par-70 layout proved tough enough, even for one of the game's great players: Crenshaw's 282 total for the four rounds was two over par.

At the finals of the 1975 Western Junior, also held at Stillwater Country Club, three-time OSU All-American Britt Harrison, of Beaumont, Texas, defeated John Jones, 2 & 1. Larry Rinker was qualifying medalist at 137. In 1979, the best female collegians in the nation came to Stillwater Country Club for the championship of the Association of Intercollegiate Athletics for Women. Women's collegiate golf would not become an official NCAA sport until 1982. Kyle O'Brien, the future coach at Southern Methodist, led the Lady Mustangs to the AIAW team title. As medalist, O'Brien shot 292; the Mustangs shot 1,208. Their coach that year was Earl Stewart Jr., winner of the 1953 Ardmore Open and the last club pro to win a PGA Tour event at his home course—the 1961 Dallas Open at Oak Cliff Country Club.

After adding nine holes in 1970 to Floyd Farley's work at Meadowbrook Country Club in Tulsa, Sechrest set his sights northeastward, to Oklahoma's Green Country, and the Grand Lake o' the Cherokees. In 1969, Charles J. Davis, an industrialist and manufacturer in Wichita, Kansas, purchased the Shangri-La Hotel, built in 1964 by Oklahoma City contractor Frank Richards. Davis immediately closed the hotel and went to work on a master plan to refurbish the hotel, adding tennis courts, condominiums, and an eighteen-hole championship golf course. The Sechrest-designed Shangri-La Blue Course, at 7,012 yards, became the crown jewel of the resort.

In 1982, a second Sechrest layout at Shangri-La, called the Gold Course, opened for play. Shangri-La's Blue and Gold courses attracted many players to northeast Oklahoma, for competitions as diverse as U.S. Amateur qualifying and the Mickey Mantle Celebrity Classic, annually benefiting the Oklahoma Make-A-Wish Foundation.

Mantle grew up in nearby Commerce. After his Hall of Fame career with the New York Yankees, the slugger returned often to Oklahoma to pursue his other sport passion—golf. According to his mentor Marshall Smith, of Miami, Oklahoma, Mantle, a switch-hitter in baseball, played golf left-handed for two years before switching over. Smith said Mantle was a quick study who loved the long ball and stout wagers.

"I never saw anybody who hated to lose more than Mickey," said Smith, who also gave lessons to Chi Chi Rodriguez, Walt Zembriski, Gary

Player, and Craig Stadler."He'd set back on his right side, just like in baseball. He had so much clubhead speed and hand action."[6]

As fourball partners, Smith and Mantle were tough customers. Average stakes were $500 to $1,000 per round, but sometimes carryovers were worth $3,000 to $5,000. While Smith played the steady role, Mantle swung for the fences. Once, at Southern Hills, he drove the 349-yard seventeenth hole on the fly. His usual strategy at the monstrous eighteenth at Southern Hills was to cut the corner of the dogleg, leaving a flip wedge to the flag. Even after Mantle's death in 1995, his charity tournament at Shangri-La continued. Over the years it drew celebrities from all walks, like Yogi Berra, Garth Brooks, Hale Irwin, Bobby Knight, Mark Fidrych, Vince Gill, James Garner, Warren Spahn, and Willie Nelson.

The Shangri-La projects put Sechrest at the forefront of Oklahoma golf course design. In 1974, he built the Windmill Course at Broken Arrow's Indian Springs Country Club, to complement the club's George Fazio–designed River Course.

In 1977, the Sechrest-designed Heritage Hills Course in Will Rogers's hometown of Claremore opened to tepid reviews. According to Dave Wilber, who became pro there in 1980, the course opened early to meet payments on the loan."It seems like everything was against the project getting off the ground," Wilber explained."Without the community of Claremore, without people wanting the golf course, it never would have flown."[7]

The first pro at Heritage was former OU player and golf coach Jim Awtrey. Awtrey later played on the PGA Tour and became executive director of the PGA of America. By 1999, the par-71 layout, managed by the Rogers University Trust Authority, was handling upwards of fifty thousand rounds annually, as a picturesque, well-maintained test of golf with abundant water, trees, sand, and rolling terrain.

The remainder of Sechrest's original work in Oklahoma included thirteen restorations, two state park courses (Boiling Springs and the second nine at Fort Cobb), and four eighteen-hole urban courses: Greens Golf and Country Club (Oklahoma City); Fire Lake (Shawnee); Page Belcher Stone Creek (Tulsa); and Coyote Canyon (Beggs).

Beginning in the late 1960s, and for the next three decades, a dozen of the most respected American course architects were hired to do design work in Oklahoma.

In an earlier era, mention of a "Fazio course" would indicate the work of George Fazio, designer of Broken Arrow's Indian Springs River Course. But as of the last two decades, a Fazio course points to the handiwork of George's nephew Tom Fazio, the preeminent designer of the late twentieth century. Indeed Tom Fazio designed what some would call two of Oklahoma's three best courses of the modern era: the Golf Club of Oklahoma, in 1982, and Karsten Creek, in 1994.

The Golf Club of Oklahoma, in Broken Arrow, hosted two Hogan Tour events. The champion of the 1991 Ben Hogan Tulsa Open was PGA Tour veteran Frank Conner, of San Antonio, who played in both golf and tennis U.S. Opens. "The Golf Club of Oklahoma was a heck of golf course, very demanding," Conner said in 1997. "It was quite similar to some of the better courses on the PGA Tour, definitely enough golf course to host a Tour Championship or USGA championship. It's tough—I shot 76 the first round and still won." Tom Fazio's other Oklahoma course—Karsten Creek in Stillwater—was named the nation's "Best New Public Course" in 1994.

Unquestionably Fazio's family name and close ties to his uncle were huge benefits to his career. Besides losing to Ben Hogan in a playoff for the 1950 U.S. Open, George Fazio designed courses in fifteen states and six foreign countries, from Hawaii to the Virgin Islands. George Fazio's River Course at Indian Springs Country Club in Broken Arrow, which opened for play in 1968, hosted the 1978 Oklahoma Open, won by Lindy Miller. The River Course was situated on prime Oklahoma bottomland,

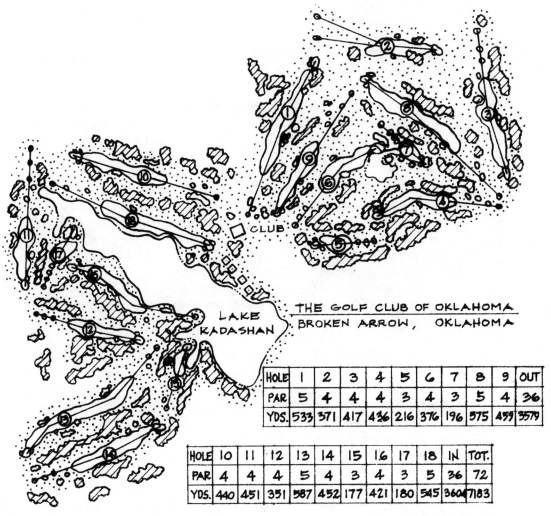

THE GOLF CLUB OF OKLAHOMA
BROKEN ARROW, OKLAHOMA

LAKE KADASHAN

CLUB

HOLE	1	2	3	4	5	6	7	8	9	OUT
PAR	5	4	4	4	3	4	3	5	4	36
YDS.	533	371	417	436	216	376	196	575	459	3579

HOLE	10	11	12	13	14	15	16	17	18	IN	TOT.
PAR	4	4	4	5	4	3	4	3	5	36	72
YDS.	440	451	351	587	452	177	421	180	545	3604	7183

Course Layout 2. The Golf Club of Oklahoma, in Broken Arrow, designed by Tom Fazio. Drawing by Jep Wille.

which was ideal terrain for a golf course and very similar to the land a few miles north of Indian Springs, where Cedar Ridge Country Club opened in 1969.

The architect at Cedar Ridge was Joe Finger, a native of Houston, who received a bachelor's degree from Rice University, where he was captain of the golf team for coach Jimmy Demaret. As a student and golfer, Finger had a wonderful combination of intellect and imagination. Some athletes found Rice's academic standards intimidating, but not Finger. By 1941 he had a master's degree from the Massachusetts Institute of Technology.

Finger worked for five years in the petroleum refining industry, then became president of a plastics manufacturing company, where he developed and patented a corrugated plastic building panel. He also owned a dairy and a turf nursery. His former coach Demaret, a three-time Masters champion, helped Finger land golf course design and remodeling jobs. He designed numerous courses for the U.S. military and wrote a book examining course design as a business.

The course at Cedar Ridge plays 7,290 yards from the back tees, the longest championship course in Oklahoma. In 1983, Cedar Ridge hosted the U.S. Women's Open, which was won by Jan Stephenson, at a 290 total of six over par. The Open was to have been the homecoming for former Tulsa University All-American Nancy Lopez. But Lopez was six months pregnant with daughter Ashley Marie and withdrew.

Another Texan, Don January, winner of the 1967 PGA Championship, codesigned two Oklahoma courses as a design partner with Billy Martindale. Martindale, a Texas A&M graduate, and January, who played at North Texas, built Yukon's Westbury Country Club in 1976 and rebuilt the old Hillcrest course in Oklahoma City, now called Willow Creek Country Club.

In 1982, January's fellow tour pro Bruce Devlin, working with architect Robert von Hagge, refurbished Shawnee Country Club. Two years later, Jay Morrish remodeled nine holes at Tulsa Country Club and designed the challenging Coves at Bird Island, on Grand Lake. Prior to the 1997 PGA Championship, Bruce Lietzke played nine holes at the Coves in even par. With that, he declared himself ready take on Winged Foot.

Texans Leon and Charles Howard collaborated on five courses in Oklahoma, including the Olde Page Belcher Course in Tulsa and the Trails in Norman. Olde Page, opened in 1977, impressed the USGA enough to bring the U.S. Women's Amateur Public Links there in 1988, which was won by Pearl Sinn.

Some consider the Howards' Trails Course in Norman (1979) one of the state's best-kept golf secrets, including PGA Tour veteran Bob Murphy. Murphy, winner of the 1965 U.S. Amateur at Southern Hills, enjoyed practicing at the Trails while visiting his daughter when she was in law school at the University of Oklahoma. Murphy said the greens at the Trails were as good as or better than most played on Tour.[8] The Howards also built Pawnee Municipal, Meadowlake in Enid, and the nine-hole Durant Country Club.

No courses in Oklahoma witnessed the coronation of more champions in a shorter period than those at the Oak Tree Golf Club in Edmond. And were it not for a broken promise, Oak Tree might never have been built at all.

In the late 1960s, while the PGA of America searched for courses to host future PGA Championships, Quail Creek Golf and Country Club pro Ernie Vossler, who had submitted a bid on behalf of Quail Creek, had every reason to believe the 1970 PGA Championship was headed to Oklahoma for the first time since 1935. Vossler was right, of course—except that the 1970 PGA would not be headed for Quail Creek. Instead, it would be played one hundred miles northeast up the Turner Turnpike, at storied Southern Hills Country Club in Tulsa.

When he heard the news that Southern Hills had been selected instead of Quail Creek, besides being heartbroken, Vossler said he felt betrayed.

A native of Fort Worth, Vossler had been head professional at Quail Creek since it opened in 1961. He had paid his dues as a Tour player, winning four times from 1958 to 1960. Quail Creek had hosted a half dozen consecutive Oklahoma City Opens, plus the 1968 PGA National Team Championship. In 1967, at Palm Beach Gardens, Florida, Vossler was voted PGA Professional of the Year, while Jack Nicklaus was voted Player of the Year. (Three decades later Vossler gave a putting lesson to Gil Morgan, who went out and won the 1997 Tradition with a record score of twenty-two under par.)

Arnold Palmer, twice winner of the Oklahoma City Open, had first suggested Quail Creek as a possible PGA Championship site as early as 1965. Encouraged by PGA officials, Vossler bid on the 1968 PGA but lost out to the Press Maxwell–designed Pecan Valley Country Club in San Antonio. Whereas Quail Creek had been campaigning since 1965 for a PGA, Southern Hills entered the picture late. The Tulsa club issued a formal bid for the 1970 PGA Championship in March of 1969. One month later, Southern Hills was awarded the 1970 PGA Championship.

The *Daily Oklahoman*'s Bob Hurt had this take: "It's sort of shocking to find the suitor you've been dancing with so happily over the past five years was, at the same time, making goo goo eyes at a beau in the background."[9] More determined than ever before, Vossler formed a partnership with his longtime friend Oklahoma City pro Joe Walser, with one mission in mind: to bring major championship golf back to the Oklahoma City area.

Walser, who had played for Labron Harris Sr. at Oklahoma State, was a native Oklahoman who had won the Oklahoma State Amateur championship and had played for several years on the PGA Tour. During the 1960s, he had been an assistant pro at Quail Creek and later head professional at both Oklahoma City Golf and Country Club and Lake Hefner. He and Vossler had been friends since traveling together during their days on the tour.

In 1971, Walser and Vossler quit their jobs at Quail Creek and Lake Hefner to form Unique Golf Concepts, Incorporated, and began scouting for the nearly two sections of land that became Oak Tree. They searched Oklahoma County for the best available land with the right blend of trees, elevation, and water. After two years and untold miles, they drove past a cattle farm north of Edmond. It had an abundance of oak and the property teemed with ponds and streams.

"There weren't any 'for sale' signs," Walser said. "We just went to work and knocked on doors, making offers, acquiring a piece here and a piece there."[10] Once they had purchased the land, they went looking for an architect who could build a course to challenge the world's best golfers. They did not look for long, settling on the most cussed and discussed architect of his era—Paul "Pete" Dye Jr.

Dye and his wife Alice had made a pilgrimage in 1963 to see the courses of Scotland. The experience, it seemed, changed Pete Dye forever. Where some visitors to the Scottish linklands saw sea, sand, and bentgrasses, Dye also saw railroad ties, sheep wallows, and gorse. If creosote timbers were good enough for the Scots to buffer their courses against the sea,

WHERE SOME VISITORS TO THE SCOTTISH LINKSLANDS SAW SEA, SAND, AND BENTGRASSES, DYE ALSO SAW RAILROAD TIES, SHEEP WALLOWS, AND GORSE. IF CREOSOTE TIMBERS WERE GOOD ENOUGH FOR THE SCOTS TO BUFFER THEIR COURSES AGAINST THE SEA, WHY WOULD THEY NOT WORK IN THE UNITED STATES?

223

why would they not work in the United States? Who said when a shot landed in a sand trap the golfer who hit it must be guaranteed a play at the green? Certainly not the Scots. There were those who suspected that Dye was enamored of the fantasy that some enraged tour pro, last seen thrashing in a Pete Dye bunker, would sell his clubs, never to be heard from again.

This made him the perfect architect for Oak Tree. If Mr. Dye could build a course tough enough, Walser and Vossler reasoned, the PGA of America would be seen as short on courage if they did not award a PGA to Oak Tree. Vossler, Walser, and Dye made a handshake agreement in 1973. Two years later construction began at Oak Tree. Within a few weeks of the startup, Unique Golf was merged with a larger corporation, Landmark Land Company.

Dye recalled: "I decided par would be 71 since I just couldn't fit in the usual four par-5s without manufacturing artificial holes. With just three par-5s and four par-3s, the eleven par-4s would mold the character of the course."[11] The Oak Tree Golf Club, at 7,015 yards from the championship tees, opened for play in 1976. Invitations were immediately extended to the U.S. Golf Association, the PGA of America, and the NCAA to consider Oak Tree as a championship site. It did not take long for the PGA to accept. First in line would be the 1980 PGA Cup Matches, between teams of club pros from the United States and Great Britain–Ireland.

The first round of the Cup Matches, scheduled for Oak Tree at 8:00 A.M. on September 19, 1980, did not get under way until 9:00. The busdriver for the Great Britain–Ireland team had overindulged the night before and was running an hour late. But Oak Tree as a test of golf measured up to its promise. Soon after the Cup Matches, the PGA made its announcement: Vossler and Walser were awarded the 1988 PGA Championship eight years in advance. This time, there would be no last-minute rug pull.

The PGA's faith was rewarded. By 1983, Oak Tree had been named one of the "50 greatest golf courses in the world," by *Golf* magazine, although the course had not yet hosted a major stroke-play championship, either professional or amateur. Architect Dye, who already had Harbour Town, the Golf Club of Ohio, and Crooked Stick on his resumé, called Oak Tree "the finest inland course I have ever built."[12]

Also in 1983, some Oklahoma touring pros were so impressed with Oak Tree that they moved their families there. Among the new residents, already being called the "Oak Tree Boys," were Gil Morgan, Mark Hayes, Doug Tewell, David Edwards, and Danny Edwards. OU golf coach David Yates, whose team practiced there often, said the course was a fair test: "Oak Tree's like anything that's great, it's controversial. Some love it and some hate it, but I've never heard anybody finish playing it and say they were lucky. It rewards good shots and penalizes bad ones."[13]

So Nathaniel Crosby was soon to discover. Crosby, the 1981 U.S. Amateur champion, came to Oak Tree for the 1984 U.S. Amateur. In the first round of qualifying he was all fours, 44-44-88. Ever the proud champion, he blamed it on too much golf. But somewhere Vossler, Walser, and Dye must have been smiling. "Obviously, I need a break from the game," Crosby said. "The course is playing about as easy as it ever will and if you shoot that bad, it's a mental lapse." William Hyndman III, a two-time U.S. Senior Amateur champion, had a different explanation for his 80. "Before I started, I thought if you hit 11 or 12 greens, you'd be decent," said Hyndman. "I did that and shot 80. I was six over after five holes. If you get behind early at Oak Tree, there's no place to catch up."[14]

Scott Verplank, from W. T. White High School in Dallas, had just completed his sophomore year at Oklahoma State University. He rolled to the U.S. Amateur title at Oak Tree, first as qualifying medalist (137), then winning six straight matches. He beat Sam Randolph 4 & 3 in the finals.

By hosting the 1984 Amateur, Oak Tree climbed even higher in the rankings, to No. 16 in *Golf Digest's* "America's 100 Greatest" courses. But by the time August of 1988 finally arrived, the tour pros had their own description for Dye's punitive style: "archi-torture." "There'll be definite criticisms about Oak Tree," said Bob Tway, 1986 PGA champion and Oak Tree member. "Everybody's got their own opinion. I don't really mind Pete Dye courses. I like Oak Tree better than some of his courses."[15]

Hubert Green, who won the 1977 U.S. Open at Southern Hills, had played an exhibition at Oak Tree in 1978. "Pete Dye gave them exactly what they asked for," said Green. "They wanted 18 unfair holes and that's what he gave them."[16]

But PGA officials claimed they were more than satisfied with Oak Tree's degree of difficulty. "This course will stand up to the best players in the world," said PGA president Patrick Reilly. "The shot value and shot balance will hold up. We wanted to select a course that will test all the clubs in a golf bag, and this course certainly does that."[17]

The fears about Oak Tree being unfair proved somewhat unfounded—instead of the usual midsummer Oklahoma winds, conditions remained calm, and the 1988 PGA turned out to play the second easiest in history. Buoyed by a 100-yard eagle shot at the par-5 fifth, which countered Paul Azinger's hole in one, one Florida State alumnus outplayed another. Jeff Sluman's twelve-under-par total of 272 held off Azinger by three strokes. The PGA was sufficiently impressed with Oak Tree and the Oklahoma hospitality to announce soon afterward that the PGA Championship would return to Oak Tree in 1994.

In 1989 Oak Tree Golf Club hosted the NCAA Championship. Among Oklahoma collegiate golf observers expectations were high. OSU had won the NCAA title in 1987 and had been runner-up in 1986 and 1988. OU had finished third in 1986 and 1987 and in 1988 had placed second, with OSU and the University of Texas at El Paso, to UCLA. With a senior-laden roster, the Sooners were favored at Oak Tree. And they had unfinished business from the year before.

Going into the 1988 NCAA Championship, at North Ridge Ranch Country Club in Westlake Village, California, the Sooners had never won a national championship in golf. At North Ridge Ranch, they had had their best opportunity ever but had self-destructed, to the tune of a thirty-five-over-par team score on the last three holes for four rounds. The Sooners finished three behind champion UCLA.

After seventeen holes of the second round at Oak Tree, the Sooners appeared in good shape once more, tied for the lead. But their five players played No. 9—their eighteenth hole of the round—a net five over par, with three bogeys and a double bogey. Instead of a tie for first, they fell five behind leader Clemson. "We should have stopped at 17," said Sooner coach Gregg Grost.

However, this was a different Sooner team than that of the year before. Instead of coming unraveled, Doug Martin, Matthew Lane, Jeff Lee, Tripp Davis, and Ricky Bell began to hole putts. While others struggled to break 290, the Sooners posted team totals of 283 and 288 for the last two rounds. They had such a commanding lead at the end that each Sooner player could have made a quadruple bogey at the last hole and OU would still have won. They finished nineteen ahead of runner-up Texas, and twenty-three better than in-state rival OSU. It was sweet redemption for the Sooners against the Cowboys, whose program, under coach Mike Holder, had captured the national title in five of the previous twelve years.

"I felt like a five-ton load of bricks was taken off my back," said Grost, in his fourth year as OU's coach. "I think our golf program can walk around the state with our head held high and receive the proper amount of recognition."[18]

Arizona State freshman Phil Mickelson, who had top ten finishes at six of his first seven collegiate tournaments, won the first of his three NCAA individual titles, with a 281 total. There was a six-way tie for second, at 285: Doug Martin (OU); Ricky Bell (OU); Kevin Wentworth (OSU); Robert Gamez (Arizona); Brian Nelson (Texas); and Dave Stockton Jr. (USC).

When Oak Tree received word that it would host the 1994 PGA Championship, Walser and Vossler were obviously elated. The news further heightened Oklahoma's enthusiasm for golf. "Those things are such a boon," said Oklahoma Golf Association Executive Director Bill Barrett. "You just can't measure how much they escalate the interest. In the past it has been a hard task for our association to get sites for our events. But the enthusiasm for golfing the last few years has blossomed so much, people are eager to offer their golf courses."[19]

However, there were troubling signs on the economic front. By August of 1991, Landmark Land Company had added another thirty-six holes at the site, and the two new courses were called Oak Tree Country Club East and West. But one month later, two years after enactment of the Financial Institutions Reform, Recovery and Enforcement Act, the Oak Tree Savings Bank of New Orleans, where Landmark Land Company's vast golf and real estate ventures were held, filed for reorganizational bankruptcy. Even though the club honored its commitment to host the 1992 Southern Amateur, won by Justin Leonard, things were so uncertain at Oak Tree that plans to host the 1994 PGA Championship had to be canceled.

Oak Tree's parent company had fallen victim to high interest rates and government rules changes for banks in the 1980s and 1990s. In June of 1994, the Resolution Trust Company liquidated Landmark's holdings, selling the East and West courses to Signature Properties, of Toronto, Canada, for $20 million, and the original Oak Tree Golf Club to a partnership of prominent Oklahoma Citians: furniture dealer Don Mathis and oilmen Ran Ricks, Art Swanson, and Walter Duncan, for $3.5 million.

Meanwhile Vossler, who had spent twenty years with the old Landmark, had already begun a new venture in Las Vegas, called Landmark Golf Company. His new partners in Nevada were former OU football coach Chuck Fairbanks, course architect Brian Curley, former Quail Creek pro Buzz Gill, former PGA Tour player Johnny Pott, and John McClure, a polished amateur player who grew up in Texas. Vossler's former partner Walser had taken a job with the PGA Tour.

"Shoot yeah," Vossler told the *Oklahoman*'s Mac Bentley when asked about the similarity of the corporate names and if he was proud of his work in Oklahoma. "What we did were good projects. Because George Bush and Ronald Reagan put in some regulations and then changed them, that bankrupted this company. There wasn't anything I was ashamed of, and I wanted to spring off of what we'd done for 20 years. I haven't had any resistance in financing, or bringing in partners, or anything, because of the name Landmark."[20]

Litigation later brought against the government continued into the year 2000. Landmark is reported to have lost $1.8 billion when Oak Tree was shut down.

Despite changes to the organization and the attendant risk that the overall condition of the courses would decline, it did not happen. Instead of being reduced, maintenance budgets at both the Oak Tree Country Club and Oak Tree Golf Club actually increased. The courses maintained their championship conditioning and continued to host the Oklahoma Open each August at the Oak Tree Country Club East Course, while looking to land another major at the Golf Club.

Of much significance to the new owners, the Oak Tree Boys remained loyal throughout the uncertain years and continued to live and raise families there. Besides three of the originals (Gil Morgan, Mark Hayes, and Doug Tewell), other Oklahomans on the PGA Tour played out of Oak

Tree: Bob Tway, Andrew Magee, Willie Wood, Scott Verplank, Brian Watts, Rocky Walcher, and Andy Dillard. David Edwards, one of the originals, built a home in 1996 at Karsten Creek Golf Club in Stillwater. His brother, Danny, moved to the Phoenix area.

Perhaps not coincidentally, there are those among the Oak Tree Boys who have played some of their best golf at other Pete Dye–designed courses. Between 1990 and 1995, David Edwards pocketed $313,817, in South Carolina's Heritage Classic, at Dye-designed Harbour Town. Tewell picked up his first victory on Tour at the same event in 1980. Morgan had top-ten finishes at Harbour Town in 1993 and 1995. In 1995, Tway won the Heritage Classic's $234,000 first prize, his first victory on the PGA Tour since 1990.

Other American architects of note designed golf courses in Oklahoma during the 1990s. Ben Crenshaw and Bill Coore brought their traditional style to Southern Hills in 1992, when they added a third nine holes to Oklahoma's best-known golf club. Crenshaw, who grew up putting on the Perry Maxwell greens at Austin Country Club, and Coore, who played the Pinehurst courses as a youngster, set about complementing the original Maxwell course at Southern Hills.

In the spring of 1997, a course designed by Atlanta architect Rocky Roquemore opened between Norman and Chickasha. Golden Eagle Golf Course is situated on 500 acres of rolling terrain, with several lakes. Rocquemore had attended the U.S. Air Force Academy and Georgia Tech, and his family is in the business of building and operating daily-fee courses in the Atlanta area. Michigan architects Raymond Hearn and Jerry Matthews designed the Traditions Golf Club in Edmond, which also opened in 1997.

In 1998, Pete Dye's youngest son, P. B. Dye, brought his design talents to central Oklahoma. As soon as it opened, P. B.'s Crimson Creek course at El Reno measured up to its advance billing as one of the finest public courses in the state. Crimson Creek has fifty-six bunkers. Redlands Community College in El Reno started a golf program in the late 1990s and made Crimson Creek its home facility.

Also in 1998, Stonebriar Golf Club opened in Bartlesville. Stonebriar was the first Oklahoma project for former tour player Bobby Clampett and Chuck Smith. Clampett and Smith were hired by Bill Shay of Bartlesville, owner of a landscaping firm. Shay brought in Dan Wood, a one-time collegiate player at South Carolina's Southern Wesleyan University, as the club's first director of golf. At one time Wood had dreamed of a career as a tour pro, but a freak accident in 1984—when he was hit in the face with a golf ball and lost an eye—had ended his career as a player. "It's a beautiful setting," Wood said of the Stonebriar site south of Bartlesville. "We've got 70 feet of elevation change and it happens several times as you play."[21]

> "IT'S A BEAUTIFUL SETTING. WE'VE GOT 70 FEET OF ELEVATION CHANGE AND IT HAPPENS SEVERAL TIMES AS YOU PLAY."

When OPUBCO Development Company decided to build a private course in northwest Oklahoma City, it hired as its course architect Arthur Hills of Toledo, Ohio. In 1991, Hills had become the first architect to have two courses honored by *Golf Digest* in the same year. In its annual ranking of the nation's top courses, the magazine named the Hills-designed Golf Club of Georgia as best new private course and his Harbour Pointe in Everett, Washington, was selected as best new public course.

Gaillardia, which opened in 1999, is situated at a fairly nondescript piece of land, a former cow pasture on the outskirts of the city. But Hills brought in eighteen hundred trees and added eighty-six bunkers. An estimated one million cubic feet of dirt were moved. The 25,000-square-foot clubhouse featured the architectural style of Normandy in France.

In Sand Springs, former British Open and Masters champion

Sandy Lyle was retained to design the Angus Valley Golf Club, with routing input from Bland Pittman.

Beginning with its first state park golf course, which opened for play at Lake Texoma in 1958, the State of Oklahoma has authorized funds for the construction of holes at twelve state parks. As of 1999, the Oklahoma state park and resort system owned and/or operated eighteen-hole courses at Lake Texoma (Durant); Sequoyah (Hulbert); Roman Nose (Watonga); Arrowhead (Canadian); Fort Cobb (Fort Cobb); Beavers Bend (Broken Bow); Fountainhead (Checotah); Boiling Springs (Woodward); Langley (Langley); Quartz Mountain (Altus); Lake Murray (Ardmore); and Chickasaw Pointe (Kingston).

Floyd Farley (108 holes) and Don Sechrest (27) designed most of the state park holes, but during the 1990s at least five other homegrown course designers have added to the collection. Of the five, Tripp Davis and Randy Heckenkemper have designed courses for the state park system. And by the final decade of the century, four other Oklahomans were trying their hand at the design game.

Heckenkemper, a Tulsa native and Oklahoma State graduate, learned the design trade with a Tulsa-based land planning company. His first two courses, South Lakes in Jenks and Forest Ridge in Broken Arrow, opened in 1989. Forest Ridge proved to be quite challenging and soon came to be considered one of the state's best tests of golf for a public course. Heckenkemper also designed Oklahoma City courses Silverhorn (1992) and Earlywine (1993). In 1994 the Heckenkemper-designed White Hawk in Bixby opened for play.

Heckenkemper's most recent work can be seen in the redesign of Perry Maxwell's Lake Hefner North Course in Oklahoma City (1994) and at Chickasaw Pointe on Lake Texoma (1999). In 1994, when asked if he was intimidated about building courses in a state where the best works were designed by the likes of Maxwell, Tillinghast, Dye, Fazio, and Farley, Heckenkemper replied: "I wasn't intimidated by that. I relished the opportunity to put my work alongside so many great architects and see if I could stack up."[22]

Davis, who played on OU's 1989 national championship golf team, was the architect of record at the nine-hole course at Langley State Park and the second nine at Roman Nose State Park in 1998. A year earlier, Davis's first Oklahoma course—the second nine at Kingfisher Municipal —opened for play. Davis, with his headquarters in Norman, also designed the eighteen-hole courses at Patricia Island—just across Grand Lake from the Shangri-La Resort—and Clary Fields in Tulsa. With Maury Miller, Davis codesigned Belmar Golf Club in Norman, scheduled to open in 2001.

Oklahoma architects of the new breed are being hired to build more and more public courses, several by municipalities. Tulsan Bland Pittman, contracted by the Owasso Public Golf Authority, designed Bailey Ranch in 1993, which was financed with $5 million in revenue bonds. The land for the course, previously a Black Angus cattle ranch, was donated to the city of Owasso by the late Larkin Bailey, a Tulsa-area philanthropist and business pioneer. Bailey Ranch has hosted numerous tournaments, including professional minitour events.

In October of 1994, the Pittman-designed Gleneagles Golf Club opened for play in Broken Arrow. Also that year, Pittman contracted with the Broken Arrow Public Golf Authority to design the Battle Creek Golf Club. Upon opening in the spring of 1997, Battle Creek immediately joined Forest Ridge, Bailey Ranch, and White Hawk on the top rung of new daily-fee courses in the Greater Tulsa area. "It's a stern test of golf," said 1996 PGA champion Mark Brooks, co-owner of the management firm hired to run Battle Creek. "A really good test from the back tees."[23] Pittman also designed Pheasant Run in Enid, the second nine holes at Shawnee Country Club, and Peoria Ridge in Miami.

Without question, the greatest player-turned-architect from Oklahoma is PGA Tour veteran Mark Hayes, twice a first-team All-American at Oklahoma State and winner of the 1976 Byron Nelson Classic and the 1977 Players Championship. Hayes, who was medalist at the 1999 Senior PGA Tour qualifying tournament, also won the Oklahoma Open twice and played on the 1979 U.S. Ryder Cup team, winning his final-day singles match against Antonio Garrido. In the first-ever matches against players from all across Europe (previously they had had to come from either Great Britain or Ireland), the United States won 17–11.

As an amateur and later a professional player, Hayes experienced many peaks and valleys. In 1972 he finished joint runner-up to Vinny Giles, with Ben Crenshaw, in the U.S. Amateur and made the World Amateur Cup team. As a pro, in the second round of the 1977 British Open, Hayes eagled the seventeenth hole at Turnberry then dropped a stroke at the last, to become the first player in 117 years of British Open history to shoot 63. Earlier that year, in the first Players Championship at Sawgrass, Hayes shot 289 to win by two strokes and gain a ten-year exemption onto the PGA Tour.

Later in his career, Hayes was labeled an inconsistent putter, based on a couple of four-putts that were as much the product of questionable pin placements as anything Hayes did with the flat blade. In 1979 at Pebble Beach, he was leading the Crosby National Pro-Am after a brilliant third-round 66 and stretched it to three after sixty-eight holes. But at Pebble's fifteenth hole, with a slick sidehiller, he left a downhill putt short, then ran the next one by, leading to a four-putt. He lost the next day in a playoff to Lon Hinkle.

In the second round of the 1982 Masters, Hayes had an eight-foot birdie putt on the eighteenth hole to move into a tie for first with eventual champion Craig Stadler and Curtis Strange. But the cup was cut on a side-hill, and after he stroked his first putt, Hayes had a 35-footer left. He rolled the second putt to within inches of the hole, only to see it roll back down the hill and leave him another 35-footer. He lagged the third putt some three feet below the hole and made his fourth.

Afterward, Hayes managed to control his frustration by refusing to talk to anyone but his wife for more than an hour. "If you're really smart, which I wasn't, you can play this hole," Hayes said after he settled down. "But the reaction of the crowd is what got me. They were laughing and snickering as the ball rolled down the hill. I understand, but it's hard to take. That's why I wasn't going to say anything to reporters when I came off the green. It was such a helpless feeling. But I've been there before and will again, probably."[24]

Hayes won more than $1 million on tour before turning his attention full-time to course architecture in the 1990s. He and partner Jerry Slack completed restorations at Sapulpa Golf Course and the Oaks Country Club in Tulsa. Their partnership dissolved in June of 1995 and Hayes, working out of Edmond, designed the critically acclaimed Sugar Creek Canyon in Hinton while also completing restorations at Stillwater Country Club, Oakwood Country Club in Enid, Earlywine South in Oklahoma City, Adams Golf Course in Bartlesville, and Oak Tree Country Club in Edmond.

Slack's most popular project in Oklahoma has been Muskogee's Lin-Lar Golf Club, completed in 1997. The privately owned, daily-fee course has greens that average 6,700 square feet, and its eighteenth hole, with an elevated green, is a throwback to the artistry of Perry Maxwell. Slack got a firsthand look at Maxwell architecture in 1997. He added nine holes to the Maxwell-designed Hillcrest Golf Course in Coffeyville, Kansas. "That's why I spent two years routing, instead of two months," Slack said of his responsibility to the Maxwell legacy.[25]

Dozens more Oklahoma landowners, golf professionals, and greens superintendents have built courses in the state, though not necessarily in business as full-time golf course builders or architects. Among them are Vince Bizik (Cherokee Grove Golf Club in Grove); Terry and Wayne Koppage, with Tom Baker, Dennis Lindeman, Don Cornelius and Wilbur Funk (Deer Run Golf Club in Broken Arrow); Kevin Benedict (Cimarron Trails in Perkins); Joe Boyer (River Oaks in Edmond); Tony Doudican with Doug Tewell (Thunder Creek in McAlester); Hamon Baker (Crosswinds Golf Club in Tahlequah); Fillmore Vaughn (Lakeview Golf Course in Ardmore); brothers Tom Harris and Labron Harris Sr.(Lakeside Memorial in Stillwater and the second nine at Woodson Park and Trosper Park in Oklahoma City); Young Bock Han (Westbury Country Club in Yukon); Jeff Woods (The Woods in Coweta); Buck Meehan (Hilltop Golf Course in Porter); Wade Meehan (Cedar Creek in Coweta); Hoot Phelan and Boyd Bibb (Okemah Golf Course in Okemah); Ab Justice (Willow Creek Golf and Country Club in Oklahoma City); Arthur Lee Schrock (Al and Em Golf Course in Marlow); Mike Gowens (the second nine at Brent Bruehl Memorial Course in Purcell); Jell Lamoreaux (Cotton Creek Golf and Country Club in Glenpool); Larry Keese (Eagle Crest Golf Course in Muskogee); Lefty Mace (Fort Sill Golf Club in Lawton); Charlie Bland (Osage Country Club in Adair); Hugh Bancroft (Pryor Municipal); Jay Driscoll (Shadow Creek Country Club in Sallisaw); Jim Housh, with Don Booher (Fairfax Golf Course in Edmond); Jeff Klaiber (consultant at Lin-Lar in Muskogee); and Andy McCormick (River Oaks Golf Club in Oklahoma City).

Also making a name as one of Oklahoma's newest course architects was Lyndy Lindsey. Lindsey designed the par-30 Links at Oklahoma City in 1998 and two courses in 1999: Broken Arrow Golf and Athletic Club and the Owasso Golf and Athletic Club. The Broken Arrow and Owasso courses represent one of the newest trends in golf. Instead of the traditional golf and country club arrangement, Lindsey's work incorporated both a golf course and a place to work out in a health club atmosphere.

NINE
Varsity

Three university golf programs in Oklahoma have won the NCAA Division I National Championship: the University of Tulsa women's team and the men's teams at the University of Oklahoma and Oklahoma State University.

TULSA UNIVERSITY

In a 1995 *South Central Golf* magazine article by Jenk Jones Jr., University of Tulsa women's golf coach Dale McNamara was asked how the Golden Hurricane, at a private school in the southern Midwest, could be consistently competitive with larger universities in warmer climates. Replied McNamara, second only to Arizona State's Linda Vollstedt as the coach with the most wins in women's collegiate golf history: "There is no city that admires, supports, and backs the game of golf like Tulsa. We have a variety of golf courses and practice facilities here unequaled by any in the country."[1]

Within a twenty-mile radius of the University of Tulsa campus, TU golf team members have access to nineteen private or daily-fee courses—342 holes of golf—designed by twelve professional architects: William Diddell (Mohawk Woodbine); Floyd Farley (LaFortune Park and Mohawk Pecan Valley); George Fazio (Indian Springs River); Tom Fazio (Golf Club of Oklahoma); Joe Finger (Cedar Ridge); Leon Howard (Olde Page Belcher); Randy Heckenkemper (Forest Ridge, White Hawk, South Lakes); Perry Maxwell (Southern Hills); Press Maxwell (Meadowbrook); Bland Pittman (Bailey Ranch, Glen Eagles, Battle Creek); Don Sechrest (Page Belcher Stone Creek, Indian Springs Windmill); and A. W. Tillinghast (Tulsa Country Club, Oaks Country Club).

It has not hurt recruiting that McNamara, whose maiden name was Fleming, was one of the top amateur players in the history of Oklahoma golf. Dale Fleming took up golf in the 1950s, after her parents joined the Oaks Country Club in Tulsa. At first she played golf left-handed. But Oaks head pro Marion Askew, who had seen her throw a ball right-handed, suggested that she switch sides.

By her teenage years, Dale began entering junior tournaments in Oklahoma and elsewhere. Her father, Lloyd Fleming, mindful of expenses, told Dale that every stroke she took cost her family twenty-five cents. "That taught me not to goof around," she said. "To me quality practice is much more important than long hours spent on the range."[2]

Beginning with the 1956 Oklahoma Women's Amateur at Oakwood Country Club in Enid, Dale dominated women's amateur golf in Oklahoma. During the next twenty years, she won seven Oklahoma Women's Amateurs. Besides at Enid, she won three Oklahoma Amateurs in Tulsa—one at the Oaks (1972) and two at Tulsa Country Club (1959, 1968); and one each at Twin Hills (1957), Muskogee Country Club (1969), and Elks Golf and Country Club in Duncan (1975). In 1983, her daughter Melissa McNamara won the Oklahoma Women's Amateur at Dornick Hills Country Club in Ardmore. Only Patty (McGraw) Coatney, with eight, has more victories in the Oklahoma Women's Amateur than McNamara.

At a time when there were no varsity women's golf programs, Dale attended the University of Oklahoma for two years before transferring to Tulsa. At TU she could have followed Susie Maxwell's example at Oklahoma City University and played on the men's team. Instead, she represented Tulsa University as an individual, competing in the few collegiate tournaments open to women. For her efforts, Fleming earned the first Hurricane varsity letter awarded to a female.

In April of 1957, Fleming was ready to turn pro. But during the 1957 North-South Amateur in Pinehurst, North Carolina, she met James McNamara, a vacationing businessman from Erie, Pennsylvania. A romance ensued and they were married two years later. After four years in Erie, the McNamaras moved to Tulsa. Even as mother to two young daughters during the 1960s and early 1970s, McNamara stayed close enough to competitive golf to keep her handicap at plus two and to qualify for several USGA events. She made the cut at the U.S. Women's Open and was a consistent contender at both the Women's Western and the Women's North-South.

The mid–1970s were the early days of Title IX, the federal law mandating equal athletic opportunities for men and women in public schools and universities. Tulsa University made a commitment to intercollegiate athletics for women by organizing golf and tennis teams. McNamara, whose daughters Cathy and Melissa had reached ages when they were more independent, accepted an invitation from TU women's athletic coordinator Karen King to serve as volunteer women's golf coach.

As coach, McNamara emphasized lessons she had learned as a competitor, developing a basic philosophy of three A's—attitude, atmosphere, and ability; and three absolutes—recruit, instruct, and support. "Recruiting is the name of the game," McNamara said. "And I tell freshmen when they come in, 'Even though I'm a dictator and this is not a democracy, you take the glory and I'll take the blame. Sure, I'll be holding their hands. And when they're seniors, they'll be holding mine.'"[3]

TU's first women's golf team (Brenda Moyers, Judy Grayston, Terri Streck, Lindsay Wetzel), organized in 1974, had a budget of $1,500 a year for recruiting, travel, uniforms, and equipment. At their first tournament, the Tucker Invitational in Albuquerque, the team wore T-shirts and blue jeans, with an assortment of bags and equipment. On returning to Tulsa, the first order of business was uniforms and matching golf bags.

Even though the Hurricane did not win at Albuquerque, the player-turned-coach had the opportunity to meet some of the game's top coaches on the men's side, such as Dave Williams of Houston and Labron Harris Sr. of Oklahoma State. Following Albuquerque, the new team wasted little time finding the winner's circle. Led by Moyers, the Hurricane won its next time out, at the Kansas Invitational.

TU's early success made an impression on at least one high school senior from Roswell, New Mexico. In early 1975, Nancy Lopez contacted McNamara (in those days coaches were not allowed to initiate contact with recruits). McNamara paid a recruiting visit to Lopez in Roswell, where she met the Lopez family, including Nancy's father, Domingo, who had taught his daughter to play. Lopez and McNamara hit it off. After a three-month recruiting process, Lopez committed to Tulsa. "Nancy was a hard recruit," McNamara said in a 2000 interview. "She could have played anywhere she wanted."

During her two years at Tulsa (she joined the LPGA Tour pro in 1977), Lopez won eleven times, including the 1976 Association for Intercollegiate Athletics for Women National Championship. "I started out as an engineering major but switched to business administration," Lopez recalled of her college days. "I finally dropped out of school after my sophomore year and turned pro. I had to. Tulsa didn't offer a degree in basket weaving, and that was about the only thing I could have passed at that point."[4]

Any ambition she lacked for the classroom was more than made up for at the golf course. After leaving Tulsa, Lopez went on to dominate the LPGA Tour. She won nine times as a rookie, including five in a row. With forty-eight career victories, Lopez was inducted into the LPGA Hall of Fame in 1987. "That's called instant credibility," said McNamara of the Lopez legacy to Tulsa. "That gave us instant tradition."[5]

Future LPGA stars followed the Lopez tradition at Tulsa. Led by Sharon Barrett and future U.S. Women's Open champion Kathy Baker (Guadagnino), Tulsa won the AIAW team championship in 1980 at the University of New Mexico South Course in Albuquerque. Two years later, the last year for the AIAW and the first year for the Women's NCAA Championship, the Golden Hurricane swept both team titles, winning the AIAW at Columbus, Ohio, and the NCAA at Stanford, California. At the NCAA, Hurricanes Baker, Jody Rosenthal (Anschutz), and Barb Thomas finished first, second, and third. Tusla's thirty-six-stroke victory margin over Texas Christian set an NCAA record.

In 1988, Tulsa won a fourth national championship under McNamara. And this time another McNamara played a pivotal role: her daughter Melissa won the NCAA individual title. During McNamara's twenty-seven seasons as coach, the Hurricane won more than seventy tournaments, with twenty-five first or second team All-Americans. At least thirty McNamara protégées went on to the professional ranks, among them daughter Melissa, Lopez, Baker-Guadagnino, Rosenthal-Anschutz, Barrett, Kelly Robbins, Carolyn Hill, Cathy Mockett, Cathy Reynolds, Barb Thomas, and

Karin Koch. In 1985, McNamara was voted by her peers as national coach of the year. Upon her retirement in 2000, McNamara was succeeded as Golden Hurricanes coach by her daughter Melissa.

UNIVERSITY OF OKLAHOMA

Until the spring of 1933, college golf in the United States had been dominated by players from eastern schools. But that year, in the University of Oklahoma's first season to field a team at the NCAA Golf Championship, Sooner player Walter Emery, a native of Duncan, won the NCAA individual title in Buffalo, New York, becoming the first NCAA men's golf champion from a university west of the Mississippi River.

Emery's feat was all the more remarkable since it was not until six years later, in 1939, that the NCAA Championship was first held at a course west of the Mississippi (Wakonda Club in Des Moines, Iowa). Stanford, in 1938, was the first school west of the Mississippi to win the NCAA team title.

The Sooners were coached in their inaugural season, and for the eighteen to follow, by Bruce Drake, who also headed the Sooner basketball team for seventeen years. In basketball, Drake led the Sooners to a second-place finish at the 1947 men's NCAA Final Four. In golf, Drake also coached OU's other NCAA champion—Jim Vickers (1952)—and Charles Coe, one of the half dozen top amateur players in the history of American golf.

An outstanding example of sports journalism was a story about Coe by James Achenbach, senior writer for *Golfweek* magazine, in 1996. It is reprinted here in its entirety, with permission of Achenbach and *Golfweek*:

CHARLIE COE: THE LAST OF THE CAREER AMATEURS

Golfweek, August 10, 1996
By James Achenbach
Castle Rock, Colorado

Long tall Charlie. He was as singular in appearance as he was in golfing ability: the cigarette-thin Oklahoma roughboy with the kill-you eyes and whiplash golf swing. When he lowered that True Temper hammer, the ball yelped as if it wanted to jump out of its balata skin.

Charlie Coe, now 73 and humbled by a stroke, is a lifelong amateur, a species practically extinct today. On the eve of the 1996 U.S. Amateur, a championship Coe won twice, there is plenty of reason to celebrate his life and times.

Coe is perhaps most famous, ironically, for a loss in the match-play final of the 1959 U.S. Amateur. Before the championship, he appeared on the cover of *Sports Illustrated*. Maybe it was the start of the *SI* jinx, as Coe met a 19-year-old hotshot named Jack Nicklaus in the 36-hole final at the Broadmoor Golf Club in Colorado Springs, Colorado.

Nicklaus and Coe came to the par-4 36th hole all square. It was getting dark. Both hit 3-woods off the tee, and both were in the fairway, Nicklaus about 10 feet ahead of Coe. Although Coe tried to feather his short-iron approach, it hit the right side of the green and took a huge hop over the putting surface. Nicklaus, seeing this, bounced his shot onto the green, 15 feet short of the hole.

Coe's ball was in a trough behind the green. The grass was eight inches high, and he faced a delicate downhill pitch. The shot he was about to hit, most observers agree, was one of the most dramatic plays ever made on the final hole of a national championship.

"It was one of the all-time great shots in one of the all-time great matches," says Jack Vickers, founder and president of Castle Pines Golf Club near Denver. "Charlie and I had been friends since high school, so I was there. He hit this beautiful pitch shot, and it looked like it stopped 10 times before it got down there. But it kept rolling and rolling toward the hole. When it finally stopped, it was maybe half an inch from the cup, dead in the middle."

Nicklaus nodded his head and said something Coe didn't clearly hear. Assuming the putt had been conceded, Coe reached down and picked up the ball.

It was then that Nicklaus told Coe he had misunderstood. Nicklaus wanted the ball left where it was, because the Rules of Golf at the time allowed a player to control his opponent's ball in match play. Nicklaus could, in effect, use Coe's ball as a backstop.

"Well, I had already picked up my ball," recalls Coe, "so I said to him, 'Jack, I concede the match to you. You win.'"

"And without hesitation he said to me, 'No, I won't take it that way.' And he got up and made his putt. He was an absolute gentleman, and he knocked the putt right in the middle of the hole. He could really putt."

Because it ended in such gentlemanly fashion, Coe has never regretted losing that match. He showed the world what he could do, yet he was tangling with a teenager who eventually would win more majors than anyone.

Today in the Castle Pines clubhouse, there is a framed letter from Nicklaus to Coe, which reads in part, "We go way back to Walker Cup days and to playing in the Amateur—when as a young boy I somehow got lucky and won. The many times I watched you play in golf tournaments, it always amazed me that a fellow who had not made golf his main interest in life could so consistently play the fantastic golf you played. You have been a great golfer and are a tremendous credit to the game."

Those who know Nicklaus know he doesn't issue praise frivolously. Even more to the point, Nicklaus once said, "There was a period of several years (in the late '50s) when Charlie Coe was one of the two or three best golfers in the world, professional or amateur."

Others think the same thing. Former PGA champion Don January says Coe was "the finest ball striker I ever saw."

Coe, along with former U.S. Golf Association president Bill Campbell and Michael Bonallack, secretary of the Royal & Ancient Golf Club, are considered the best lifelong amateurs since Bobby Jones. But of the three, only Coe competed successfully against top professionals.

At a time when he captured every major amateur title in this country (U.S. Amateur, Western Amateur, and Trans-Mississippi) and once recorded 27 consecutive match-play victories, Coe also tied for second in the 1961 Masters and posted three top–10 finishes in a four-year span at Augusta. Altogether he played in 19 Masters.

Coe was tall and sinewy, with a determined look in his eyes that matches the more famous concentration of Ben Hogan. "He has the most intense eyes," says Keith Schneider, head professional at Castle Pines. "You can see how much he wants to win, but he's so nice at the same time. He's almost like a second father to me." Coe and Hogan, the two great concentrators, were paired once at the Colonial Invitational. Coe complimented Hogan after brilliant shots on both the first and second holes.

"And he didn't say a word," Coe recalls.

There followed a few more words of praise from Coe, with no response from Hogan, so long tall Charlie zipped his lip. "I got put out because he didn't say anything. He didn't say, 'Thank you,' or 'Kiss my fanny.' So I just made up my mind that was it. I wouldn't say anything more."

They got to the 15th tee without another word being spoken, when suddenly Hogan addressed Coe. "You got a cigarette, Charlie?" he asked.

One sentence, five words. Those were the only words Coe would hear from Hogan during the round. When it came to competitive golf, Coe was the strong and silent type, but he was outsilenced by the best of them—the Iceman.

Later, in the locker room, Hogan approached Coe and said wholeheartedly, "I appreciate playing with you, Charlie. That was the most enjoyable round of golf I've ever played."

Most enjoyable, as in hit the ball and keep your mouth shut. Coe and Hogan would become close friends, their friendship cemented by excellent golf rather than a flurry of words. When they spoke, both were straightforward.

What Hogan was to professional golf, Coe was to amateur golf. Coe let his clubs do the talking. Even today, as he is honored at the Charlie Coe Invitational at Castle Pines, he speaks concisely, saying what's on his mind and sitting down before the applause has a chance to start.

"I want to thank you all for being here," he drawls at a ketchup-stuck-in-the-bottle pace, talking like a man who is embarrassed that so many of his friends are here to celebrate his life and career. "It is because of people like you that golf remains the wonderful game that it is."

End of speech. Long tall Charlie, the human 1-iron, was always resolute—decide on a strategy, do it, then get out of the way.

And he always believed that golf is a gentleman's game (gentlewomen, too, for he was never a chauvinist). Swear words rarely escape his mouth, but if they do, they are always followed by an "excuse me." Yet this gentleman was one of the fiercest competitors ever to lace on a pair of spikes. He played to win.

There is a story of touring pro Bo Wininger, who, when asked how he played in a tournament, responded, "Pretty damn good. I shot 64 and only got beat by five shots. That amateur (Coe) shot 59."

Coe's son, Rick, executive director of the Oklahoma Golf Association, remembers a friendly round of golf about 12 years ago at Oklahoma City Golf & Country Club that suddenly didn't seem so friendly.

"There was a new assistant pro, so he and I played my father and one of his friends," said Rick. "This pro was playing pretty good, and we were beating them every way imaginable. We were killing them. The pro made a birdie putt at 9, and my father asked, 'What was that?' And the pro said, 'That was a 3. It's the 9th hole, isn't it?'

"That made Dad mad. He pulled me aside and told me he didn't like the pro's attitude. Then he birdied 10, 12, 14, 16, and 18 on the back side, and, of course, we lost money."

In summing up his father, Rick says, "He's the nicest guy in the world, but he is very blood-thirsty on the course. His idea of playing golf was to beat his opponent—even if it was a close friend—as badly as possible. Then the match would be over, and he would forget about it. He would continue to be the nicest guy in the world."

Coe always enjoyed a challenge, like the time he first visited New Jersey's Pine Valley Golf Club. Many first-time players at Pine Valley have been suckered into bets that require them to break 90 or 80, but Coe was ready.

Though he was a Walker Cup player, some were prepared to bet him he couldn't break 80. "Save your money, boys," he said charitably, as he played entirely with irons to avoid trouble and shot 71. The second time he played, he used his woods and shot 70. Coe always hit the ball a long way, but he rarely practiced. "I detested hitting practice balls," he explains. "The reason was that you were always hitting off the same lie. When you play, every lie is different. My definition of an idiot is a guy who gets a bad lie on the practice tee. Everybody hits nice shots off nice lies."

Coe's practice routine was to stick three balls in his pocket and play alone. Every time he hit an unsatisfactory shot, he would throw down another ball "while it was fresh in my mind."

Growing up in Ardmore, Oklahoma, Coe first played golf at six. At nine, he won a junior tournament for boys 17 and younger. He won the Oklahoma State High School Championship and was off to the University of Oklahoma, where he majored in business administration.

"My father was in the oil business, and it was only natural that I would go into it," he says. "We've got five generations in the oil business. My wife's great-grandfather was on the crew that discovered the first oil well in the United States."

The only time he considered leaving the business was in the early 1950s. He said to his wife, Elizabeth, "I think I'll turn pro." To which she replied, "You can do anything you want, but if you think I'm going to raise a family (they had three boys) and live out of a suitcase, you're crazy."

And that was it. He never again thought of turning pro. "I respect her advice and wisdom," Coe says of his wife. "I'm very grateful for the fact that she made that comment to me. It was cut and dried in 15 minutes."

Oil and water may not mix, but Coe proved that oil and golf certainly do. "We've been in the business so long (Rick runs the family business in addition to his duties with the state golf association) that we know we're gonna have ups and downs. The only way you prepare for this is not to be greedy. You have to be prepared for slumps, so we conserve a little money when things are good and then we can ride it out when they aren't. That's the way we've done it, and we've been moderately successful."

Once, Coe points out, he discovered a "little field" in which he drilled for 52 wells and ended up with 49 producers. That was the oil business equivalent of winning the U.S. Open.

Association with winners is a Coe hallmark. He has remained close to Byron Nelson over the years, and he calls Nelson "the purest striker of the ball I've ever seen. I'm not trying to take anything away from Hogan, but Nelson could maneuver the golf ball as well as any man. In my opinion, he had the best set of hands."

The instructor who knew Coe's swing best was Tony Penna. "He could watch me swing a few times and tell me what was wrong," Coe says. "He was a genius."

For years Coe played with MacGregor clubs, designed by Penna. Later, when Penna started his own equipment company, Coe switched out of loyalty. Now he uses Cobra.

He has seen most of the great golf courses in this country, and he quickly names his personal top four: Augusta National, Olympic Club, Southern Hills, and Castle Pines.

"Of course," he adds, "I'm a little prejudiced about Southern Hills. Years ago they had a dinner for me and my wife and made me an honorary lifetime member. They gave Elizabeth a charm bracelet for most miles behind the ropes (in the gallery). She always goes with me to tournaments. I think she's missed three in her life."

Coe played Dick Chapman in the final of the 1951 British Amateur. After the morning 18, he said to Elizabeth, "If I win this, I'm going to hang my clubs on a rusty nail and retire."

He swears he would have done it, but he lost to Chapman. "I guess it was a blessing I didn't win," he says with a laugh.

After leaving OU in 1948, Coe remained activee as an alum. Due in large measure to Coe's successes, in 1950 the university commissioned Perry Maxwell and his son Press Maxwell to design and construct a championship course on the OU campus. The new course reinforced OU's dominance in the Big Seven Conference. The Sooners won five of eight conference titles from 1950 to 1957 and saw Jim Vickers win the 1952 NCAA individual title at the Purdue University Course.

During the 1950s, 1960s, and 1970s, under coaches Ted Gwin, Pete Elliot, Bob James, Clyde "Bud" Cronin, Raymond Thurmond, Jim Awtrey, and Robert O. Smith, the Sooners qualified for seven NCAA Championships. Beginning with coaches Lynn Blevins (1980–81) and David Yates (1982–85), and continuing under Gregg Grost, OU fielded fifteen All-Americans during a run of qualifying for fifteen consecutive NCAA Championships. The streak was punctuated by the Sooners' 1989 NCAA team title, under Grost, at Edmond's Oak Tree Golf Club (see chapter 8). Grost retired following the 2000 season.

While the OU golf program had been to the mountaintop, the OU Golf Course had deteriorated after four decades. The course had never been irrigated and greens and tees were in disrepair. In the early 1990s a fund-raising effort was begun to restore and remodel the course. In 1996, Seminole businessman and golf enthusiast Jimmie Austin contributed $1 million to the $2.5 million fund-raising effort. Soon afterward, the OU regents voted to name the course for Austin. "The university is grateful for the extraordinary generosity of Jimmie and Marie Austin," said OU president David Boren. "Their most recent gift to the universiy will help create a golf course of national and international stature and bring increased attention to our outstanding golf program."[6]

To oversee the project, OU brought in Atlanta course architect Robert Cupp, a 1961 University of Miami graduate, who had worked for twelve years for the Jack Nicklaus design team. In 1985, Cupp had established his own firm, building a series of highly regarded courses with 1976 U.S. Open champion Jerry Pate. Among other PGA Tour pros Cupp enlisted as consultants were Sam Snead, Fred Couples, Fuzzy Zoeller, Hubert Green, and Tom Kite. The OU course renovation committee members were particularly impressed by two Cupp courses of note: Oregon's Pumpkin Ridge, voted best new private course by *Golf Digest*, and Old Waverly in West Point, Mississippi, site of the 1999 U.S. Women's Open.

After visiting the OU course, Cupp summarized the magic of Maxwell and the challenge that lay ahead. "If his bunker is against the edge of a green, the collar rises up over the green's shape, so that the putting surface is not just a straight line as you see it from the fairway," said

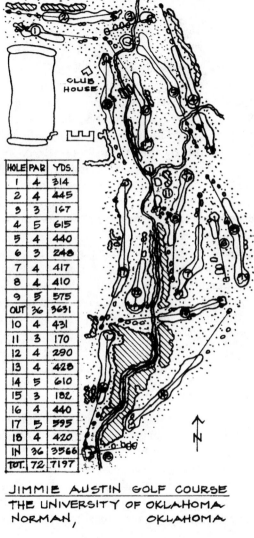

HOLE	PAR	YDS.
1	4	314
2	4	445
3	3	167
4	5	615
5	4	440
6	3	248
7	4	417
8	4	410
9	5	575
OUT	36	3631
10	4	431
11	3	170
12	4	290
13	4	428
14	5	610
15	3	182
16	4	440
17	5	395
18	4	420
IN	36	3566
TOT.	72	7197

JIMMIE AUSTIN GOLF COURSE
THE UNIVERSITY OF OKLAHOMA
NORMAN,   OKLAHOMA

Course Layout 3. The Jimmie Austin Golf Course at the University of Oklahoma, Norman, designed by Perry Maxwell and Robert Cupp. Drawing by Jep Wille.

Cupp. "It's broken by these rises and falls above the bunkers. It's a wonderful look. The best example I think is at Prairie Dunes in Kansas, which I think is vintage Maxwell. It's nice to be able to bring that Maxwell look back, let people experience it, and be proud of it."[7]

Just to be certain, the university sought advice from Press Maxwell, who had worked with his father when the course was originally built. "I'm sure there is some concern remodeling will destroy the Perry Maxwell image," said Press, after reviewing the plans. "But you can't do that. The routing remains essentially the same. Given the same topography, the same background of trees and creek, they can't hurt that any. The changes are perfectly feasible, all of them."[8]

The most noticeable changes were to the front side, where the par-5 second hole was divided into a par 4 and par 3, just the opposite of the par-4 eighth and par-3 ninth, which were combined into a par 5. Lines of play for holes 5, 6, 7, and 8 remained the same but played in the opposite direction. Cupp also added eighty-seven bunkers, lengthened the course to 7,197 yards from the back tees, and replaced all the turf. The Jimmie Austin–University of Oklahoma Golf Course, following the $4.8 million restoration, reopened to the public on August 14, 1996, to positive reviews.

"IF THE GUYS BACK IN THE 1950S COULD SEE THIS THING NOW, THEY'D NEVER BELIEVE IT."

Tour pro and OU alumnus Andrew Magee said, "If the guys back in the 1950s could see this thing now, they'd never believe it." Former OU All-American Grant Masson called it a "championship course waiting to happen." Director of golf Stan Ball compared the new version to attending a class reunion: "For those who played the original course, the redesign may be like seeing classmates at a 20-year high school reunion," said Ball. "Some holes are unchanged, others vaguely recognizable, and the rest are brand new."[9]

Golf people had confidence that the project would be a success even before the course reopened. In July of 1996, a few weeks after Bartlesville's Hillcrest Country Club withdrew its bid for the 1997 Men's NCAA Central Regional, the NCAA awarded the regional to OU. Subsequently, the 1998 Women's Big 12 Conference Championship was held there, along with the Susie Maxwell Berning Classic. "It's everything you would want in a golf course," said OU women's coach Carol Ludvigson. "It can be as easy for the general public or as hard as we want for tournaments. From a college or professional standpoint, you can find all the difficulty that you would out on tour." [10]

In June of 1997, the OU regents announced a permanent tribute to its best-known golfing alumnus by naming a new golf learning center after Charlie Coe. Located on the west edge of the golf course, the 7,000-square-foot, all-weather facility was designed by former Sooner All-American Tripp Davis, in conjunction with Cupp and OU coach Gregg Grost. In addition to teaching bays with video setups, the Coe Golf Learning Center houses the offices of the OU men's and women's golf coaches, team locker rooms, meeting rooms, and administrative areas. There is a practice area 90 yards wide and 225 yards deep, with a 12,000-square-foot practice green.

"'THIS AIN'T FAIR. IT JUST AIN'T FAIR.'"

"I call this the cherry on top of the sundae," said Grost. "This building has already been a recruiting tool," said Ludvigson. "We signed four outstanding freshmen just from the construction." Said OU athletic director Joe Castiglione: "I had a friend of mine come through here whose son will be a freshman on a fellow Big 12 team in golf, and he was speechless. The only words he uttered as he walked through the facility were, 'This ain't fair. It just ain't fair.'" [11]

OKLAHOMA STATE UNIVERSITY

In the summer of 1946, Oklahoma State (then called Oklahoma A&M) head basketball coach and athletic director Henry P. Iba was coming off consecutive basketball national championships and had the go-ahead from OSU regents to hire coaches for other sports at the Stillwater campus. When one of Iba's first hires was Labron Harris to be OSU's first paid golf coach, it was almost as if Iba had hired half a dozen individuals for the price of one.

In addition to his coaching responsibilities at OSU, Harris, a native of Dardanelle, Arkansas, who grew up in Wewoka, Oklahoma, taught full-time in the OSU business school, built Stillwater's Lakeside Memorial Golf Course and oversaw its maintenance, conducted summer camps for kids, and still found time to play tournament golf.

It was Harris's success as a competitor that initially caught Iba's attention. Harris had taken up golf in 1930, while he was a student at Southwestern Oklahoma State College in Weatherford. He was such a fast learner that within three years he won the Oklahoma Collegiate Conference championship. He followed that with three consecutive Oklahoma Sand Greens titles, beginning in 1936. Harris soon took over as head professional at Guthrie Country Club and oversaw the course's conversion from sand greens to grass.

Once Iba offered Harris a job, the decision was an easy one for Harris. "I guess I always had coaching in the back of my mind," Harris recalled. "I was teaching at Guthrie High School when I got the chance to go to Stillwater. I jumped at it without asking any questions."[12]

His success at OSU was immediate. Beginning in 1947, the Cowboys won nine Missouri Valley titles in a row and finished in the top five at the NCAA Championship in each of his first three seasons. In 1953 at

Colorado Springs, Earl Moeller became the first player from OSU to win the NCAA individual crown.

Later that summer, at Oakwood Country Club in Enid, Harris showed that he could play as well as he coached. Competing in the Oklahoma Open, Harris fired back-to-back 69s, beating former OSU player Richard Turner by a stroke (65-74). Ten years later, in October of 1963, Labron Harris Jr. duplicated his father's feat, winning the Oklahoma Open at Muskogee Country Club, after winning the 1962 U.S. Amateur.

Under Harris, OSU won twenty-four conference titles and the 1963 NCAA Championship and had twenty top-five finishes at the NCAAs. He coached twenty-seven All-Americans, including Ab Justice, Dave Eichelberger, Bob Dickson, Grier Jones, Danny Edwards, and Mark Hayes, and served as head professional at a course he designed, Lakeside Memorial Golf Course in Stillwater. He made lasting impressions on both collegians and junior players who attended his summer golf camps.

"Coach Harris would help you with your golf swing if you asked," recalled Bob Dickson, the last player in history to win both the U.S. and British Amateurs in the same year. "But he was strong in the mental part of the game. And this was back before you ever heard of such thing as a sports psychologist—but he was one." An avid proponent of fast play, Harris insisted that his players practice even in the rawest Oklahoma weather. There were stories about Harris sending his charges out with ice on the ground, running between shots to get in eighteen holes in ninety minutes, "so they wouldn't catch cold." It is still a perception OSU does not necessarily want to live down.

"We take a beating on that every year," said former Cowboy assistant Bruce Heppler, four decades later. "Some of our more southerly rivals recruit like the Arctic Circle begins at Ardmore and that the entire state turns into an ice block from November through March. But if people insist on believing that we practice other than when it's sunny and 72 degrees, that's OK too. Coach Holder tells recruits the same thing Coach Harris told him, 'If our weather is so bad why is our record so good?'"

For twenty-seven years, the business professor-turned-golf coach Harris made the golf course his outdoor classroom. "I have no idea where I'd be today if it weren't for Labron," said Dave Eichelberger, a native of Waco, Texas, a two-time Cowboy All-American, and winner of the 1999 U.S. Senior Open. "OSU was the best school to go to if you wanted to learn golf. Houston had better players and they didn't require as much instruction. Their coach (Dave Williams) was a great recruiter, but Labron was an excellent coach and teacher."[13]

Harris was a self-taught golfer, as serious about his own game as he was about coaching. It was reported that Harris won more than 150 tournaments in Oklahoma and elsewhere. "Even in his sixties, during the heat of summer, Mr. Harris practiced a lot harder than we did," recalled former OSU golf camper Marcus Lemon, a low-handicap player who became a banker in Tulsa. "Everybody called him Labe the Babe. He claimed he could hit it straighter than any man alive. And we didn't doubt it. He was a genius from 100 yards in. He would set up old tires as targets and walk the line, barking out, 'Spin the rod!' To say Mr. Harris believed in strong left-side control would be an understatement. He taught us to backhand the blade through impact."

Lemon said Harris was a trick shot artist and an innovator. "He'd spin a club in his hands and say, 'Whaddya wanna see me do?' Then he'd turn it upside down or hit shots left-handed. He was always talking things like muscle memory, dominant eye, stretching, stuff you read about now in *Golf Digest*. One time he showed up with a pair of reverse gravity boots and hung from a door jamb, upside down."

In the days of mandatory retirement, Harris stepped down from coaching in 1973. He picked as his successor a former player, three-time OSU All-American Mike Holder, a Texas native who had graduated in 1966 from Ardmore High School. When Holder took over the OSU program, he was still clinging to a dream of playing professional golf. "I took the job planning to stay one year," Holder recalled in 1997. "I needed a job where I could make a little money and play a lot of golf." He got half his wish, earning $6,500 his first year in Stillwater.

"I had this master's degree and thought I could do better than $6,500. I remember how amazed I was that Labron had stayed for 27 years. Now I look up and realize I've been here for 24."[14]

Initially, Holder's mission was as basic as the Hippocratic oath: first do no harm. At OSU, this meant keep winning. Under Harris, OSU had won five consecutive Big Eight Conference championships and fifteen of the last sixteen. Holder was more than up to the challenge. He started a streak of his own: ten conference titles in a row, a second-place finish in 1984, followed by twelve of the next thirteen. Only Missouri (1984) and OU (1992) interrupted OSU's Big Eight Conference title streak, which continued in the Big 12 Conference.

Holder's success on the course mirrored his successes as a recruiter. Tom Jones of Tulsa signed first with Holder, followed by Brazilian Jaime Gonzalez. The next season Holder landed the most coveted junior player in the nation: Lindy Miller from Fort Worth. In the next fifteen years, Holder signed an impressive succession of future All-Americans: David Edwards (younger brother of former OSU star Danny Edwards), Rafael Alarcon, Bob Tway, Willie Wood, Tommy Moore, Andy Dillard, Scott Verplank, Brian Watts, Michael Bradley, Alan Bratton, Chris Tidland, E. J. Pfister, Trip Kuehne, Edward Loar, and Charles Howell, to name a few.

"Getting Tom Jones that first year was the key to it all," Holder said of the Tulsa Rogers star, who would one day become director of golf at Karsten Creek. "He gave us stability during the transition. Then getting Lindy out of Texas, at a time when Houston was such a powerhouse, was a big deal."[15]

At the national level, Holder took OSU's golf program straight to the top—winning eight NCAA team championships in twenty-seven years, including a stretch from 1975 through 1988 when OSU finished first or second at the NCAAs in thirteen years out of fourteen. During the Harris and Holder tenure, seven OSU players (Earl Moeller, Grier Jones, David Edwards, Verplank, Watts, Pfister, and Howell) won NCAA individual crowns.

In June of 2000, Howell, an OSU junior from Augusta, Georgia, led the Cowboys to their ninth NCAA team title, the eighth in the Holder era, with the most dominating team and individual performances in 104 years of NCAA Golf Championship history. Competing at the Robert Trent Jones Grand National Lake Course in Auburn, Alabama, Howell sank a putt at the seventy-second hole of regulation to send OSU into a playoff against Georgia Tech, which OSU won. Both OSU and Georga Tech had team totals of thirty-six under par, setting the all-time NCAA tournament scoring record.

The twenty-year-old Howell, whose season scoring average of 69.57 also set an NCAA record, posted four rounds in the 60s at the NCAA, which included a school-record-tying 63 in round two. He played the final fifty holes without a single bogey, and his eight-stroke margin of victory over runner-up Chris Morris of Houston was five better than Tiger Woods's three-stroke NCAA Championship victory margin in 1996. Howell's twenty-three-under-par total for the seventy-two holes obliterated by six shots the prevous tournament scoring record of seventeen under par, held jointly by North Carolina's John Inman (1984), Arizona State's Phil

Mickelson (1992), Texas's Justin Leonard (1994), and Minnesota's James McLean (1998).

"Charles played golf like I have never seen before," Holder said at a press conference afterward. "I've been privileged to coach some great players, but the performance he put on for four days was unreal."

In the weeks before the NCAA Championship began, Howell won the Big 12 Conference title and the prestigious Perry Maxwell Invitational. Soon after the NCAA, he was named the Big 12 Conference Male Athlete of the Year and received the Jack Nicklaus Award as the national collegiate player of the year. One month after the 2000 championship season, Howell entered a Buy-com Tour event as an amateur, finishing in second place. The next week he gave up his amateur status and began his professional career at the Greater Hartford Open.

In his first twenty-four years as OSU coach, Holder's golfers won 155 team titles and had eighty runner-up finishes, meaning that the Cowboys finished first or second 68 percent of the time. Through 2000, Holder combined with Harris to continue the most impressive team streak in collegiate golf history, qualifying for fifty-four consecutive NCAA Championships without missing a single cut. No other school even came close. Like his predecessor, Holder brought more to the OSU program than coaching ability. Seventeen of his players made Academic All-American and nine were first team both academic and athletic.

Even with all the Cowboy team and individual honors, Holder's most enduring legacy to OSU may be Karsten Creek Golf Course, a project of immense pride to his alma mater. In 1993, Holder said: "The way I see it is I've already coached for 20 years and I'll probably coach a few more. But I'll only build one golf course. I want to be there to see it built. Because whatever we end up with, I'm going to have to live with it for a long time."[16]

OSU's original home course was Stillwater's Lakeside Memorial, designed by Coach Harris. In 1983 the team moved its base to Stillwater Country Club, which had hosted the 1973 NCAA Championship. About the same time, Holder began a fund-raising effort to build a university course on acreage west of Stillwater that Wiley T. McCollum donated to the OSU Foundation. This was followed by the acquisition of adjacent parcels, which eventually totaled 960 acres.

Holder's goal was to raise enough funds from friends of the university to construct a championship course on the land seven miles west of Stillwater and provide an endowment for maintenance costs. Donors were secured, including eighteen who sponsored holes at $150,000 each. But the reality was that the course probably never would have been built without the generosity of Karsten Solheim, inventor and manufacturer of Ping golf clubs. Solheim's unconventional line of investment-cast, cavity-backed irons and heel-toe weighted putters, eventually revolutionized the clubmaking industry. But in the 1960s and early 1970s, his company was struggling for an identity, hoping to find a niche in the market for an investment-cast alloy in a world of forged steel.

One of the first collegiate players to experience success with the new irons was OSU's Danny Edwards, a two-time conference medalist and low amateur at the 1973 British Open. Holder was impressed enough that soon thereafter, Pings became the unofficial clubs of the OSU golf program. Although this was not mandatory, by 1976 other OSU golfers were using the irons and carrying Ping bags, among them Edwards's younger brother David, who won the 1978 NCAA Championship at Eugene (Oregon) Country Club playing Ping irons and a Ping golf ball.

Less than a decade later, former OSU player Bob Tway used Pings to win the 1986 PGA Championship, a victory that gave Solheim's company a boost of much-appreciated publicity. When word of Holder's fund-

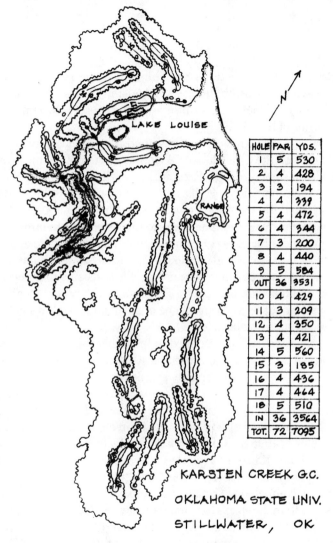

HOLE	PAR	YDS.
1	5	530
2	4	428
3	3	194
4	4	339
5	4	472
6	4	344
7	3	200
8	4	440
9	5	584
OUT	36	3531
10	4	429
11	3	209
12	4	350
13	4	421
14	5	560
15	3	185
16	4	436
17	4	464
18	5	510
IN	36	3564
TOT.	72	7095

KARSTEN CREEK G.C.

OKLAHOMA STATE UNIV.

STILLWATER, OK

Course Layout 4. Oklahoma State University's Karsten Creek Golf Club, Stillwater, designed by Tom Fazio. Drawing by Jeff McMillian, © LEW Graphics, Inc., Stillwater, Oklahoma.

raising efforts reached the Solheim family, they welcomed the chance to help, eventually contributing several million dollars. The course was named in honor of Solheim and its primary water source was named Lake Louise, in honor of his wife.

Holder knew who he wanted as architect from the moment he laid eyes on the Golf Club of Oklahoma, a championship layout in Broken Arrow designed by Tom Fazio in 1981. With courses like Shadow Creek, PGA National, Indian Wells, and Pinehurst No. 6 to his credit, Fazio was considered the top American course architect of his generation. So much in demand was Fazio that it was to OSU's benefit to bring him on site as soon as possible. "My concern was that the longer it took us, the more famous he got," said Holder. "His concern was that we wouldn't have enough money to build the kind of course people had come to expect him to build. When people come to play a Fazio course, they don't want to hear any excuses about weather problems or small budgets. If it's got his name on it, they expect the best."[17]

Karsten Creek opened to the public on March 9, 1994. At par 72, it played 7,194 yards from the tips. Keeping in mind the variability of the Oklahoma winds, two separate practice areas were built with target greens and tees at all points on the compass. Within a year, *Golf Digest* named Karsten Creek the best new public course in the United States.

As a test of golf, the new course played long and tough. In the summer of 1995 the Oklahoma State Amateur Stroke Play championship was held at Karsten Creek. The average score was 83. Less than a year later, players from eleven of the top twenty-five collegiate programs in the country competed at Karsten, where the course was set up in less extreme fashion than the state's top amateurs saw. Medalist was OSU's Trip Kuehne, the 1994 U.S. Amateur runner-up to Tiger Woods, with a five-under-par total of 211. Florida won the team title at three-over-par 867.

In June 2000 OSU restructured its golf programs. Holder, while continuing his position as men's head coach, also became assistant athletics director for golf operations. Women's head coach Ann Pitts, who led the Cowgirls to fifteen conference championships and fifteen NCAA appearances during the twenty-four-year history of the women's program, announced her retirement following the 2000 season. Pitts was succeeded by former Cowgirl Amy Weeks, the 1995 Big Eight Conference medalist. Men's assistant coach Mike McGraw, a former NAIA All-American at the University of Central Oklahoma and coach of nine state championship teams in Edmond, was named associate head coach of both the men's and women's teams.

"We're going to try to be the absolute best we can be in men's and women's golf, and neither program will be more important than the other," said Holder."Nothing would make me happier than to see us win national championships in women's golf."

TEN
Oklahoma
and the
USGA

Half a century after golf was first played in the state, Oklahoma was awarded its first United States Golf Association championship. From the end of World War II through the year 2001, only four states west of the Mississippi River hosted more USGA championships than did Oklahoma.

All USGA championships were canceled during World War II. At the end of the war, the USGA began to hold more of its national championships away from the East Coast. At the behest of Ben Hogan, John M. Winters, and others, the USGA selected Southern Hills to host the 1946 U.S. Women's Amateur. The 1946 Women's Amateur was the first of sixteen USGA championships Oklahoma would host during the next fifty-five years.

In 1953, two USGA championships were conducted in Oklahoma. The 1953 U.S. Junior Amateur, won by Rex Baxter Jr., was held in late August at Southern Hills. Notable in the 128-player field were five Oklahomans—Jack Moore and Bob Richardson of Duncan and Bob Kappus, John Hyden, and Jerry Pittman of Tulsa; future PGA Tour commissioner

Deane Beman; future swing instructors Phil Rodgers and Davis Love Sr.; future PGA champion Bobby Nichols; and the youngest player in the field, thirteen-year-old Jack Nicklaus of Columbus, Ohio. Nicklaus, who would eventually win eight USGA and twenty major championships, was competing at his first USGA competition. Nicklaus lost in the round of sixteen, 5 & 4, to Robert G. Ruffin of Winston-Salem, North Carolina.

Six weeks later, the USGA returned to Oklahoma for the granddaddy of them all, the U.S. Amateur, which Gene Littler won at another Perry Maxwell course—Oklahoma City Golf and Country Club. Out of 1,284 entries nationwide, two hundred advanced to Oklahoma City, including many of the top amateur players in Oklahoma: Charlie Coe, Walter Emery, Dee Replogle, H. H. Edwards, Bill Parker, Glen Fowler, Bo Faulkenberry, Troye Kennon, Ed Hamilton, Lynn Burrus, Paul Reitz, Chris Gers, J. C. Hamilton, Fred Mock, Loy Martin, Bill Winslow, Emmett Rogers, and Joe Walser.

There were four future USGA presidents in the field for the 1953 Amateur: C. Grant Spaeth, Hord Hardin, Harry Easterly, and William C. Campbell. Campbell, who would go on to win the 1964 U.S. Amateur, won four matches in Oklahoma City, losing to eventual runner-up Dale Morey. Of three future Masters winners in the 1953 U.S. Amateur field—Gay Brewer, Billy Casper, and Arnold Palmer—Palmer fared best. In the fourth round, Palmer dueled future U.S. Open champion Ken Venturi before prevailing 2 & 1. Then Palmer, who would win the championship a year later, was defeated one up in the quarterfinals by Don Albert of Alliance Golf Club in Ohio.

The most compelling match of the championship was a third-round battle of titans featuring two of the best amateurs in the history of American golf: Harvey Ward, who would win back-to-back Amateur crowns in 1955–56, and Oklahoma Citian Charlie Coe. All square after eighteen,

Ward finally defeated Coe away at the twenty-third hole. One match pitted a legend against a legend's brother. Chick Evans, winner of both the U.S. Open and U.S. Amateur in 1916, was paired against Royal Hogan, brother of Ben Hogan. Evans, who had won his first tourna-ment in 1907, was sixty-three years old at the 1953 Amateur. He lost to Hogan 4 & 3. The champion turned out to be Californian and future U.S. Open champion Gene Littler, who defeated Morey one up in the thirty-six-hole final.

It was not long before the USGA looked to Oklahoma again, awarding Southern Hills the 1958 U.S. Open (see chapter 4). Also that year, Southern Hills member John Winters was appointed to the USGA executive committee. Winters went on to serve as USGA president in 1962–63. By 1960, the USGA had discovered two more courses in Tulsa suitable for national championships: the Oaks Country Club and Tulsa Country Club. They conducted the 1960 U.S. Girls' Junior and U.S. Women's Amateur at the two clubs on consecutive weeks.

The twelfth U.S. Girls' Junior, at the Oaks, was won by seventeen-year-old Carol Sorenson (Flennikin) of Janesville, Wisconsin. Future Hall of Famer Sandra Haynie lost to runner-up Iowan Sharon Fladoos in the third round. Missouri's Judy Torluemke (Rankin), a future member of the LPGA Hall of Fame, lost to Sorenson one up in the semifinals. Tulsan Jeannie Thompson, the state junior champion, lost to Sorenson one up in the second. Thompson, Sorenson, Torluemke, and Haynie stayed in Tulsa to compete the following week in the sixtieth U.S. Women's Amateur at Tulsa Country Club.

The Women's Amateur, entirely at match play, had 109 entries, including seventeen Oklahomans. Thompson and Muskogee's Beth Stone, the state amateur champion, both lost in the second round. Future three-time U.S. Women's Open champion Susie Maxwell (Berning), of Okla-homa City, and future Tulsa University women's coach Dale Fleming (Mc-

Namara), also lost in the first round, as did two-time state junior champion Patty David of Tulsa. Former state junior and amateur champion Betsy Cullen, of Tulsa, was beaten in round one by the eventual champion, JoAnne Gunderson (Carner).

By 1960, "the Great Gundy" had already won two USGA titles (the 1956 Girls' Junior and 1957 Women's Amateur). By week's end, Gunderson had so dominated the blue-ribbon field that four of her seven match victories, including the thirty-six-hole final against Jean Ashley of Chanute, Kansas, were by a margin of 6 & 5 or greater. Indiana's Alice Dye, a course architect and wife of Oak Tree architect Pete Dye, won three matches. Anne Quast (Sander), a seven-time USGA champion, lost in the quarterfinals. Future LPGA player Sandra Spuzich lost to Gunderson one up in the fourth round. Future LPGA Hall of Famer Carol Mann lost in the third.

Two of the most impressive wins were by future USGA president Judy Bell, then of Wichita, Kansas. In the second round, by one up, Bell beat Sandra Palmer, who would go on to win twenty-one times on the LPGA Tour (including a U.S. Open). Then Bell defeated another future U.S. Women's Open champion, Sandra Haynie, 4 & 3, in the third. But the week belonged to Gunderson. She needed only 122 holes to win seven matches, including the thirty-six-hole final.

After marrying Don Carner, JoAnne remained an amateur until after winning the LPGA's Burdine Invitational in 1969. A year before, Gunderson had won her fifth U.S. Women's Amateur title. She went on to win forty-two times on the LPGA Tour, including two U.S. Women's Opens, and was inducted into the LPGA Hall of Fame in 1982.

In 1961 at Southern Hills, Dexter Daniels of Winter Haven, Florida, won the U.S. Senior Amateur on his first attempt. Also entered were

Oklahomans Lewis Lacey and Clarence Kay of Twin Hills and USGA vice president John Winters of Southern Hills.

The 1965 U.S. Amateur at Southern Hills (see chapter 4) snapped a seventy-year tradition of match play. Instead, entrants played seventy-two holes of stroke play, with Floridian Bob Murphy totaling 291, one stroke fewer than Bob Dickson of Muskogee. Jim Vickers, the 1952 NCAA champion at OU, placed fifth (294), while two-time Amateur champion Charlie Coe of Oklahoma City, the fifty-four-hole leader, tied for twelfth (296).

In 1967, the USGA returned to Oklahoma City for the first time since 1953. The twentieth U.S. Junior Amateur, at Twin Hills Golf and Country Club, featured a pair of future U.S. Open champions—Andy North and Tom Kite—but it was North Carolinian John Crooks who came away with the championship trophy. He beat North 2 & 1 in the finals. Oklahomans who qualified were Ted Goin of Seminole; Joey Dills of Muskogee; Eddie Vossler of Oklahoma City; and Tulsans Vic Benson, Pete Harpster, and Jack Steinmeyer.

A record 131 players entered the 1970 U.S. Women's Open at another Perry Maxwell–designed course, the Muskogee Country Club. Forty golfers shot eight over par or better (150) on the first two rounds to make the cut, including seven of the first ten players elected to the LPGA Hall of Fame: Sandra Haynie (288), Kathy Whitworth (289), Carol Mann (292), Betsy Rawls (295), JoAnne Carner (298), Patty Berg (300), and Mickey Wright (306). Oklahomans Betsy Cullen and Nancy Hager also made the thirty-six-hole cut. Cullen's 299 tied for twenty-sixth place, earning $455. Hager, an amateur, shot 301, a tie for thirty-second.

At the end, Donna Caponi, a native of Detroit, successfully defended her Open title, becoming only the second player to win U.S. Women's Opens back to back. Caponi's 287 tied Mickey Wright for the lowest total ever. First-place prize money was $5,000. Haynie and Sandra Spuzich tied for second at plus four, 288.

Following Hubert Green's U.S. Open victory at Southern Hills in 1977 (see chapter 4), the USGA returned to Oklahoma six years later. By all accounts, the 1983 U.S. Women's Open at Tulsa's Cedar Ridge Country Club presented a starting field of 150 with a significant challenge. "It felt like I was in a washing machine out there, banging my head against the sides," said Patty Sheehan, the eventual runner-up. "Playing this golf course in that kind of heat was so hard. I never felt like I had an advantage or any momentum."[1]

Cedar Ridge, a par-71 designed by Joe Finger in 1969, was a demanding test in the best of conditions. With its series of relentless par 4s, and at 6,298 yards, Cedar Ridge could easily have been stretched to play as the longest course in U.S. Women's Open history. But that would not be necessary. With daily temperatures in excess of one hundred degrees, the players called it the "Oven Door Open" and any hope of shooting par golf was a pipe dream. Of the championship's 434 complete rounds, only nine broke par. For the four-day total, nobody came close to breaking par.

"IT FELT LIKE I WAS IN A WASHING MACHINE OUT THERE, BANGING MY HEAD AGAINST THE SIDES. PLAYING THIS GOLF COURSE IN THAT KIND OF HEAT WAS SO HARD. I NEVER FELT LIKE I HAD AN ADVANTAGE OR ANY MOMENTUM."

Twelve players with Oklahoma ties qualified for the 1983 Women's Open, and four made the cut: Lauren Howe (former TU player, 297); Val Skinner (OSU All-American, 298); Kathy Baker (TU All-American, 1985 U.S. Open winner, 303); and Jody Rosenthal (TU All-American, 305). Oklahoma players to qualify but miss the cut of 157 were three-time Open champion Susie Maxwell Berning (159); Melissa McNamara (162); Patty Coatney (162);

Adele (Lukken) Peterson (164); Robin Hood (166); Sharon Barrett (166); and Tammy Welborn (167).

From the moment in Thursday's opening round when she holed out a 6-iron for eagle at the par-4 eleventh, Australian Jan Stephenson handled the heat best, literally and figuratively. As the reigning LPGA champion, if Stephenson was concerned that overconfidence or self-promotion might doom her chances, she never let on.

"I want the U.S. Open desperately," said Stephenson, "and that's putting it mildly. To go with winning the LPGA and the Australian Open. Not to mention the bonuses. Pretty much all my endorsements have a bonus clause, and if I win it will be worth well over $100,000."[2]

As the most celebrated centerfold in the history of the LPGA's official publication, *Fairway* magazine—(LPGA veteran Jane Blalock described the *Fairway* lingerie photos of Stephenson on an antique bed as "pornography")—Australia's best-known player had been fodder for the tabloids well before she arrived in Tulsa. During the early 1980s, after divorcing her husband, Stephenson had married her business manager, who then tried to have a judge declare her mentally incompetent. Stephenson went back to court to have the second marriage annulled. She subsequently returned to her first husband, after which her career took off.

At the 1983 U.S. Women's Open, some five hundred glamour photos of Stephenson were sold at a concession stand near the eighteenth green. When USGA officials heard about it, they closed down the stand. However, all the extraneous commotion apparently had little effect on Stephenson. She remained focused and consistent.

Pat Bradley used a third-round ace at the sixth on Saturday to shoot 31 and tie Judy Bell's Open record for nine holes, but finished bogey-bogey-bogey for a 71. Kathy Whitworth signed an incorrect scorecard and was disqualified. JoAnne Carner opened with an 81, then played the final fifty-four holes in three under par, explaining, "That's the hardest I ever worked in my life." But she scored one stroke too many. "I passed 100 players," said Carner, "but I hoped to pass 101."[4] Both Donna Caponi and Beth Daniel withdrew after eighteen holes. Four other players were penalized for slow play.

Stephenson, however, played almost mistake-free golf. She was in such command that bogeys on the final two holes were inconsequential. She tapped in a 1-foot putt for the victory, completing a six-over-par 290 total, with rounds of 72-73-71-74. Carner and Sheehan tied for second at 291.

"I love Tulsa," Stephenson said afterward. On her way to the pressroom she received a phone call. "It was President Reagan, and talking to him gave me goosebumps," Stephenson told the media. "He said he thought Patty was going to catch me and he thanked me for an enjoyable afternoon. Of course, I said, 'You're welcome.'"[4]

Including the 1983 U.S. Women's Open, nine of the first twelve USGA championships in Oklahoma had been held in Tulsa. In 1984, the USGA returned to Oklahoma for the U.S. Amateur Championship, 100 miles west of Tulsa at Oak Tree Golf Club in Edmond. The eighty-fourth Amateur Championship had a contingent of future PGA Tour winners, among them Davis Love III, Scott Verplank, Rocco Mediate, Bob Estes, Nolan Henke, Dillard Pruitt, and Jeff Maggert.

Maggert, then a student at Oklahoma State, was one of nineteen players with Oklahoma ties to qualify for the 282-player field, from an original 3,679 entries. Qualifying rounds were held at Oak Tree Golf Club and Oak Tree Country Club, from which sixty-four players advanced to match play. Besides Maggert, who squeezed in at the 150 cut line, six other players with Oklahoma ties qualified for match play: medalist Scott Verplank (137, OSU); Darryl Donovan (144, Oklahoma City); Greg Turner (144, OU); Todd Hamilton (147, OU); Brian Watts (150, OSU); and Cliff Pierce (150, OU).

Oklahoma qualifiers who did not advance to match play were Phillip Aickin (OU), Grant Waite (OU), Rocky Walcher (Woodward), Doug Bailess (Yukon), Mike Hood (Oklahoma City), Michael Davidson (Oklahoma City), William Lavender (Oklahoma City), Chris Hutchens (Bartlesville), Mike Houpe (Edmond), Roger Brown (Ponca City), Jim Unruh (Tulsa), and future OSU All-American Bob May 15 of La Habra, California, at fifteen the youngest player in the field. Other nonadvancers were 1981 Amateur champion Nathaniel Crosby (88 at the Golf Club) and former NFL quarterback John Brodie.

Floridian Scott Dunlap and Pennsylvania amateur legend Jay Sigel set the day-one qualifying pace with 64s at the Oak Tree Country Club, tying David Edwards's course record. But Sigel could do no better than 78 at the Oak Tree Golf Club, and he exited in the first round of match play, 3 & 1 to Rocco Mediate of Greensburg, Pennsylvania. Mediate lost to Peter Persons in his next match. Maggert lost to Love in the third round. Love was beaten by Randy Sonnier in the fourth. Verplank beat Estes, two up, in the first.

Verplank, about to begin his junior year at OSU, was the dominant amateur player in the country. He had already won the Porter Cup and Sunnehanna Amateur and two of his final three collegiate events that spring, including the 1984 Big Eight Conference championship. With his coach Mike Holder caddying, Verplank shot 137 in qualifying, the only player to break 140. After defeating Estes and Turner, Verplank took one-up matches over Persons and Sonnier, advancing to the finals against Sam Randolph of Santa Barbara, California.

In the thirty-six-hole final, Verplank caught Oak Tree in a soft drizzle and began to pour in birdies. Tied after the morning round, Verplank birdied the twenty-sixth (10 feet), twenty-seventh (15 feet), twenty-eighth (15 feet), and thirtieth (12 feet), cilminating with a thirty-footer putt at the thirty-third to close out Randolph, 4 & 3. "For that period of time I've never seen putting like it," said Randolph. "I couldn't keep up with that." Said Verplank: "I've gone six months on this course where I didn't make five birdies, much less in eight holes."[5]

Three years later the USGA brought the first-ever U.S. Women's Mid-Amateur Championship, for players aged twenty-five and older, to Tulsa's Southern Hills. Californians Cindy Scholefield of Malibu and Pat Cornett of Corte Madera met in the finals, with Scholefield winning, 6 & 5. Muskogee's Susan Kennedy qualified for match play (176) but lost in the first round.

A year later at the Leon Howard–designed Page Belcher Golf Course, Pearl Sinn of Bellflower, California, won her second consecutive U.S. Women's Public Links Championship, 2 & 1, over Tami Jo Henningsen of Colorado Springs. Lee Ann Hammack of Oklahoma City was qualifying medalist at 141 but lost in the third round.

The only Oklahomans to have been three-time USGA champions were women. In 1939, Betty Jameson, who was born in Norman, won the first of two U.S. Women's Amateurs. She also won the 1947 U.S. Women's Open. Susie Maxwell Berning, of Oklahoma City, won U.S. Women's Opens in 1968, 1972, and 1973 (see chapter 7). Since then, eighteen other native Oklahomans or players who have lived in the state have won USGA championships.

Chickasha-born Orville Moody, Oklahoma Citian Charles Coe, and three Oklahoma collegiate players—Nancy Lopez, Cathy Mockett, and Jo Jo Robertson—have won two USGA championships each. Lopez, from Roswell, New Mexico, starred at the University of Tulsa and won the

U.S. Girls' Junior in 1972 and 1974. Mockett, a two-time All-American at Tulsa, won the 1984 U.S. Girls' Junior and the 1990 U.S. Women's Public Links. Robertson, like Lopez a native of Roswell, won the U.S. Women's Public Links in 1995 and 1997, while a team member at Oklahoma State.

Coe, twice a winner of the U.S. Amateur (1949, 1958), barely missed a third, losing in the final match of 1959 to Jack Nicklaus (see chapter 9). Moody, winner of the 1969 U.S. Open and the 1989 U.S. Senior Open, joins Jameson, Maxwell Berning, Haworth-born Tommy Bolt, and Tulsa All-American Kathy Baker Guadagnino as National Open champions.

Only in 1997, when the University of Texas renamed its football stadium in honor of Oklahoma-born OU graduate Darrell K. Royal, did an Oklahoma sports figure make a greater splash south of the Red River than when Moody stood over a 14-inch putt at Houston's Champions Golf Club to win the 1969 U.S. Open.

To most pros, a 14-inch tap-in was little more than a formality. Not so with Orville James Moody, the son of a greenskeeper, especially when it was for a U.S. Open title. Any time Moody had a flatblade in his hands, anything was possible. As fellow pro Randy Petri recalled in 1990, "Orville was so good, he used to play for money against me and my partner's best ball. But the only time we gave him a putt was if he marked it and it fell in the hole."

As a touring professional in the spring of 1969, Moody was more anonymous than prominent. Nicknamed "Sarge" by his fellow pros, he had been a touring pro for exactly thirteen months when he arrived in Houston for the 1969 U.S. Open.

It was said that he knew more about the PX than about the practice tee. But Moody had earned his stripes both on and off the golf course. After winning the 1952 state high school golf championship for Oklahoma City's Capitol Hill, Moody enrolled that fall at the University of Oklahoma, on a football scholarship from Bud Wilkinson. Six weeks later he enlisted with Uncle Sam. "Coach Wilkinson wanted to jump start the golf program," recalled Moody, "but I didn't stay long enough for them to see me. That's when I quit and went into the Army."[6]

During his years in the army Moody won three Korean Opens and every major military golf championship there was. In 1967, at age thirty-three, he entered the PGA Tour qualifying school. Moody played well enough to get his tour card, then earned the grand sum of $12,959 in 1968. During the first five months of 1969, he played better, with four top-five finishes, including a playoff loss at Greensboro, North Carolina.

But it was something of a wonder that Moody even qualified for the 1969 U.S. Open. At local qualifying, in Dallas, Moody birdied the thirty-fifth hole from out of the sand to shoot 149. The cut was 150. In the sectional qualifier at Memphis, Moody's 140 total was the highest score to qualify for Champions.

Without fail, at every U.S. Open, there are players who qualify as virtual unknowns—Cinderella stories—except to family and close friends. At Champions, were it a horse race instead of a golf tournament, Moody might have carried the longest odds in the race. However, a former marine named Lee Trevino, who had butted heads with Moody during golf championships in the military, had a hunch about the Sarge. Two days before the first round, Trevino was quoted as saying, "My choice to win the title is Orville Moody."[7]

Had Trevino made such a prediction one year earlier, nobody would have paid any attention. But in June of 1969, with the world's best players in town, anything from Trevino's mouth was duly noted. In 1968 Trevino, then himself an unknown driving-range pro from El Paso, had shocked the golf world by capturing the U.S. Open in Rochester, New York.

Moody started out quietly enough at the 6,967-yard, par-70 Champions course, shooting 71, good for a fourteenth-place tie with past and future major championship winners Sam Snead, Gary Player, Julius Boros, Tony Jacklin, Tommy Aaron, Johnny Miller, and former U.S. Amateur champion and Oklahoma State All-American Labron Harris Jr.

In the second, Moody shot 70, moving into a tie for eighth with Miller, Jacklin, and Jack Nicklaus (74-67), four behind leader Deane Beman. Among the players who missed the cut at 149 were Trevino and Oklahomans Chris Gers (154), Jerry Pittman (155), Skee Riegel (155), and Dave Eichelberger (155). Wewoka native Dale Douglass was still in the hunt at 145.

On Saturday, Moody torched Champions in 68 strokes, which vaulted him into second place (209), leaving in his wake more celebrated names like Palmer (212), Nicklaus (216), and Player (218). But he was still three shots behind Miller Barber, who had also had 68. After that round, reporters could no longer ignore the Oklahoma pro, who was living in Killeen, Texas. "Orville James Moody promises to remain calm in the National Open windup," wrote Jack Gallagher of the *Houston Post*, "He says he can win."[8]

What Moody lacked in experience, he made up for with self-confidence. "I came here with every intention of winning this tournament," said Moody, who putted ninety-nine times in the first three rounds. "I can win." When informed by a reporter that leader Miller Barber of Sherman, Texas, was an unfamiliar name to most golf fans, Moody was asked where he might rank. "Three shots back of Barber," retorted the Sarge.

While others struggled on Sunday (Barber 78, Player 77), Moody played steady if not spectacular golf. He started with seven consecutive fours, then went 3-4 at eight and nine to shoot even par 35 on the front (one birdie, one bogey). He bogeyed No. 10 and No. 14, but then made three pars in row. With Deane Beman, Al Geiberger, and Bob Rosburg having already posted totals of 282, Moody came to the Champions 431-yard eighteenth hole needing a par 4 to give him a 281 total and a permanent place in golf history.

His drive split the fairway and his 8-iron approach stopped just thirteen feet from the pin. But with Moody and putting, anything was possible. Just trying to two-putt, Moody left the first one 14 inches short of the hole. He took out a coin and marked. Moody stood at the edge of the green, watching playing partner Barber hole out. Then, in front of a national television audience, and a gallery of seventeen thousand lined up ten deep around the eighteenth green, Moody "treated his second putt as if the weight of the universe rested on his shoulders."[9]

After studying matters carefully from both sides of the hole, Moody lined up, addressed the ball, then stood over it for what seemed an interminably long time, even for a player with a history of putting woes. Finally he drew the putter back and holed it. And just like that, Orville James Moody of Chickasha, Oklahoma, became the fifty-first player to win the U.S. Open.

After signing his scorecard, Moody was asked why he spent so much time over the final putt. "That was a long 14-incher," he said weakly, shaking his head. "A million dollar 14-incher."[10]

Less than two years earlier, Staff Sergeant Moody had cleared $508 a month, after deductions. At the press conference, attended by 250 reporters, he held up a white cap, its crown decorated by an alligator. "A fellow told me he'd give me $2500 if I wore this today," said Moody. And that was *before* he became champion.

"Orville could have signed with First Flight (a club manufacturer) not long ago for $5,000," said his agent Bucky Woy. "His price now for the same endorsement will be between $50,000 and $100,000." Added Woy: "He isn't as talkative as Trevino, but he does have color, and that Army background should be helpful in promoting him. Orville's signature golf clubs oughta make a fortune in Army PX's alone."[11]

On his way to the interview room, Moody was told he had a phone call, which turned out to be President Richard Nixon. Observed columnist Jim Murray of the *Los Angeles Times*: "The last time Moody got a missive from the President of the United States, it started out 'Greetings.'" Moody said the call shook him up and that true to his GI background, about all he could think of to say was "Yes sir," and "No, sir."

"It isn't often that a retired Army sergeant wins the U.S. Open," the President told Moody.

"Sir, it's *never* happened before," Moody said politely, not trying to be funny. When Moody told the story at the press conference, one observer said you could hear the laughter out on Jackrabbit Road.

Asked how it felt to win the Open, Moody replied, "I felt a little wet-eyed when it was over. The feeling was for everyone back in Oklahoma, my family, my sponsors in Killeen, my Army buddies, and everyone who wanted me to win." Asked what his future plans were, Moody's thoughts turned to American soldiers half a world away. "I wouldn't mind goin' to Viet Nam to see the troops if someone asked me," Moody said.[12]

"I'VE GOT BLISTERS ON THE BACKS OF BOTH FEET, BUT I'D WALK ANOTHER 18 HOLES RIGHT NOW WITH MR. MOODY. I ALMOST CRIED WHEN HE MADE THAT PUTT."

Nobody was happier—or more relieved—with the victory than Moody's caddie, seventeen-year-old Michael Ashe, a senior at Houston's Saint Pius high school. "I've got blisters on the backs of both feet, but I'd walk another 18 holes right now with Mr. Moody," said Ashe. "I almost cried when he made that putt."[13] Ashe had been the 122nd caddie applicant selected from a total of 150. In those days, no professional caddies were allowed at the U.S. Open. Ashe's only previous caddying experience had been for his father.

His initial reaction to drawing Moody was: "I'd never heard of him. But then I talked with Mr. (Jack) Burke and some others and they told me Mr. Moody was a super player. I started caddying for him last Sunday and he hit the ball great. I got to going over to the practice tee and watching Mr. Palmer and Mr. Nicklaus and the others and I told everybody Mr. Moody was the best."

Before the third round Ashe suffered a caddie's nightmare. During practice, Moody and Ashe had paced off distances all over the course, from tee boxes to sand traps, from Moody's tee shots to the edges of greens, from pins to the back of greens. The information was penciled in, filling a small notebook, which Ashe kept in his top coverall pocket. But early on Saturday morning, before the third round, Ashe accidentally dropped the notebook into a portable toilet. Some pros would have fired that caddie on the spot, but not Moody.

"That's why I almost cried," Ashe said on Sunday. "I could have cost Mr. Moody the whole tournament. But he just laughed when I told him what happened and said not to worry. I still think losing those distances sort of bothered him on the front side Saturday." Before the final round, Moody's then wife Doris had told Ashe to "'talk to him, keep him relaxed.' Funny, but he talked more today than he had any of the other days. He had so many pressures on him, but he wouldn't let them get him down."[14]

The 1969 U.S. Open would be Moody's only victory ever on the regular PGA Tour. However, on the Senior PGA Tour, he flourished, winning thirteen times, including a second USGA championship—the 1989 U.S. Senior Open at Laurel Valley Golf Club in Ligonier, Pennsylvania.

Three other players with Oklahoma ties—all women—won two USGA championships each.

The only guarantee going into the 1972 U.S. Girls' Junior at Jefferson City Country Club in Missouri was that Hollis Stacy of Savannah, Georgia, would not win the championship a fourth consecutive time. Stacy, Girls' Junior champion in 1969, 1970, and 1971, had turned eighteen years old in March of 1972, making her no longer eligible. Amazingly, Stacy's name would be followed immediately on the Girls' Junior Championship Trophy by two players who made it to the LPGA Hall of Fame before she did. Amy Alcott was Girls' Junior medalist in 1972, the champion in 1973. Nancy Lopez of Roswell won in 1972.

Lopez, who became 1976 AIAW National Champion as a freshman at the University of Tulsa, defeated Catherine Morse one up in the final at Jefferson City. Two years later, in 1974, a seventeen-year-old Lopez repeated the feat, downing Lauren Howe, who would also play for Tulsa, 7 & 5, at Columbia–Edgewater Country Club in Portland, Oregon.

In 1984, a future two-time Tulsa All-American won the U.S. Girls' Junior. Cathy Mockett of Newport Beach, California, defeated future U.S. Women's Amateur champion Michiko Hattori of Nagoya, Japan, one up, at Mill Creek Country Club in Bothell, Washington. Mockett was also medalist. Six years later, after graduating from Tulsa, Mockett earned her USGA double, winning the 1990 U.S. Women's Amateur Public Links at Hyland Hills Golf Club in Westminster, Colorado. Mockett defeated Barbara Blanchard in the finals, 5 & 4.

Like Lopez two decades earlier, Jo Jo Robertson, also from Roswell, attended college in Oklahoma. Following her freshman season at Oklahoma State, Robertson captured the 1995 U.S. Women's Amateur Public Links Championship, defeating Elizabeth Drambour, 3 & 1, at Hominy Hills Golf Course in Colts Neck, New Jersey.

Robertson, nineteen years old when she won at Hominy Hills,

had played in the U.S. Women's Amateur Public Links since she was thirteen. In June of 1997, her USGA experience paid off once more. At Center Square Golf Club in Center Square, Pennsylvania, Robertson became only the fourth player to win two U.S. Women's Amateur Public Links. She defeated Angie Yoon of San Diego, 3 & 2, in the finals. Robertson's father, Andy, an assistant coach at Hopewell High in Aliquippa, Pennsylvania, conducted an off-season football workout, then rode a bus all night from Pittsburgh, arriving at 5 a.m., to watch his daughter win her second Public Links.

Robert B. (Bob) Dickson of McAlester was not the first player to win both the U.S. and British Amateurs in the same year, but as of this writing nobody has done it since. In May of 1967 Dickson, twice a first-team All-American at OSU, was the reigning champion of both the Oklahoma Open and the Oklahoma Amateur. As runner-up to Bob Murphy at the 1965 U.S. Amateur, Dickson earned a place on the 1967 U.S. Walker Cup team for the biennial matches against Great Britain at Royal St. George's in Sandwich, England. Dickson went undefeated in his matches (3–0), leading the U.S. team to victory. Afterward he stayed in England to compete in the 1967 British Amateur at Formby Golf Club.

"FORTY-EIGHT HOURS AFTER I WON THE BRITISH AMATEUR, I'M AT ARMY BASIC TRAINING AT FORT BLISS IN EL PASO, TEXAS. THAT'S GOING FROM ONE EXTREME OF LIVING TO THE OTHER."

After his first six matches at Formby, Dickson was a perfect 9–0 in England. In the final thirty-six-hole match, Dickson met Californian Ron Cerrudo. "I remember hitting a good drive on No. 17, the 35th hole of the match, and winning the championship on that hole," Dickson recalled of 2 & 1 victory over Cerrudo. "But that was my last drive for a while."[15]

Years later, as a member of the Senior PGA Tour, Dickson remembered what followed as "that incredible summer." He was automatically exempt into the 1967 U.S. Amateur, set for late August at the Broadmoor in Colorado Springs. But first Dickson took a detour—by enlisting in the U.S. Army.

"Forty-eight hours after I won the British Amateur, I'm at Army basic training at Fort Bliss in El Paso, Texas," Dickson recalled in 1997. "That's going from one extreme of living to the other. Then about six or seven weeks into basic, I got out on a Sunday afternoon, played 18 holes, shot 78. Once I got through basic, they stationed me at Fort Huachuca, Arizona, for AIT (Advance Individual Training). After class was over every day at 5:00, I'd go to the course, hit a few balls or whatever, and play nine holes."

Dickson explained that his muscles "had been re-arranged" but that he was in the best physical shape he had ever enjoyed in his life. "At the British Amateur, I'd been hitting the ball really well and really long," Dickson said. "But by the time I got out of basic I had lost some of that length and was stiff from a golf standpoint. I went to the Broadmoor with absolutely no expectations other than not embarrassing myself. And what do you know, I won."

That year the U.S. Amateur was at stroke play. Dickson and Vinny Giles were paired together the entire seventy-two holes of the championship, neither player gaining a significant advantage. After seventy-one holes, Dickson had a one-shot lead. Then he hooked his tee shot at the seventy-second, took a free drop from television cables, and played back to the fairway. When Dickson's third came to rest seven feet from the pin, Giles was already thirty feet from the pin in two, in position to make birdie. Giles missed, giving Dickson a seven-footer for the championship. He rolled it in right into the middle of the cup.

"I was the most surprised of anybody that I played well," said Dickson. "I mean the odds on that were very slim."[16] For his incredible summer, Dickson was presented the USGA's most prestigious honor—the 1968 Bob Jones Award.

In addition to Bolt, Dickson, and Verplank, eleven other players with Oklahoma ties each captured one USGA championship: Robert H. (Skee) Riegel, Billy Maxwell, Hunter Haas, Labron Harris Jr., Willie Wood, Carolyn Hill, Doug Martin, Kathy (Baker) Guadagnino, Dale Douglass, Brian Montgomery, and Dave Eichelberger.

Riegel, who moved to Tulsa from Pennsylvania, won the 1947 U.S. Amateur at Pebble Beach, defeating John Dawson, 2 & 1, in the finals. In 1947–48 school year, Texan Billy Maxwell played for Coach Labron Harris on OSU's first-ever golf team, which won the Missouri Valley Conference title. Maxwell subsequently transferred to North Texas State, winning the 1951 U.S. Amateur at Saucon Valley Country Club (Old Course) in Bethlehem, Pennsylvania. Maxwell defeated Joseph Gagliardi, 4 & 3, in the finals. Labron Harris Jr., a two-time OSU All-American, won the 1962 U.S. Amateur at Pinehurst Country Club (No. 2 course), defeating Downing Gray one up in the finals.

At age sixteen, Willie Wood, a future four-time OSU All-American from Tucson, Arizona, defeated David Grimes, 4 & 3, to win the 1977 U.S. Junior Amateur at the Ohio State Scarlet Course in Columbus, Ohio. In 1979, University of Tulsa All-American Carolyn Hill defeated future LPGA Hall of Famer Patty Sheehan, 7 & 6, in the finals of the U.S. Women's Amateur at Memphis Country Club. In 1984, Ohio native and future OU All-American Doug Martin claimed both medalist honors and the champion's trophy at the U.S. Junior Amateur. Martin defeated Texan Brad Agee, 4 & 2, in the final match at Wayzata Country Club in Wayzata, Minnesota.

An astute handicapper of the 1985 U.S. Women's Open at Baltusrol might have wagered a dollar on Kathy (Baker) Guadagnino, the 1982 NCAA champion from the University of Tulsa. Guadagnino, a native of Albany, New York, had finished as low amateur at both the 1982 and 1983 U.S. Women's Opens. After turning pro in late 1983, she finished her 1984 LPGA rookie season strongly, with a second-place finish at Portland in September. At New Jersey's Baltusrol Country Club the following July, Guadagnino dominated a field of the world's best players, shooting a four-round total of 280, eight under par. Judy (Clark) Dickinson finished second, three shots back. The U.S. Open was Guadagnino's first victory as a professional.

Dale Douglass, who was born in Gil Morgan's hometown of Wewoka and later learned to play at Oklahoma City's Twin Hills Golf and Country Club, only won three times on the regular PGA Tour. But he caught fire after turning fifty. Tops among Douglass's ten victories as a senior pro was the 1986 U.S. Senior Open at Scioto Country Club in Columbus, Ohio. Douglass, at five under par for seventy-two holes, held on for a one-stroke victory over Gary Player (280).

In the summer of 1986 Brian Montgomery, from Bristow, Oklahoma, won both the PGA Junior Championship and the U.S. Junior Amateur. In the U.S. Junior at Muirfield Village in Dublin, Ohio, Montgomery, who later played for four years at OSU, defeated Nicky Goetze, 2 & 1, in the final.

In July of 1999, former OSU All-American Dave Eichelberger joined the fraternity of USGA champions with a three-shot victory margin over Ed Dougherty, in the U.S. Senior Open at Des Moines Golf and Country Club in Iowa. Eichelberger later called the final round 3-wood shot he hit into the par-5 fifteenth hole the greatest shot of his life. Later that month, the University of Oklahoma's Hunter Haas captured the U.S. Public Links Championship at Alton, Illinois. Haas, the Big 12 champion and a U.S. Amateur semifinalist later that year, defeated South African Michael Kirk in the final, 4 & 3.

Six golfers with Oklahoma connections have played on U.S. Curtis Cup teams: Amy Benz, Kathy Baker Guadagnino, Nancy Lopez, Jody Rosenthal Anschutz, Carolyn Hill, and Nancy Hager. Twenty Oklahomans have played on U.S. Walker Cup teams: Alan Bratton, Charles Coe, Kris Cox, Bob Dickson, Danny Edwards, Dave Eichelberger, Brad Elder, Walter Emery, Hunter Haas, Labron Harris Jr., Trip Kuehne, Edward Loar, Doug Martin, Bob May, Lindy Miller, Brian Montgomery, Joey Rassett, Skee Riegel, Scott Verplank, and Willie Wood.

Three Oklahomans have received the USGA's highest honor, the Bob Jones Award: Charles Coe in 1964, Bob Dickson in 1968, and Nancy Lopez in 1998.

The late John M. Winters, longtime member at Tulsa's Southern Hills Country Club, served on the USGA's executive committee (1955–57) and was secretary in 1958, vice president in 1959–61, and president in 1962–63.

Doug Sanders, winner of the 1962 Oklahoma City Open, missed the Wednesday Pro-Am at Quail Creek because of a pulled thigh muscle but lit it up on Sunday with a 67.

OPPOSITE PAGE: Pete Brown and admirers at the Colonial National Invitation Tournament in Fort Worth, Texas, one week after Brown captured the 1964 Waco Turner Open in Burneyville, becoming the first African-American PGA member to win a PGA Tour event. *Sepia.*

Courtesy Moorland-Spingarn Research Center, Howard University.

Anthony David "Champagne Tony" Lema leans into one at the 1964 Oklahoma City Open, two months before winning the British Open. In 1966 Lema returned to Quail Creek, scene of the final triumph of his meteoric career.

Copyright, *The Daily Oklahoman.*

Defending champion Jack Rule, nemesis of Jack Nicklaus, demonstrates the croquet stroke, later outlawed, that won him the 1965 Oklahoma City Open.

Copyright, *The Daily Oklahoman.*

Caddies for the 1966 Oklahoma City Open, at Quail Creek,
wait in hope of the caddiemaster calling their names.
Copyright, *The Daily Oklahoman.*

Oklahoma Office of Tourism and Recreation Executive
Director Jane Jayroe, one of four Miss Americas from
Oklahoma, was honoree for the 1967 Oklahoma City Open at
Quail Creek. Today Jayroe enjoys putting the bentgrass greens
at Oklahoma City Golf and Country Club.
Photo: Fred Marvel. Courtesy Jane Jayroe.

In 1977 Mark Hayes, a two-time All-American at Oklahoma State, won the Players Championship and became the first golfer in history to shoot 63 at the British Open.

Courtesy Oklahoma State University.

Arnold Palmer, the only player to win the Oklahoma City Open twice, at the site of the second, Quail Creek Golf and Country Club.

Copyright, *The Daily Oklahoman.*

Hat trick: Juan "Chi Chi" Rodriguez covers up the hole after a Quail Creek birdie at the 1966 Oklahoma City Open.

Photo: Bill Dixon, *Lawton Constitution.*

Jack Nicklaus at the 1967 Oklahoma City Open, three weeks before winning the second of four U.S. Opens.

Photo: Bill Dixon, *Lawton Constitution.*

In August 1970 Dave Stockton quieted even the rowdiest members of Arnie's army with shots like this at the PGA Championship.

AP/Wide World Photos.

Count it: Dave Stockton watches another putt drop en route to winning the 1970 PGA Championship at Southern Hills.

AP/Wide World Photos.

Only an ant bed could slow down the "General of the Army" the day before Arnold Palmer marched to his second Oklahoma City Open crown.

Photo: Bill Dixon, *Lawton Constitution*.

Even before LPGA Hall of Famer Nancy Marie Lopez turned
professional, winning suited her to a tee, as it did in 1976,
when the Tulsa University star was medalist at the AIAW
National Championship.
Courtesy University of Tulsa.

Future Southern Methodist coach Kyle O'Brien and teammate celebrate on the eighteenth green at Stillwater Country Club after O'Brien's putt clinched the 1979 Association of Intercollegiate Athletics for Women National Championship for SMU.

Photo: Charles Turman. *Stillwater News-Press.*

OPPOSITE PAGE: Full finish: Tulsa University All-American Adele Lukken with her Ben Hogan persimmon driver, circa 1985.

Courtesy *South Central Golf.*

TEXAS	11	72	38
CLEMSON	15	72	40
OKLAHOMA ST	17	72	42
ARIZ	19	72	46
ARI	18	72	50
GE	22	72	52

ABOVE LEFT: Oklahoman Bob Tway, a three-time OSU All-American and one of the "Oak Tree Boys," holds the Wannamaker Trophy for winning the 1986 PGA Championship. (ABC's Al Trautwig at right.)
AP/Wide World Photos.

LEFT: Bob Tway holed this bunker shot at the seventy-second hole to win the 1986 PGA Championship at the Inverness Club in Toledo, Ohio.
AP/Wide World Photos.

ABOVE: At Oak Tree Golf Club in Edmond, the team that won the 1989 NCAA Championship for OU (left to right): Coach Gregg Grost, Tripp Davis, Ricky Bell, Jeff Lee, Matthew Lane, and Doug Martin.
Courtesy University of Oklahoma.

At impact: four-time Oklahoma State All-American Scott Verplank won the 1984 U.S. Amateur, the 1986 NCAA Championship, and the 1985 Western Open—the first amateur in thirty-one years to win a PGA Tour event.

Courtesy Oklahoma State University.

Epilogue

At the time of this writing, as Oklahoma prepared to host its third U.S. Open in forty-three years, there were indications that the second century of golf history in the state could be as memorable as the first:

- Edmond's Oak Tree Golf Club hosted the first PGA of America Club Professional Championship of the new century.

- Groups such as Golf Incorporated, First Tee, South Central PGA, the Oklahoma Golf Association, the Women's Oklahoma Golf Association, and the Tiger Woods Foundation were continuing to involve more Oklahomans with golf.

- Word emanating from LPGA headquarters at Daytona Beach, Florida, placed Tulsa Country Club at the top of their list to host a new LPGA Tour event, perhaps in the fall of 2001.

- Oklahoma State's Karsten Creek Golf Club was named as host of the 2003 NCAA Championship.

- The 2000 Oklahoma Open secured a new title sponsor and distributed a purse of $150,000, matching the largest payout in its ninety-one-year history.

- Oklahoman Doug Tewell won the 2000 PGA Seniors' Championship.
- In May of 2000, Tiger Woods sponsored and conducted a junior clinic at Oklahoma City's James E. Stewart Golf Course, where one of those in attendance was fifteen-year-old Treas Nelson, the first African American to win an Oklahoma state high school golf championship.
- One month later, the OSU men's team, led by Charles Howell, shattered 104 years of scoring records at the 2000 NCAA Championship.
- Several new upscale daily-fee courses, including the Oklahoma state park system's highly acclaimed Chickasaw Pointe on Lake Texoma, had opened for play or were under construction.
- The New York Times Magazine Group, in conjunction with *Golf Digest* and the personal finance editors at *Business Week,* published a two-hundred-page *Golf Retirement Planner,* which ranked Oklahoma's Payne County, population 61,507, as the nation's ninth best retirement destination for golfers.

In 1990 there were approximately 150 golf courses in Oklahoma with some 200,000 persons who golfed at least once each month. Ten years later the numbers had risen to 220 and 300,000. In decades to come the golf industry in Oklahoma should have numerous opportunities, perhaps as cooperative endeavors among statewide golf associations, media, municipalities, and the departments of commerce, tourism, and recreation, to increase public awareness about the game in a sector of the U.S. heartland that could rightfully call itself the crossroads of American golf.

The foundations for promoting Oklahoma as a golf destination are already in place—thanks to such visionaries as Jackson, Maxwell, Phillips, Winters, Turner, Farley, Ferguson, Proctor, and Holder. No doubt the next generation of Oklahoma golf promoters and course architects will have gained inspiration from those who came before, thereby introducing new golfers to the old styles and older golfers to the new. In addition to the new courses, high levels of volunteerism and enormous interest in golf as a spectator sport should assure that Southern Hills, Oak Tree, and Karsten Creek continue bringing major golf championships to Oklahoma, both professional and amateur. Furthermore, the national publicity surrounding the collegiate programs at OSU, TU, and OU means these programs should merit serious consideration each year by the nation's top junior golfers as they make decisions about their futures.

In naming Payne County the nation's ninth best retirement destination for golfers, the *Golf Retirement Planner* recognized a trend. With its affordable golf options, clean air and rivers, low crime rate, reasonable living costs, accessible health care, central geographic location, efficient turnpike system, commitment to historic preservation, and moderate climate (more than 300 golfing days per year) with four distinct seasons, Oklahoma is drawing more out-of-state players searching for bentgrass greens at less crowded courses; it is increasingly being considered as a realistic alternative to the pricier, if better known, retirement resorts in nearby sunbelt states. Even Oklahoma state government has joined the effort.

"Golf is an eighteen-hole sport," Art Proctor said in 1989.[1] Since that comment by Proctor, then golf director of the state tourism department, several state park courses have been expanded or modernized, increasing the number of eighteen-hole courses in the park system from four to eight. By the millennium, the crown jewel of the state park system's thirteen courses was Chickasaw Pointe on Lake Texoma. Since it opened in the fall of 1999, Chickasaw Pointe has regularly attracted players from Oklahoma City, Dallas, Fort Worth, Wichita Falls, Texarkana, and Shreveport.

Oklahoma's golf boom during the 1990s saw the construction of at least half a dozen other championship caliber courses in the state that would compare favorably—in quality of maintenance and degree of difficulty—with Chickasaw Pointe. Still, a statement by the man who designed nine Oklahoma state park courses, retired course architect Floyd Farley of Sedona, Arizona, rings as a challenge and suggests that much remains to be done.

Said Farley in a 1998 interview: "I think Oklahoma's greatest golf course has yet to be built. One of the reasons Oklahoma already has so many good courses is you haven't had a lot of developers demanding things, because of population. But greens fees are still too high. Too often you can't get on the golf courses in the first place and the ones you can get on you can't afford. It sounds romantic for someone to build such a course in Oklahoma. But it always comes back to money. It costs so much nowadays to keep a golf course up. That's the big thing. But with greens fees as high as they are, and municipalities having the ability to get funds, I don't know why more cities and counties don't get involved with the golf. Sure a private promoter could do it, but they're always going to be looking for homesites. If they can't get homesites, they don't go."

As regards potential sites for new courses, Farley mentioned "out in the country," especially north and east of Oklahoma City. "The secret is the rivers. You can find a lot of nice land if you follow the rivers. The Cimarron would be ideal. The Canadian River is the same way." Farley compared portions of the rolling dune country and sandbottoms of the Cimarron River watershed, which traverses the state from west to east, including just north of the Tulsa–Oklahoma City corridor, to similar topography in Kansas, Nebraska, and even the British linksland. The Perry Maxwell–designed

Prairie Dunes Country Club in Hutchinson, Kansas, and the Ben Crenshaw and Bill Coore–designed Sandhills Club near Mullen, Nebraska, make anyone's list of top fifty golf courses in the world.

Were such a course to take life in central Oklahoma, positioned to draw customers from the golf populations of both Oklahoma City and Tulsa, a moderate-fee public facility with state-of-the-art environmental protections, Oklahoma would further secure its position among the dozen or so best golfing destinations in the United States. At that point the icing on the cake, perhaps on the same site as the golf course, would be a state golf hall of fame and library, a repository showcasing the first century of Oklahoma golf history.

When your state has hosted three U.S. Opens, two U.S. Women's Opens, three U.S. Amateurs, and two U.S. Women's Amateurs, plus 175 other prominent professional and amateur tournaments, it could be well served by a state golf hall of fame and library.

When your state has produced forty-three different winners of major American professional and amateur golf championships, plus three universities with a total of fourteen national championship team titles, it could justify a state golf hall of fame and library.

When your state has twenty-eight courses—designed by some of the finest course architects in American golf history—that have hosted a century's worth of open, professional tour, and major amateur championships, it would surely attract even out-of-state visitors to an Oklahoma golf hall of fame and library.

When your state boasts bentgrass greens and ever-changing weather conditions and regularly features the world's best players on some of the most suitable terrain for golf this side of Scotland, the golfers there would support a golf hall of fame and library.

Near the south steps of the Oklahoma State Capitol is a towering bronze statue of a Native American woman, sculpted by native Oklahoman Allen Hauser. The inscription at its base reads: "As Long as the Waters Flow." May someone be enjoying golf in beautiful Oklahoma for as long as the waters flow.

DEL LEMON

Austin, Texas
December, 2000

PLAYER LIST

The players briefly profiled here were born in Oklahoma or have been residents. Because All-American selections were not made until 1958, for earlier years players earning three or more varsity letters are included.

Jerry Abbott—Abbott won the South Central PGA Section Championship in 1970.

John Adams—Adams, whose father was a golf professional, was born in Altus on May 5, 1954. He won the 1975 Arizona State Amateur. Adams, was co-medalist in the 1973 PGA Tour School, and earned almost $2 million in two decades as a PGA Tour pro. He is known for excellent tee-to-green skills, leading the 1988 Tour in greens in regulation (73.9 percent) and third in driving distance in 1992 (275.8).

Rafael Alarcon—A native of Guadalajara, Mexico, Alarcon was a three-time All-American at OSU (1978–80) and played on two NCAA championship teams. He won the 1979 Southern Amateur, the 1980 Big Eight individual title, the 1984 Indian Open, and the 1990 Mexican PGA Championship and led the Mexican PGA Tour in earnings in 1989–92. He played on four World Cup teams for Mexico.

Mike Alsup—Alsup was Missouri Valley Conference champion and All-American at Tulsa in 1978.

Jim Awtrey—Awtrey played at OU in 1962–64, where he was captain as a senior and finished second individually in the Big Eight Championship. Awtrey played on the PGA Tour in 1969–72. He returned to his alma mater in 1982 as head golf coach. In 1988, Awtrey was named CEO of the PGA of America.

Kathy (Baker) Guadagnino—The 1982 NCAA Champion at the University of Tulsa, Baker finished low amateur at the U.S. Women's Open in 1982 and 1983, then won the U.S. Women's Open in 1985 at Baltusrol. She won the Eastern Amateur twice (1979, 1982), the 1979 PGA Junior Championship, and the 1980 Western Amateur and was a two-time All-American at Tulsa.

Ralph Baker—Baker was Missouri Valley Conference champion for Tulsa in 1961.

Steve Ball—Ball won the South Central PGA Championship in 1986.

Dave Barr—A native of Kelowna, British Columbia, Barr was an All-American at Oral Roberts (1973) and won the 1973 Oklahoma Amateur. A two-time winner on the PGA Tour and four-time winner of the Canadian Order of Merit, Barr played on thirteen Canadian World Cup teams. He won thirteen times on the Canadian PGA Tour and earned $2.5 million on the PGA Tour.

Sharon Barrett—An All-American at Tulsa (1980), Barrett won the first five tournaments she entered as a collegian and played on TU's 1980 AIAW national championship team. A native of San Diego, she won three consecutive California state high school championships and both the California Junior and Junior World Championship in 1978 and 1979. Barrett won the 1984 Potamkin Cadillac Classic and earned a quarter of a million dollars on the LPGA Tour 1980–97.

Jenny Bartley—Bartley was All-American at OSU in 1997.

O. S. "Sandy" Baxter—Baxter came to Oklahoma from Scotland in the early 1900s and was pro at Oklahoma City Golf and Country Club. He won the 1921 Oklahoma Open.

Sara Beautell—Beautell was All-American at Tulsa in 1996.

Jim Begwin—Begwin was an OU All-American in 1984.

Ricky Bell—Bell, an OU All-American in 1989, led the Sooners to a nineteen-stroke victory in the 1989 NCAA Championship at Oak Tree, by finishing tied for second individual, at 285, four behind Phil Mickelson.

Johnny Bench—A Baseball Hall of Fame catcher from Binger, Bench competed unsuccessfully in the 1997 Senior PGA Tour qualifying tournament, shooting twenty-seven-over-par 315, in second-stage qualifying, at Arizona's Rio Rico Resort.

Susie Maxwell Berning—Susie Maxwell was the first woman to receive a golf scholarship at Oklahoma City University, where she played on the men's golf team and graduated with a business degree. She is one of only four players to win three U.S. Women's Opens (1968, 1972, 1973); the others are Mickey Wright, who won four, Betsy Rawls, and Hollis Stacy. Maxwell, born in Pasadena, California, came to Oklahoma as a schoolgirl and learned the game in Oklahoma City from U. C. Ferguson at Lincoln Park. She won three straight Oklahoma state high school championships and three straight Oklahoma City Women's Amateurs. In 1968 she married Dale Berning. Between 1965 and 1976, she won eleven times on the LPGA Tour. Her first victory as a pro was at the 1965 Muskogee Civitan Open. Later that year, she won her first major championship—the 1965 Women's Western Open. Maxwell Berning later taught at the Nicklaus–Flick Golf Schools and is a member of four halls of fame, including the OCU Hall of Fame and the Oklahoma Sports Hall of Fame.

George Bigham—Bigham earned three letters at OSU (1950–52).

Patti Blanton—Blanton captured four Oklahoma Women's State Amateur Championships between 1931 and 1948.

Lynn Blevins—Blevins, OU golf coach in 1979–81, earned four letters as a player for the Sooners and was twice named team captain. He finished in the top five at the 1975 and 1977 Big Eight Conference Championships. Blevins later competed on the European PGA Tour and a series of U.S. minitours.

Don Bliss—Bliss was Big Eight individual champion for OSU in 1973.

Joan Blumenthal—Blumenthal coached the OU women's golf team from 1975 to 1982. Under Blumenthal the Sooners won three Big Eight Conference Championships.

Maria Boden—Boden, twice an OSU All-American, was Big 12 Conference champion for OSU in 1999. In 2000, she tied for tenth place at the NCAA Championship.

Tommy Bolt—Born in Haworth in the southeastern part of the state on March 31, 1918, Bolt became the second native Oklahoman to win a U.S. Open, at Tulsa's Southern Hills Country Club in 1958. He did not join the PGA Tour until he was thirty-two, having served in World War II and worked in the construction business. But Bolt went on to win fifteen Tour events, including at the Colonial NIT in Fort Worth (1958) and the Los Angeles Open (1952). In 1969 Bolt won both the PGA Senior and World Senior championships. In 1980, he partnered with Art Wall to win the Legends of Golf in Austin, Texas. Bolt is a member of the Texas Golf Hall of Fame.

Andre Bossert—Bossert was a 1987 All-American at Tulsa and Missouri Valley Conference champion in 1988.

Heather Bowie—A three-time state champion at Bishop McGuinness in Oklahoma City (1991–93), Bowie was a four-time All-American (Arizona State and University of Texas) and the 1997 Big 12 and NCAA individual medalist as a senior at the University of Texas.

Michael Boyd—Boyd, the 1994 state high school champion from Tulsa Union, was a two-time Missouri Valley Conference champion for Tulsa (1995–96). In 1994 Boyd, a two-time junior All-American, won the Jim Thorpe Award for Outstanding Male Golfer in Oklahoma. In 1996 Boyd won the Rice Planters Championship. In 1997 he was quarterfinalist at the U.S. Amateur.

Michael Bradley—A three-time All-American at OSU (1986–88), Floridian Bradley played on OSU's national championship team of 1987 and was individual medalist six times as a Cowboy, including the 1987 Big Eight title. After joining the PGA Tour in 1992, Bradley won the 1996 Buick Challenge and the 1998 Doral-Ryder Open and has had two victories on the Canadian PGA Tour. In 1983, Bradley won the PGA Junior Championship. He once shot 59, at the Willows Classic Pro-Am in Saskatoon, Saskatchewan.

Alan Bratton—Bratton, a Jack Nicklaus Award winner from Bryan, Texas, was a four-time All-American at OSU (1992–95) and played on the Cowboys' 1995 national championship team. Bratton was Big Eight Champion in 1992 and 1995 (with Chris Tidland) and twice Big Eight player of the year. Seven times a collegiate medalist, Bratton shared the 1994 college player of the year award with Justin Leonard and was a rookie on the 1999 PGA Tour.

Jaxon Brigman—A native of Abilene, Texas, Brigman was an honorable mention All-American at OSU in 1992 and played on OSU's NCAA championship team the year before. He won the LaJet National Amateur twice and the 1993 Sunnehanna Amateur.

Maria Brink—Brink was Missouri Valley Conference champion and All-American at Tulsa University in 1994.

Ted Brodzik—Brodzik was Missouri Valley Conference champion for Tulsa in 1982.

Bill Brogden—In three decades as a collegiate golf coach at four universities (Memphis State, Louisiana State, Oral Roberts, Tulsa), Brogden coached nineteen All-Americans and won thirteen conference championships. At Oral Roberts (1977–86), Brogden's Titans finished in the top six at the NCAAs in four consecutive years. ORU was NCAA runner-up in 1981. After he took over at Tulsa in 1986, Brogden teams won seven Missouri Valley Conference championships. A native of Wilmington, North Carolina, Brogden played varsity golf and basketball at East Carolina University. A nine-time conference coach of the year, Brogden was voted national coach of the year in 1980. In 1991, Brogden was elected to the Coaches' Hall of Fame.

Roger Brown—Brown was honorable mention All-American at OSU in 1967.

Dave Bryan—Bryan, while head professional at Southern Hills, won the South Central PGA Championship in 1991.

Jimmie Bullard—Bullard won the South Central PGA Championship in 1976.

Janice (Burba) Gibson—Born in Tulsa on February 24, 1961, Gibson earned All-American honors twice at OSU (1982–83) and won the 1983 Big Eight Championship. After winning twice on the Futures Tour, Gibson qualified for the LPGA Tour on her second attempt and earned over $300,000 in thirteen years as a pro. In 2000, she joined the teaching staff at Baker's Golf Learning Center at Broken Arrow.

Lynn Burrus—Burrus earned three letters at OSU (1937–39).

Dick Canon—Canon was the Big Eight individual champion at OSU (1962).

Keefe Carter—One of the state's pioneer amateur golfers, Carter won the 1925 Western Amateur and three Oklahoma Amateur Championships between 1924 and 1930. He was instrumental in bringing the PGA circuit to Oklahoma and attracting sponsorship for the first four Oklahoma City Opens (1926–29).

Clarence Clark—Winner of seven PGA events plus the 1930 Oklahoma Open, this pro at Tulsa's old McFarlin Golf Club won the 1932 Texas Open and had a top-ten finish in the 1936 U.S. Open at Baltusrol. Clark won back-to-back South Central PGA championships in 1929–30.

Mrs. Hulbert Clarke—Ms. Clarke won back-to-back Oklahoma Women's Championships (1924–25) and the 1930 Women's Trans-National Amateur.

Patty (McGraw) Coatney—Outdistancing all others in Oklahoma Women's Amateur Championship victories, Coatney captured eight State Amateur titles between 1977 and 1991 as well as the 1976 Oklahoma Junior Girls' Championship. She played collegiate golf for Oklahoma State.

Charles Coe—Coe, born in Ardmore on October 26, 1923, is considered one of the half dozen greatest career amateurs in the history of American golf. After being taught the fundamentals by pro Harrell Butler at Dornick Hills, Coe blossomed into an outstanding junior player, winning the Oklahoma state championship at Ardmore High in 1941. At the University of Oklahoma (1946–48), Coe won three Big Seven Conference Championships. Forgoing a professional golf career to be a father and operate the family's Oklahoma City oil business, Coe won two U.S. Amateur Championships (1949, 1958), four Trans-Mississippi titles (1947, 1949, 1952, 1956), and the 1950 Western Amateur. During one stretch, he won twenty-seven consecutive matches in major amateur tournaments. In the 1949 U.S. Amateur at Oak Hill Country Club in Rochester, New York, Coe defeated Rufus King of Wichita Falls, Texas, 11 & 10 in the final, second only to Charles Macdonald's 12 & 11 over Charles Sands in the very first Amateur in 1895 as the most lopsided victory margin in Amateur history. Coe won his second U.S. Amateur at San Francisco's Olympic Club in 1958, defeating Tommy Aaron in the final. As the defending champion in 1959, at the Broadmoor in Colorado Springs, thirty-five-year-old Coe had his hands full with a player barely half his age. Coe birdied the first three holes of the final match, but this was only good enough for a one-hole lead. He led by two after eighteen but lost by one up at the thirty-sixth and final hole, to a birdie by then teenager Jack Nicklaus. Competing in 17 consecutive U.S. Amateurs, from 1947 through 1963, Coe won 55 of 70 matches. Only one golfer (Chick Evans) had more Amateur match wins. Coe was also runner-up in the 1951 British Amateur and low amateur in the 1958 U.S. Open at Southern Hills. In the 1961 Masters, Coe tied Arnold Palmer at 281 to finish in second place, a stroke behind Gary Player. Coe owned fourteen amateur records at the Masters—more than any other player—including most cuts made (8); most career eagles (6); most rounds played (67); most rounds par or better (22); most times low amateur (6); lowest total (281); best finish (second, tied with Frank Stranahan and Ken Venturi); and most starts (19, tied with Dick Chapman). Coe, a six-time member of the U.S. Walker Cup team, is a member of the Oklahoma Sports Hall of Fame. One of his sons, Rick Coe, became executive director of the Oklahoma Golf Association. In September of 1998, the University of Oklahoma's Charlie Coe Golf Learning Center was dedicated in his honor. He is a member at Augusta National, Southern Hills, Olympic Club, and Oklahoma City Golf and Country Club and a founder at Colorado's Castle Pines. Coe received the game's highest honor—the USGA's Bob Jones Award—in 1964.

Hulen Coker—Coker, born on July 24, 1924, in Lynn, Oklahoma, won the 1966 New Mexico State Open and joined the Senior PGA Tour in 1982.

Chris Cole—Cole was a two-time All-American at OSU (1972–73). He won the South Central PGA Championship in 1980.

Sean Collard—Collard was Missouri Valley Conference champion at Tulsa in 1987.

J. G. "Jock" Collins—Winner of the 1917 Oklahoma Open, Collins, a native of Scotland, was teaching pro at Tulsa Country Club.

Jeff Combe—Combe was a two-time All-American at Oral Roberts (1982–83) and won the South Central PGA Championship in 1992.

Kris Cox—Cox, a three-time All-American at OSU (1994–96), played on OSU's 1995 NCAA championship team and won the 1996 Big Eight Conference Championship individual title, as a senior, at Prairie Dunes Country Club in Hutchinson, Kansas. Ten months earlier, his mother, Valerie Cox, a high school athletic director, golf coach, and English teacher in San Antonio, had died at age forty-eight, of a heart illness. Prairie Dunes had always been Valerie's favorite course to walk with her son. Cox was Big Eight Newcomer of the Year in 1993.

Craig Cozby—A two-time All-American at OU (1994–95), Cozby is the son of Jerry Cozby, 1985 PGA Golf Professional of the Year and longtime director of golf at Hillcrest Country Club in Bartlesville. Cozby's brothers, Cary and Chance, both played on the golf team at OU.

Billy Craig—Craig earned three letters at OU (1937–39).

William Creavy—As head pro at Oklahoma City Golf and Country Club, Creavy won the 1923 Oklahoma Open and the South Central PGA section championship in 1925.

Betsy Cullen—Cullen, winner of three Oklahoma Women's Amateur Championships and two Oklahoma Junior Girls' titles between 1953 and 1961, won the 1972 Women's World Classic on the LPGA Tour and the 1973 Alamo Ladies Classic. She later became a top teaching professional in Texas.

Eva Dahllof—A native of Ornskoldsvik, Sweden, Dahllof was a three-time All-American at OSU (1987 89) and the first winner of three consecutive Big Eight individual crowns. As a professional she competed in two World Cups for Sweden. Dahllof joined the LPGA Tour in 1993.

Tripp Davis—Davis, an All-American on OU's national championship team of 1989, became a golf course architect.

David Dawley—Dawley, of Chandler, won the 1991 PGA Junior Championship.

Glen Day—A two-time All-American at OU (1987–88), Day finished second at the 1998 Players Championship and MCI Classic. Day joined the PGA Tour in 1994 and earned more than $2.5 million in his first five years. He won the 1993 South Central PGA Championship and the 1999 Heritage Classic, for his first victory on the PGA Tour.

J. C. DeLeon—OSU's DeLeon sank the winning birdie putt to defeat Georgia Tech in a playoff for the 2000 NCAA team title.

Henry DeLozier—DeLozier won the 1972 Oklahoma Amateur and was an All-American at OSU in 1973.

Scott DeSerrano—DeSerrano, a two-time All-American at OSU (1990–91), played on the Cowboys' 1991 NCAA Championship team.

Ben Dickson—Dickson earned four letters at OSU (1950–51, 1954–55), twice winning the Missouri Valley individual title (1951, 1955).

Bob Dickson—Born in McAlester on January 25, 1944, Dickson was twice a first-team All-American at OSU (1965–66) and in those same years won back-to-back Oklahoma Amateur Championships. He also won the Big Eight individual title in 1965. In 1966, Dickson won the Oklahoma Open as an amateur, and he repeated the feat as a pro in 1971. In 1967 Dickson became one of only four players ever—and the last since 1935—to win both the U.S. Amateur and British Amateur in the same year. He was a member of the victorious Walker Cup team that year and won the USGA's Bob Jones Award in 1968. Medalist at the Tour's spring 1968 qualifying school, Dickson won twice on the PGA Tour and joined the Senior PGA Tour in 1994. Dickson began working for the PGA Tour in 1979 as the director of marketing at Sawgrass, Florida. He was instrumental in the founding of the Hogan Tour. In June of 1998, Dickson sank a 20-foot putt on the first playoff hole to defeat Jim Colbert and Larry Nelson in the Senior PGA Tour's Cadillac NFL Golf Classic.

Andy Dillard—A three-time All-American at OSU (1982–84), Dillard played for OSU's 1983 national championship team. He won the 1979 American Junior Golf Association Tournament of Champions. As a pro, Dillard set a USGA record by making birdie at each of the first six holes of the 1992 U.S. Open at Pebble Beach.

Joey Dills—Dills, winner of both the Oklahoma Junior (1969) and the Oklahoma Mid-Amateur (1984), was medalist at the 1975 PGA Tour National Qualifying Tournament.

Sheila (Luginbuel) Dills—Dills won four Oklahoma Women's Amateur Championships between 1989 and 1996, including three in a row.

Dale Douglass—Born in Wewoka on March 5, 1936, Douglass learned to play at Twin Hills Golf and Country Club in Oklahoma City, where his father was a member. After attending college at the University of Colorado, Douglass turned pro in 1960 and won three times on the PGA Tour. He saved his best golf for the Senior PGA Tour, winning ten times, including the 1986 U.S. Senior Open. He partnered with Charles Coody to two Legends of Golf wins.

Karen Dowd—Dowd coached the first OU women's golf team in 1974–75.

Bruce Drake—Drake was OU's first golf coach, coaching the Sooners from 1933 to 1951. Under Drake, Sooner Walter Emery won the 1933 NCAA Championship. Drake also coached two-time U.S. Amateur champion Charlie Coe and OU's other NCAA champion, Jim Vickers. Drake coached OU in basketball as well, taking the Sooners to the Final Four in 1947. He was inducted into both the Helms Foundation and College Basketball halls of fame.

Estelle Drennan—Drennan won six Oklahoma Women's Amateur Championships, including four in a row (1926–29).

Ed Dudley—With his smooth swing, Dudley had seventeen professional victories from 1925 to 1948, including the 1925–26 Oklahoma Opens. For many years he was head professional at Tulsa Country Club, before taking the same job at

Augusta National Golf Club. Dudley played on three Ryder Cup teams and was president of the PGA in 1942–48. He was leading the Masters in 1937, only to have his drive at the thirteenth hole on Sunday ricochet into Rae's Creek, off the head of a man who had wandered into the fairway. Dudley made seven at the par-5, finishing third —three shots behind Byron Nelson. Dudley won the first South Central PGA section championship in 1924.

Zell Eaton—Oklahoma Citian Eaton, who tied for twenty-eighth at the 1934 U.S. Open as an amateur, won the 1934 Western Amateur at Twin Hills. After turning professional, Eaton captured the 1936 Illinois Open and the 1939 Oklahoma Open at Lincoln Park.

Danny Edwards—A three-time winner of the Oklahoma Open and three-time All-American at OSU (1971–73), Edwards won two Big Eight Conference championships and claimed four victories on the PGA Tour. After winning the 1972 North and South Amateur at Pinehurst and making the 1973 Walker Cup team, Edwards qualified for the 1973 British Open at Troon. Tom Weiskopf won the Open; Edwards was low amateur, an accomplishment he called his greatest thrill in golf.

David Edwards—Younger brother to Danny Edwards, David Edwards won two Oklahoma Opens and was a two-time All-American at OSU (1977–78). He also won the 1973 Oklahoma Junior title and the 1978 NCAA Championship. Edwards has four victories on the PGA Tour, including the 1984 Los Angeles Open and the 1992 Memorial. In 1980, the Edwards brothers won the National Team Championship at Walt Disney World.

Dave Eichelberger—Eichelberger won the 1999 U.S. Senior Open at Des Moines Golf and Country Club. A native of Waco, Texas, and a two-time All-American at OSU (1964–65), Eichelberger played on OSU's national championship team of 1963. He went on to win four times on the PGA Tour, later winning the 1994 Quicksilver Classic and 1997 Transamerica Championship on the Senior PGA Tour.

Brad Elder—Tulsa native Elder was a two-time All-American at the University of Texas, the 1997 Jack Nicklaus college player of the year, 1997 NCAA runner-up, and a member of the 1997 Walker Cup team. He won twice on the Nike Tour prior to earning a PGA Tour card for the year 2000.

Charlotta Eliasson—Eliasson was a two-time All-American at OSU (1991, 1994) and five-time medalist, including the 1994 Big Eight title.

Walter Emery—Emery won the Oklahoma state high school championship in 1931. In 1933, playing for the OU Sooners, he became the first player from a university west of the Mississippi River to win the NCAA individual title. Two years later, at the Country Club in Cleveland, Ohio, Emery lost 4 & 2 in the finals of the U.S. Amateur to Lawson Little. Also in 1935, Emery became the second amateur to win the Oklahoma Open. He won the Oklahoma Amateur in 1936 and 1939.

Jake Engel—In 1996, Engel, a retired hatchery owner and convenience store manager from Oklahoma City, played 10,374 holes of golf, most of them at Lincoln Park and all by walking, to break South Carolinian Ollie Bowers's twenty-seven-year-old record for most holes of golf played in one year. In the process, Engel wore out a Bag Boy pull cart and five pairs of golf shoes.

Sofie Eriksson—Eriksson, of Sweden, was a four-time All-American at Tulsa (1992–95).

Floyd Farley—Farley, the most prolific golf course architect in Oklahoma history, won the South Central PGA Championship in 1937 and 1942.

Robert "Bo" Faulkenberry—Playing out of Lincoln Park, Faulkenberry was a quarterfinalist at the 1953 U.S. Amateur.

Larry Field—Field, from Oklahoma City, won the 1976 PGA Junior Championship and later played at the University of Texas.

Tim Fleming—Fleming was a first-team All-American for the 1987 NCAA champions Oklahoma State and won the South Central PGA Championship in 1994 and 1999.

Terry Forcum—Long drive specialist "White Lightnin'" Forcum of Ponca City was the 1983 National Long Driving champion. His longest drive ever measured was 475 yards; his longest in competition was 369 yards, at the 1982 World Championships in Japan.

Glen Fowler—Fowler won three consecutive Oklahoma Amateur Championships (1958–60).

Robin Freeman—Freeman, a two-time NAIA All-American at the University of Central Oklahoma (1981–82), is the only two-time medalist in PGA Tour qualifying tournament history (1988, 1993). In 1995, Freeman tied for second at the Byron Nelson Classic, three strokes behind Ernie Els.

Vene Fry—Fry earned three letters at OSU (1936–38).

Larry Fryer—Fryer won the South Central PGA Championship in 1967.

Kim Gardner—Gardner earned All-American honors at Tulsa in 1984.

John Gatherum—Head professional at Tulsa Country Club in 1924–25, Arkansas native Gatherum won the 1919 Oklahoma Open at Muskogee Country Club.

Jimmie Gauntt—One of only two five-time winners of the South Central PGA Championship (Bob Ralston of Little Rock, Arkansas is the other), Gauntt is the only person to have won the Oklahoma Open five times, including three years straight, 1954–56. A native of Ardmore, a former caddie at Dornick Hills, and long-time pro at Twin Hills, Gauntt also won three consecutive Texas PGA Championships (1942–44). During Byron Nelson's streak of eleven consecutive victories in 1945, Gauntt finished third to Nelson at the Durham Open in North Carolina. In the spring of 1999, at age eighty-five, Gauntt shot 74 at Yaupon Golf Course in Austin, Texas.

Chris Gers—Gers, a native Oklahoma Citian and club pro at Dornick Hills in Ardmore, won back-to-back Oklahoma Opens in 1969–70. He also won the South Central PGA Championship in 1964.

George Getchell—This Oklahoma City Golf and Country Club assistant pro won the 1947 Oklahoma Open at the Oaks Country Club in Tulsa.

Scott Gibson—Gibson was an All-American at Tulsa in 1994 and won the Missouri Valley Conference individual title in 1996.

Bill Glasson—After joining the PGA Tour in 1984, California native Glasson, a three-time All-American at Oral Roberts University (1980–82) and a resident of Stillwater, became known as a tenacious competitor who battled chronic knee problems and an ailing lower back. He won seven Tour events in fifteen years. In 1997 he won the last regular season PGA Tour event, his first victory in three and a half years, to jump from fifty-fourth to twenty-seventh place on the season money list and earn a spot in the Tour Championship. In the first ever World Match Play Championship (1999), Glasson defeated David Duval—the player ranked number two in the world—2 & 1, in the second round.

Robert (Bob) Goetz—Goetz, from Lynn, Massachusetts, lettered four years at OSU (1952, 1955–57), won the 1956 Missouri Valley individual title and the 1957 Oklahoma Amateur, and finished sixteenth at the 1958 U.S. Open.

Dick Goetz—Goetz won the South Central PGA Championship in 1974 and 1981.

Ted Goin—Goin was a two-time All-American at OSU (1971, 1973).

Jaime Gonzalez—A four-time All-American at OSU (1974–77), Gonzalez is from São Paulo, Brazil. He won five individual titles as a collegian, including the 1974 Big Eight Championship, and played on OSU's 1976 NCAA Championship team. He won the 1980 Oklahoma Open at Kickingbird and has played on Brazil's World Cup team and on the European, South American, Mexican, PGA, and Nike tours.

Jamie Gough—In 1967 U.S. Air Force Academy graduate Gough, a twenty-three-year old second lieutenant at Vance Air Force Base in Enid, strung together five straight birdies in the final round to win the Oklahoma Open at Enid's Oakwood Country Club. Gough was the seventh and last amateur to win the Oklahoma state open.

Skip Graham—Graham won the Big Eight individual crown for OU in 1969.

Pat Grant—Grant, from Shawnee, won six Oklahoma Women's Amateurs between 1939 and 1949, including four in a row (1939–42). She was medalist at the 1941 Women's Trans-National.

Morrie Gravatt—Gravatt won the South Central PGA Championship in 1948.

Quinton Gray—Born in Mangum, Oklahoma on October 18, 1934, Gray played for seven years on the PGA Tour and joined the Senior PGA Tour in 1984. He was runner-up at the 1987 PGA Senior Tour National Qualifying Tournament. Gray also won the 1976 South Central PGA Championship.

Gregg Grost—Grost, who coached OU to the national title in 1989, is a four-time conference coach of the year (three Southland, one Big Eight) and has twice been named national coach of the year (at Lamar in 1984 and OU in 1989). After graduating from Texas Christian University, Grost played professionally on the South African Tour and on U.S. minitours. In the fall of 1980 at age twenty-four, Grost took the top job at Lamar, becoming the youngest Division I head golf coach in the nation. After fifteen seasons at OU, Grost retired as Sooner coach in 2000. Grost's OU teams had sixteen tournament victories, including the 1992 Big Eight

Conference title. He coached twenty-six All-Americans and his teams participated in thirteen NCAA Championships.

Dick Grout—One of six members of Oklahoma City's Grout family to become professional golfers, Dick Grout, the pro at Okmulgee Country Club, won two Oklahoma Opens (1927, 1929) and the 1926 South Central PGA Championship.

Jack Grout—Younger brother of Dick Grout, Jack Grout played on the PGA circuit during the 1930s and 1940s. In 1950, as the golf professional at Scioto Country Club in Columbus, Ohio, Grout began to teach eleven-year-old Jack Nicklaus, a relationship that continued until Grout's death in 1989.

Brian Guetz—Guetz, winner of the 1994 Colorado Open as an amateur, was a two-time All-American at OSU (1996–97).

Jimmy Gullane—Gullane, a Scot, was head pro at Hillcrest Country Club in Bartlesville when he won back-to-back Oklahoma Opens (1932–33). In the 1933 Oklahoma Open at Hillcrest, Ben Hogan finished tied for third, three back of Gullane. Gullane won the South Central PGA section championship three times.

Ted Gwin—A three-year letterman at OU and Sooner golf coach in 1952, Gwin guided the Sooners to the Big Seven title and Jim Vickers to the individual championship at the 1952 NCAAs. Gwin won the South Central PGA Championship in 1952 and 1958. He tied for fiftieth at the 1958 U.S. Open.

Harry Gwinnup—Gwinnup won the first three Oklahoma Amateur Championships (1910–12) and a fourth in 1916.

Hunter Haas—Haas, winner of the 1999 U.S. Amateur Public Links Championship and the 1999 Porter Cup, was All-American at OU in 1998 and 1999, and won the 1998 Big 12 Conference individual title. He also played on the 1999 U.S. Walker Cup team.

Nancy Hager—An Oklahoma native, Hager won back-to-back Texas Girls' Championships (1967–68) and was low amateur at the 1968 Dallas Civitan Open. Hager, who played at the University of Texas, was a semifinalist at the 1969 U.S. Women's Amateur.

Craig Hainline—Hainline, who won the first collegiate tournament he ever entered, was a three-time All-American at OSU (1990–92), finishing runner-up in the Big Eight (1991) and fourth at the 1991 NCAA Championship. He played on the Cowboys' 1991 NCAA championship team.

Art Hall—Hall earned four letters at OSU (1955–58).

Todd Hamilton—Hamilton was a three-time All-American at OU (1985–87).

Lee Ann Hammack—Hammack, of Oklahoma City, was qualifying medalist at the 1988 U.S. Women's Public Links in Tulsa and medalist and runner-up at the 1986 Women's Trans-National.

Jim Hardy—Hardy was an OSU All-American in 1966.

Labron Harris Jr.—Harris won the 1962 U.S. Amateur (defeating Downing Gray in the final), the 1960 Western Junior, and the 1963 Oklahoma Open (as an amateur). Born in Stillwater on September 27, 1941, he became a two-time All-American at Oklahoma State (1961–62), where his father, Labron Harris Sr., was coach. Harris Jr. played on the 1963 Walker Cup team and won the 1971 Robinson Open on the PGA Tour. He and Harris Sr. are the only father and son to win both the Oklahoma Open and the South Central PGA Championship.

Labron Harris Sr.—Harris Sr., who grew up in Wewoka and Guthrie, founded the OSU golf program in 1947 and went on to coach the Cowboys to twenty-four conference titles and one national championship (1963). Harris coached twenty-seven All-Americans in Stillwater, one of whom, Mike Holder, succeeded him as coach. Harris was himself a superb player, winning the 1953 Oklahoma Open at Oakwood Country Club in Enid and tying for twenty-seventh at the 1958 U.S. Open. He also won the 1954 South Central PGA Championship. Harris was instrumental in building Lakeside Memorial Golf Course in Stillwater and Weatherford Golf Course (with Ward Maynard). His son Labron Jr. won the 1962 U.S. Amateur, and an older son, James Lee, also played for him at OSU (1959–61).

Britt Harrison—Harrison, a three-time All-American at OSU (1976, 1978–79) from Beaumont, played on two national championship teams (1976, 1978) and won the 1975 Western Junior at Stillwater Country Club.

E. J. "Dutch" Harrison—When the PGA Tour commissioned a statistical survey in 1989 to determine the top one hundred PGA Tour professionals in the history of American golf, Harrison, a native of Conway, Arkansas, and longtime pro at Dornick Hills in Ardmore, was ranked number nineteen all-time, ahead of Gary Player, Julius Boros, Tommy Armour, Jack Burke Jr., and Johnny Miller. Nicknamed the "Arkansas Traveler," Harrison won eighteen PGA events between 1939 and 1958. He was the 1954 Vardon Trophy winner, is a member of the PGA Hall of Fame, and had 213 top-ten finishes in his career. He won the South Central PGA Championship in 1953.

Holly Hartley—Hartley was a first-team All-American at Tulsa in 1978.

Mark Hayes—Hayes, a Stillwater native and two-time All-American at OSU (1970–71), won the Oklahoma Amateur twice and the Oklahoma Open three times. He captured the 1972 Sunnehanna Amateur and also made the World Amateur Cup team that year. Hayes won three times on the PGA Tour, including the 1977 Players Championship. In 1976 he led the Byron Nelson Classic wire to wire, for his first victory on the PGA Tour. Hayes was a member of the victorious 1979 U.S. Ryder Cup team. In 1977 at Turnberry, he became the first player ever to shoot 63 in the British Open. Hayes won the 1999 Texas Senior Open and was medalist at the 1999 Senior PGA Tour qualifying tournament. Hayes learned the game under U. C. Ferguson at Lincoln Park and became a golf course architect between years on the regular and senior PGA Tours.

Flippa Helmersson—Helmersson was 1996 Missouri Valley Conference individual champion and All-American at Tulsa in 1998.

Phil Hessler—Hessler, professional at Tulsa Country Club, won the 1922 Oklahoma Open.

Bob Higgins—Higgins won back-to-back South Central PGA Championships in 1931–32.

Carl Higgins—Higgins was an All-American at OU in 1970.

Frank Higgins—Higgins won the South Central PGA Championship in 1940.

Bill Hildebrand—Hildebrand was an All-American at OU in 1982.

Carolyn Hill—Hill, a 1978 All-American at the University of Tulsa, won the 1979 U.S. Women's Amateur at Memphis Country Club, defeating Patty Sheehan in the final, 7 & 6. On the LPGA Tour, Hill won the 1994 McCall's Classic at Stratton Mountain, Vermont. She was a member of the 1978 U.S. Curtis Cup team.

Dennis Hillman—Hillman was a 1995 All-American at Tulsa.

George Hixon—Hixon, a member of the Cowboys' 1963 NCAA championship squad, earned All-American honors twice at OSU (1963–64), won two Big Eight individual titles (1963–64), and in 1964 won the Oklahoma Amateur.

Carin (Hjalmarsson) Koch—Koch, from Kungalv, Sweden, was All-American at Tulsa in 1990. She turned pro in 1992 and finished third at the 1993 Women's British Open.

Mike Holder—A native of Odessa, Texas, Holder grew up in Ardmore. He won the Big Eight Conference individual title in 1970 and was a three-time All-American at OSU (1968–70). In 1973, Holder succeeded Labron Harris Sr. as Cowboy head golf coach. Holder's teams at OSU won eight national championships in his first twenty-seven years. He coached ninety-eight All-American selections in twenty-seven years and his players won twenty-four conference team titles, twenty conference individual titles, and five NCAA individual crowns. During the first fifty-four seasons under Harris and Holder, Cowboy golf teams never failed to qualify for the NCAA Championship (1947–2000) nor missed the cut—both NCAA records. During the early 1990s, Holder raised funds from private donors to build Karsten Creek Golf Club, as home course for the OSU golf teams. Holder won the Oklahoma Amateur in 1968.

Robin Hood—A three-time All-American at OSU (1984, 1986–87), Hood won eight individual titles in college, including the 1984 and 1986 Big Eight Conference titles, plus winning the Indiana Amateur three times. In her second year on the LPGA Tour, Hood won the 1989 Pat Bradley International in High Point, North Carolina.

Lauren Howe—Howe, who played for one year at the University of Tulsa (1977), turned pro at age eighteen. As an amateur she won the 1977 Women's Western Amateur and the 1976 Mexican Amateur. She was medalist twice at the U.S. Junior Girls' and won the 1983 Mayflower Classic on the LPGA Tour. Howe tied for fifteenth in the 1983 U.S. Women's Open at Tulsa's Cedar Ridge Country Club.

Charles Howell—Howell, the 2000 NCAA individual champion from Oklahoma State, won four times during his record-setting junior season, including the 2000 Big 12 Conference individual title by ten strokes. Following his fourth career victory, at the Perry Maxwell Intercollegiate, Howell, a native of Augusta, Georgia, recorded the best performance by an individual in 104 years of NCAA Golf Championship history. Howell's rounds of 67-66-63-69 broke by six strokes the previous NCAA record held by four players and led the Cowboys to the NCAA team title. He finished runner-up at the 1996 U.S. Junior, was fifth in the 1999 NCAA Championship, and earned All-American honors in each of his first three seasons at OSU (1998–2000). In 2000 Howell was named Big 12 Golfer of the Year, Big 12 Men's Athlete of the Year, and recipient of the Jack Nicklaus Award for being the nation's outstanding collegiate golfer. He turned professional in June 2000.

Kenny Huff—A 1977 graduate of TCU, Huff took a job as assistant pro at Oak Tree in 1983. The following summer he won the Oklahoma Open, at Kickingbird in Edmond, defeating Gil Morgan in a playoff.

Anders Hultman—Hultman, an OSU All-American, played on the Cowboys' 2000 NCAA Championship team.

Laura Hurlbut—A member of Tulsa's 1980 national championship team, Hurlbut played on the LPGA Tour 1981–94.

Yoshitko Ito—Ito was an All-American at OSU (1985) and joined the Japanese LPGA Tour in 1987.

Darryl James—James was a 1982 All-American at Oral Roberts.

Jennifer James—At the 2000 Big 12 Conference Championship in Lubbock, Texas, James, an OU sophomore from Edmond North High, sank a two-foot putt at the final hole to finish as Big 12 individual runner-up and to secure the Sooner women's program its first Big 12 Conference team title.

Betty Jameson—Born in Norman on May 9, 1919, Jameson is a founder of the LPGA Tour and a charter member of the LPGA Hall of Fame. She had a brilliant fourteen-victory amateur career, including winning the 1932 Texas Public Links at age thirteen and the 1934 Southern Championship when she was fifteen. In addition to winning the 1947 U.S. Women's Open at Starmount Forest Country Club in Greensboro, North Carolina, Jameson won two U.S. Women's Amateurs, two Women's Trans-Nationals, two Women's Western Amateurs, and two Women's Western Opens. Her 295 total for the 1947 U.S. Women's Open marked the first time a female golfer scored lower than 300 in a seventy-two-hole tournament. She has thirteen official victories on the LPGA Tour.

Jim Jamieson—Jamieson, a native of Kalamazoo, Michigan, played on OSU's 1963 national championship team. He joined the PGA Tour in 1969 and three years later won the Western Open, the oldest tournament on the PGA Tour. At the 1973 Masters, Jamieson (73-71-70-71) tied for third with Jack Nicklaus and Peter Oosterhuis, two behind Tommy Aaron.

Clint Jensen—Jensen was Missouri Valley Conference champion in 1994 and All-American at Tulsa in 1996.

Brandt Jobe—Jobe, originally from Oklahoma City, went to college at UCLA and has been successful on the Japanese PGA Tour.

John Johnson—Johnson earned four letters at OU (1952–55).

Grier Jones—A native of Wichita, Kansas, Jones, was one of OSU's seven NCAA individual champions (1968, at Las Cruces, New Mexico) and won the Big Eight Conference individual title in 1967 and 1968. Jones also captured the 1968 Oklahoma Open at Dornick Hills and had three victories on the PGA Tour. He was medalist at the 1968 Tour qualifying school and was voted the 1969 PGA Tour Rookie of the Year. In 1995, Jones became head golf coach at Wichita State.

Jerry Jones—Jones won the South Central PGA Championship in 1977.

Tom Jones—A four-time All-American at OSU (1974–77), Jones won the 1974 Trans-Mississippi Amateur and had six individual championships as a collegian, including the 1975 Big Eight Conference title. He was Big Eight runner-up three times. Jones also was medalist at the 1979 PGA Tour school, won the 1983 Oklahoma Open, and played on OSU's 1976 NCAA Championship team. Later he became director of golf at Karsten Creek.

Ab Justice—Justice, winner of the 1955 Oklahoma Amateur and the inaugural Big Eight Conference championship (1958), was OSU's first official All-American (1958).

Jim Kane—Kane, a four-time All-American at Oral Roberts (1979–82), won back-to-back Oklahoma Amateurs (1979–80) and the 1991 Oklahoma Open.

Spike Kelley—Kelley, a native of Shawnee, won the 1973 Oklahoma Open at Lakeside Municipal in Ponca City.

Loddie Kempa—Kempa, a Stillwater native, who played for three years at OSU, won the 1948 National Lefthanded Amateur Championship.

James Kennedy—Tulsan Kennedy won four consecutive Oklahoma Amateurs (1920–23) and finished runner-up to Wild Bill Mehlhorn at both the 1920 and 1923 Oklahoma Opens.

Palmer Kise—Kise was Missouri Valley Conference champion for Tulsa in 1941.

Brandon Knight—Knight was honorable mention All-American at OSU in 1993.

Lou Kretlow—An Enid pro and former American League pitcher, Kretlow set a world record in a 1961 tournament with a 421-yard hole in one at Lake Hefner Golf Course in Oklahoma City.

Trip Kuehne—Kuehne, a three-time OSU All-American (1994–96) from Dallas, played on OSU's national championship team of 1995. Kuehne won the 1991 Western Junior and came close in the 1994 U.S. Amateur, losing to Tiger Woods, two up, in the final at the Sawgrass Stadium Course in Ponte Vedra, Florida. In 1995, Kuehne received college golf's Ben Hogan Award for academic and athletic excellence.

Christina Kuld—Kuld was All-American at Tulsa in 1997.

Ky Laffoon—Born on December 23, 1908, in Zinc, Arkansas, Laffoon moved with his family to Miami, Oklahoma, at the age of seven. His first pro job was at age nineteen at the Miami Golf Club. So strong that he could tear a deck of cards in half, Laffoon with his good looks and raven black hair became a legend of sorts on the early days of the PGA. As profiled by Al Barkow in *Golf* magazine's 1978 yearbook issue, he won ten tournaments between 1933 and 1946, including the Atlanta and Phoenix Opens.

Niina Laitinen—Laitinen, a 1999 All-American, won back-to-back Western Athletic Conference individual crowns for Tulsa in 1998–99.

Matthew Lane—Lane, a three-time All-American at OU (1988–90), played on the Sooners' 1989 NCAA Championship team. On the 1994 Canadian Tour, he finished ninth on the Order of Merit.

Jeff Lee—Lee, a three-time All-American at OU (1989–91), played on the Sooners' 1989 NCAA Championship team. He finished tied for second at the 1993 Nike Wichita Open.

Patrick Lee—Lee was a two-time OU All-American (1992, 1994) and winner of the 1995 Western Amateur. Lee had three top-five finishes on the 1996 Nike Tour.

Bruce Lietzke—During the 1980s, Lietzke, born in Kansas City, Kansas, lived in both Jay and Grove, Oklahoma, while playing out of the Shangri-La Resort on Oklahoma's Grand Lake O' the Cherokees. Lietzke, called the "pro's pro" for his winning ways with minimal practice, grew up in Beaumont, Texas, and played at the University of Houston (1970–74). He won the 1971 Texas State Amateur. In nearly five hundred tournaments on the PGA Tour, Lietzke won thirteen times.

Edward Loar—Loar, a Rockwall, Texas, native and four-time All-American at OSU (1997–2000), won the 1997 Southern Amateur, the 1998 Golf World Invitational, the 1999 U.S. Collegiate Championship, and consecutive Sunnehanna Amateurs (1999 and 2000). In 1999 Loar played for the U.S. Walker Cup team. He was a member of OSU's 2000 NCAA Championship team.

Harold Long—While head professional at Oklahoma City's Lakeside Golf and Country Club, Long won the 1928 Oklahoma Open.

Nancy Lopez—As a University of Tulsa freshman out of Roswell, New Mexico, Lopez was the 1976 AIAW National Champion. A year earlier, she tied for second at the U.S. Women's Open as an amateur. Recruited by Tulsa University coach Dale McNamara, Lopez medaled ten out of nineteen collegiate tournaments. She won three LPGA Championships, two U.S. Girls' Juniors, three Western Juniors, and the 1975 Mexican Amateur. As a pro, Lopez required only ten years to play her way into the LPGA Hall of Fame. Her victory count for her first nineteen years as a professional was fifty-one. Lopez received the USGA's Bob Jones Award in 1998.

Carol Ludvigson—The women's golf coach at the University of Oklahoma from 1985 to the time of writing, Ludvigson won the Big Eight Conference team championship both as a player (1981) and as a coach (1991). A native of Flossmoor, Illinois, she was a walk-on at OU in 1978. In 1995, Ludvigson shared national coach of the year honors with Linda Vollstedt of Arizona State. Under Ludvigson, the Sooners won the Big 12 Conference Championship in 2000.

Adele (Lukken) Peterson—A first-team All-American for Tulsa (1986) and two-time Oklahoma Junior champion, Lukken won the 1986 Harder Hall Invitational and the 1986 U.S. vs. Japan NCAA Competition in Tokyo. She tied for fifteenth at the 1991 U.S. Women's Open.

Don Maddox—Don Maddox won the 1972 Oklahoma Open at Lakeside Municipal in Ponca City and the 1984 South Central PGA Championship.

Andrew Magee—Magee, a three-time All-American at OU (1982–84) and winner of the 1983 Big Eight individual crown, lost to Jeff Maggert, in thirty-eight holes, at the inaugural World Match Play Championship (1999). In 415 career starts (1985–98), Magee earned four PGA Tour victories. In 2000 Magee received the first Payne Stewart Professionalism Award, in memory of the 1999 U.S. Open Champion.

Jeff Maggert—Maggert played at OSU in 1983–84 and finished his collegiate career at Texas A&M. In 1999, he defeated Andrew Magee (in thirty-eight holes) in the final of the first World Match Play Championship.

Landry Mahan—Mahan, an OSU All-American, played on the Cowboys' 2000 NCAA Championship team.

Jack Malloy—In 1937 at Oklahoma City Golf and Country Club, Tulsa's Malloy became the third amateur to win the Oklahoma Open.

Martin Maritz—Maritz, the 2000 Western Athletic Conference medalist, earned All-American honors at Tulsa University in 1999 and 2000 and was named WAC player of the year in 2000.

Doug Martin—Martin, a three-time OU All-American (1987–89), led the Sooners to a nineteen-stroke victory in the 1989 NCAA Championship at Oak Tree Golf Club in Edmond, finishing runner-up medalist at 285, four behind Phil Mickelson. Later that summer, Martin was semifinalist at the U.S. Amateur and was named a member of the U.S. Walker Cup team. A PGA Tour member since 1992, he won the 1989 Oklahoma Open and the Nike Tour's South Texas Open in 1993. Martin won the 1984 U.S. Junior Amateur.

Stephanie Martin—Martin was a two-time All-American at OSU (1992–93) and four-time medalist.

Wendy Martin—The Oklahoma state high school champion in 1996, OU freshman Martin won the 1999 Susie Maxwell Berning Classic and tied for medalist honors at the 1999 Big 12 Conference Championship.

Grant Masson—Masson was a three-time OU All-American (1994–96).

Billy Maxwell—A Texas native, Maxwell played for coach Labron Harris Sr.'s Missouri Valley Conference Championship team in 1947–48, the first year OSU fielded a varsity golf team. Maxwell, who later transferred to North Texas State, went on to win the 1951 U.S. Amateur and played on a national championship at North Texas State University. He won eight times on the PGA Tour and was a member of the 1963 U.S. Ryder Cup team.

Bob May—May was a three-time OSU All-American (1989–91), a member of the 1991 Walker Cup team, and on OSU's national champion team in 1991. He won the 1999 British Masters and was second to Tiger Woods at the 2000 PGA.

Mike McGraw—A 1981 NAIA honorable mention All-American at the University of Central Oklahoma, McGraw finished sixteenth at the 1981 NAIA Championship. McGraw coached nine state championship teams in Edmond before taking a position as assistant golf coach at Oklahoma State. Following OSU's NCAA Championship in 2000, McGraw was named associate head coach of both the Cowboy men's and women's programs.

Marnie McGuire—A native of Auckland, New Zealand, McGuire won the 1986 British Women's Amateur and made first-team All-American at OSU (1990). She was Big Eight Conference individual champion in 1990. After turning pro in 1992, McGuire played five years on the Japanese LPGA Tour, winning four times. She also won the 1991 Queen Sirikit Cup.

Carolyn McKenzie—McKenzie was an All-American at OSU (1990).

Jeff McMillian—McMillian, an OSU player (1979–82) and later a golf professional, won two Oklahoma Junior Championships and two Oklahoma Amateurs, the youngest winner of both championships.

Dale (Fleming) McNamara—McNamara, a seven-time Oklahoma Women's Amateur champion, coached the University of Tulsa women's team to four national championships during the 1980s (two AIAWs and two NCAAs). In 1988, her daughter, Melissa McNamara was crowned NCAA individual medalist. In her first twenty-four years as coach (beginning in 1974), she had eighteen All-Americans, including national champions McNamara, Nancy Lopez, and Kathy (Baker) Guadagnino. McNamara retired as TU's coach in 2000 and was succeeded by her daughter Melissa.

Melissa McNamara—A four-time All-American at Tulsa (1985–88), McNamara won the 1988 NCAA individual title. In 1983, she joined her mother, Tulsa head coach Dale (Fleming) McNamara, as a winner of the Oklahoma Women's Amateur. McNamara, who was born in Tulsa, also won two Oklahoma Junior Girls' titles (1981–82), the 1991 Stratton Mountain LPGA Classic, and the 1993 JC Penney Mixed Team Classic (with Mike Springer). In 2000, she succeeded her mother as TU women's golf coach.

Robert Meek—Meek earned three letters at OU (1950–52).

William "Wild Bill" Mehlhorn—Mehlhorn grew up in the Chicago suburbs to become one of the great technicians in the evolution of the golf swing. He served as head professional at Tulsa Country Club during the early 1920s and won the 1920 and 1923 Oklahoma Opens. He had twenty-one career victories as a pro and was a member of the 1927 Ryder Cup team. Ben Hogan once called Mehlhorn the best tee-to-green player he had ever seen.

Marvin Mesch—Mesch earned three letters at OU (1938–40).

Lindy Miller—A four-time All-American at OSU (1975–78), Miller is the leading individual medalist in Cowboy golf history, with eleven, including three consecutive Big Eight titles (1976–78). He had a brilliant amateur career, winning the 1977 Southern and Pacific Coast Amateurs, was low amateur at the 1977 U.S. Open, and was a Walker Cup choice. In 1978, Miller was low amateur at Augusta, his 286 total the lowest score ever posted by an amateur in his first Masters. Miller also played on two OSU national championship teams (1976, 1978) and won the Haskins Award in 1978, as the nation's outstanding collegiate golfer. As a pro, Miller won the Oklahoma Open in 1978 and 1986 and the 1990 Ben Hogan Amarillo Open.

Dorea Mitchell—Mitchell was Big Eight Conference champion for OU in 1981.

Cathy Mockett—Mockett, champion of the 1984 U.S. Girls' Junior, the 1990 U.S. Women's Amateur Public Links, and the 1990 Trans-National, was a two-time All-American at Tulsa (1989–90) and played on the Hurricane's 1988 NCAA championship team.

Earl Moeller—As an OSU sophomore in 1953 from St. Louis, Moeller became the Cowboys' first NCAA individual champion, winning the title at the Broadmoor Golf Club in Colorado Springs.

Brian Montgomery—Montgomery, from Bristow, played at OSU in 1987–91. He won the U.S. Junior Amateur and the PGA Junior Championship in 1986.

Orville Moody—Moody's only victory on the regular PGA Tour was a major—the 1969 U.S. Open, at Champions Golf Club in Houston. Moody, the youngest son of a greens superintendent, was born on December 9, 1933, in Chickasha. In 1952, he won the Oklahoma state high school championship. Known as Sarge to his fellow pros, Moody captured the 1958 All-Army championship and the All-Service championship in 1962. After the U.S. Open victory, Moody had success internationally, winning opens in Morocco, Hong Kong, Australia, and the Caribbean. Moody joined the Senior PGA Tour in 1984 and had much success. Included among eleven Senior Tour victories were the 1989 U.S. Senior Open and the 1989 Senior Players Championship. Moody also won the Legends of Golf twice, with Bruce Crampton (1987–88).

Jack Moore—Moore was Big Eight Conference champion for OU in 1957.

Tommy Moore—A three-time All-American at OSU (1982–84), Moore played on the Cowboys' 1983 NCAA championship team and earned his first PGA Tour card on his sixth attempt (1989). In 1980 he was the number one–ranked junior player in the country. At age seventeen, Moore and future OSU teammate Tracy Phillips captured the Junior World Cup at St. Andrews, Scotland. Moore won the 1993 Nike Boise Open and tied for fourth at the 1990 Buick Southern Open. He died in May of 1998, at age thirty-five, from complications of a rare blood disease.

Gil Morgan—Morgan was born in Wewoka on September 25, 1946. Even though no one offered him a golf scholarship out of Wewoka High School, Morgan went on to become an NAIA All-American at East Central State (1968) in nearby Ada. Immediately after earning a Doctor of Optometry degree in 1972, Morgan turned professional and joined the PGA Tour a year later. In 1977 he won the BC Open and a year later the World Series of Golf, the first two of eight PGA Tour victories. Morgan set the all-time Oklahoma Open record (198, later tied by Bob Tway) at Kickingbird in 1981. During the second round of the 1992 U.S. Open at Pebble Beach, Morgan became the first player in U.S. Open history (Tiger Woods was the second) to be more than nine strokes under par (he got it to twelve). But Morgan lost ground the final two rounds, finishing twelfth behind Tom Kite. After joining the Senior PGA Tour in 1996, Morgan dueled Hale Irwin for supremacy. At the end of three full Senior Tour seasons, Morgan had sixteen victories (and over $5 million in earnings), including three Senior majors: the 1997 and 1998 Tradition and the 1998 Senior Players Championship. Morgan also won a second Oklahoma Open, at the Oak Tree Country Club East course, in 1997. Morgan played on two Ryder Cup teams (1979, 1983). He has been voted into two halls of fame: the NAIA Hall of Fame (1982) and the Oklahoma Sports Hall of Fame (1998).

Linda (Melton) Morse—Linda Morse won four Oklahoma Women's Amateur Championships between 1962 and 1974.

Chester Nelson—Nelson, a Scottish pro who came to Oklahoma City Golf and Country Club in 1912, won three of the first six Oklahoma Opens.

Treas Nelson—In April 2000 at age sixteen, Nelson, a junior at Lawton Eisenhower High School, won the individual title at the class 5-A State Golf Championship, becoming the first African-American prep golf champion in Oklahoma history.

Donald Nichols—Nichols earned three letters at OSU (1952, 1954–55).

William Nichols—Nichols, Scottish pro at Muskogee Town and Country Club, won four of the first seven Oklahoma Opens.

Joe Nick—Beginning in 1989, Nick won three Oklahoma Amateurs, four Oklahoma Men's Stroke Play Championships, and one Oklahoma Mid-Amateur Championship.

Robert Noever—Noever earned three letters at OU (1952–53, 1955).

Bryan Norton—Born in Salina, Kansas, Norton was a two-time All-American at Oral Roberts (1980–81). He played on the European, Nike, and PGA Tours and won the 1984 Kansas Open and the 1992 Oklahoma Open.

Richard Norville—Norville earned four letters at OU (1946–49).

John O'Neill—O'Neill, a member of OSU's 1987 NCAA championship team, won back-to-back Southwestern Amateurs (1985–86).

William Oliver—Oliver won the South Central PGA Championship in 1944.

Alicia Ogrin—Ogrin won four individual titles, including back-to-back Big Eight Conference titles for OSU in 1978–79.

Johnny Palmer—While serving as head professional at Tulsa Country Club, Palmer won the 1957 Oklahoma Open at Twin Hills. Palmer, a native North Carolinian, notched seven PGA Tour victories, five Carolina Opens, the 1947 Western Open, the 1949 World Championship of Golf, the 1952 Canadian Open, and the 1954 Mexican Open; he also played on the 1949 U.S. Ryder Cup team. In 1979 Palmer was elected to the North Carolina Sports Hall of Fame.

Owen Panner—Panner earned three letters at OU (1947–49).

Jack Parnell—Parnell earned three letters at OSU (1955–57).

Tom Parnell—Parnell earned four letters at OSU (1953–56).

Craig Perks—Perks was an All-American at OU in 1987.

E. J. Pfister—Pfister, a three time All-American at OSU (1986–88), won both the Big Eight and NCAA individual titles in 1988. He was a member of OSU's 1987 national championship team and won the 1990 Philippine Masters.

Tracy Phillips—Phillips, a 1982 All-American at OSU, played on the Cowboys' 1983 national championship team. The 1982 Big Eight runner-up, he had won the 1980 PGA Junior Championship and paired with Tommy Moore to win the World Junior Cup at St. Andrews, Scotland. The son of a golf pro, Phillips was a four-time Junior All-American and a state high school champion and became one of Oklahoma's top teaching pros.

Jerry Pittman—As a student at Tulsa's Rogers High School, Pittman won the 1953 National Caddie Championship (at age sixteen). At SMU, Pittman won the 1957 Southwest Conference Championship. He tied for seventeenth at the 1958 U.S. Open and won the 1964 Oklahoma Open at Elks Country Club in Shawnee.

Ann Pitts—Pitts, elected to the National Golf Coaches Association Hall of Fame in 1995, became the first Oklahoma State women's golf coach in 1975, winning fifteen conference titles before her retirement in 2000. Three times the West Region coach of the year, Pitts was named Big 12 Conference coach of the year following both the 1998 and 1999 seasons. In her twenty-four seasons at OSU, Pitts coached nineteen All-Americans and led the Cowgirls to fifty-six team titles. In 1994 Pitts filed and won a sexual discrimination lawsuit against OSU, claiming her salary was not equal to the salary a male collegiate golf coach would receive; the result was renegotiation of her contract. In 2000 Pitts became the second coach to receive the National Golf Coaches Association's highest honor—the Rolex–Gladys Palmer Meritorious Service Award—for a second time. The Palmer Award honors a coach for outstanding service and contributions to women's collegiate golf.

Buddy Poteet—Tulsa Northridge club pro Poteet won the 1941 Oklahoma Open, in a playoff with Kansan Mike Murra, at Tulsa's Oakhurst Country Club. He won the South Central PGA Championship in 1939.

Stacy Prammanasudh—Enid's Prammanasudh, a first-team All-American in each of her first two seasons at Tulsa, won five consecutive Oklahoma Junior Girls' Championships, 1993–97. As a TU freshman she won the 1998 Mercedes-Benz Women's Collegiate. In May 2000 she tied for seventh place at the NCAA Championship in Sunriver, Oregon, and was named Western Athletic Conference player of the year.

Dale Pringle—Pringle, who played at Tulsa, was the Missouri Valley Conference individual champion in 1947.

Art Proctor—Proctor, winner of the 1973 and 1983 South Central PGA Championship, earned a conditional Senior PGA Tour card in 1992. He once played 414 holes for charity in one day, and he tied for seventh in the 1991 Senior British Open at Royal Lytham.

Joey Rassett—A four-time All-American at Oral Roberts (1978–81), Rassett was semifinalist at the 1979 U.S. Amateur and low amateur in the 1981 U.S. Open at Merion.

Dee Replogle—Replogle, instrumental in bringing professional golf to Oklahoma City during the 1950s, won the 1942 and 1949 Oklahoma Amateurs.

Cathy Reynolds—Reynolds, a native of Springfield, Missouri, and a former player at the University of Tulsa, won three Missouri Junior Championships, the 1976 Missouri Amateur, the 1977 Mexican Amateur, and 1977 the Trans-National. During a twenty-year career on the LPGA Tour, she won the 1981 Golden Lights Championship in Greenwich, Connecticut.

Robert H. "Skee" Riegel—A Pennsylvania native who moved to Tulsa for a few years beginning in 1948, Riegel did not start playing golf until 1940, at the insistence of his golfing wife. But seven years later, he won the 1947 U.S. Amateur at Pebble Beach. Riegel also won the 1946 and 1948 Trans-Mississippi Amateurs and the 1948 Western Amateur. In 1949, Riegel was low amateur at the U.S. Open at Medinah. He finished runner-up to Ben Hogan in the 1951 Masters.

George Rives—Rives was a 1969 All-American at OU.

Kelly Robbins—Robbins, a two-time All-American at Tulsa (1990–91), played on the 1988 Tulsa national championship team and won seven times as a collegian. Robbins also won the 1991 North-South and that year shared NCAA player of the year honors with Annika Sorenstam of Arizona State. In 1995, Robbins won her first professional major, the 1995 LPGA Championship.

Jo Jo Robertson—A native of Roswell, New Mexico, Robertson played at OSU (1995–99) and is a two-time winner of the U.S. Women's Amateur Public Links Championship. While at Roswell's Goddard High, Robertson was a three-time state girls champion. Her first U.S. Women's Amateur Public Links came in 1995 at Hominy Hill Golf Course in Colts Neck, New Jersey. She won a second Women's APL in 1997, at Center Square, Pennsylvania, only the fourth player in the championship's forty-eight-year history to win it twice. She was a member of the 1998 U.S. Curtis Cup team.

Scott Robertson—Robertson was a two-time Missouri Valley Conference champion at Tulsa in 1990–91.

Ashley Roestoff—Roestoff earned All-American honors at Oral Roberts in 1982.

Emmett J. Rogers—In 1931, Rogers, of the Oklahoma City Golf and Country Club, became the first amateur to win the Oklahoma Open. He also claimed two Oklahoma Amateurs (1932, 1940).

Art Romero—Romero won the South Central PGA Championship in 1990.

Jody (Rosenthal) Anschutz—As the first four-time All-American golfer at Tulsa (1982–85), Rosenthal won seven tournaments, played on TU's 1982 national championship team, and was NCAA individual runner-up in 1982 and 1985. She also won the 1984 British Amateur, the 1983 Broadmoor Invitational, and the 1981 American Junior Golf Association Tournament of Champions and played on the 1984 U.S. Curtis Cup team. In 1987 Rosenthal won twice on the LPGA Tour, her second win being the du Maurier Classic, which was her first professional major.

Charles Rotar—Rotar won the South Central PGA Championship in 1965.

Andy Schaben—Schaben won the South Central PGA Championship in 1988.

Francis Scheider—Scheider won the South Central PGA Championship in 1935.

Tom Sieckmann—Born in York, Nebraska, Sieckmann, who played at OSU in 1976–77, won the 1981 Philippines, Thailand, and Brazilian Opens, the 1982 Swiss Open, the 1984 Singapore Open, and the 1992 Mexican Open. He was medalist at the PGA Tour's 1985 qualifying school. In 1988, Sieckmann won the Anheuser-Busch Classic at Kingsmill, Virginia.

Billy Simpson—Simpson, a Bartlesville amateur who played at OU (1936–38), is the only amateur to have won the Oklahoma Open twice (1938, 1940).

Arantxa Sison—Sison was an OSU All-American and winner of the Big Eight individual title in 1992.

Val Skinner—A two-time Big Eight champion and twice All-American at OSU (1980, 1982), in 1982 Skinner was named Big Eight Female Athlete of the Year. At OSU she won nine collegiate events, more than any female player in OSU history, and led the nation in scoring average two years in a row. Skinner, who began playing golf at age four, won twenty high school titles, including two Nebraska Junior Girls', two Nebraska state high school titles, and the 1980 Nebraska Match Play Championship. In her first twelve years on the LPGA Tour, she won six times and was a member of the 1996 U.S. Solheim Cup team. In 1999 Skinner became the first woman inducted into the OSU Athletic Hall of Honor.

Robert O. Smith—A 1963 All-American at OU, Smith was the Big Eight Conference individual champion as a sophomore (1961). He coached the OU golf team in 1978–79.

Wayne Speegle—Speegle earned four letters at OU (1947–50).

Bill Spiller—Spiller, born in Tishomingo in 1913, worked in 1931 with his father as a clubhouse attendant at Hillcrest Country Club in Bartlesville. A basketball and track star in high school, Spiller graduated from Wiley College, in Marshall, Texas, with a teaching certificate. He did not start playing golf until 1942, at age twenty-nine. By 1946, Spiller had won all the black tournaments in southern California. He turned professional in 1947. Since Spiller was African American and because of the PGA's "Caucasians only" membership clause, he was banned from joining the PGA and competing against whites. So Spiller and others started the

United Golf Association, a professional tour for blacks. In 1948, the Los Angeles Open—this and George S. May's Tam O'Shanter in Chicago were the only two PGA events to invite blacks voluntarily—extended an invitation to Spiller. He shot 68 at Riviera Country Club. But instead of playing the Tour, Spiller devoted his energies during the prime of his life to fighting racism and bringing down the PGA's offending clause. In the late 1950s, California Attorney General (and future California Supreme Court Justice) Stanley Mosk filed suit on behalf of Spiller and Charlie Sifford against the combined PGA Tour/PGA of America, for civil rights violations. After the PGA first threatened to hold all PGA tournaments at private courses, Mosk sent letters to all other attorneys general in the United States. Finally, in 1963, the PGA submitted to the law of the land, and thanks to Spiller and others, the doors of professional golf were opened to all players.

Ed Stanard—Stanard won the South Central PGA Championship in 1938.

Cathy Stevens—Stevens was Big Eight Conference champion for OU in 1991.

Beth Stone—Muskogee's Stone, winner of two Oklahoma Junior Girls' and the 1960 Oklahoma Women's Amateur, played on the LPGA Tour during the 1960s and 1970s. In the 1967 U.S. Women's Open at Hot Springs, Virginia, Stone tied for second (to French amateur Catherine Lacoste) with fellow Oklahoman Susie Maxwell Berning.

Lisa Stone—Stone was Big Eight Conference champion for OSU in 1985.

Ron Streck—Streck, a two-time All-American at Tulsa (1975–76), was twice Missouri Valley Conference medalist. In the second round of the 1978 Texas Open at Oak Hills Country Club in San Antonio, Streck saved par from a bunker at the eighteenth hole, just making the cut. In the third round, he went out in 29 and came back in 34 for a 63. The next day he totaled 62, establishing a PGA Tour record (125) for the lowest final thirty-six holes ever shot and winning the Texas Open. However, Streck was not finished with his 62s in the Lone Star state. At the 1981 Houston Open, Streck shot 62 in the third round to lead by two. When the final round was washed out, Streck had his second PGA Tour victory in Texas. He also finished tied for third at the 1982 Players' Championship and won the 1993 Nike Yuma Open. He is a member of the TU Athletic Hall of Fame.

J. H. "Jack" Taylor—Taylor, winner of the 1918 Oklahoma Open, was a native of Scotland and head professional at the Oklahoma City Golf and Country Club.

Ralph Terry—Born in Big Cabin, Oklahoma, on January 9, 1936, Terry rose to fame as a major league pitcher and the 1962 World Series Most Valuable Player of the New York Yankees. He earned a card on the 1989 Senior PGA Tour, won two Midwest PGA section titles, and won two Midwest PGA section senior titles.

Doug Tewell—Tewell, who grew up in Stillwater and played three years at OSU (1969–71), won the 1966 Oklahoma Junior, the 1971 Tulsa Intercollegiate, and the 1982 Oklahoma Open. As a junior, he learned the game from Labron Harris Sr. at Stillwater's Lakeside Memorial Golf Course. As a professional, Tewell became one of the state's top players, winning four times on the PGA Tour. He led the PGA Tour in driving accuracy in 1992 and 1993. Tewell won the South Central PGA Championship in 1978. Upon joining the Senior PGA Tour in 2000 Tewell won twice in six months—at the PGA Seniors' in April and the Dominion Senior Classic.

Barb (Thomas) Whitehead—A 1982 All-American at Tulsa, Thomas won twice as a collegian and placed third individually at the 1982 NCAA Championship, where Tulsa was team champion. Thomas won two Iowa Juniors and two Iowa state high school championships. On the LPGA Tour, she won the 1995 Hawaiian Ladies Open. She earned her Tour card in 1983 by holing a bunker shot on the final hole of the qualifying tournament.

Jeannie Thompson—Thompson, of Tulsa, won the 1962 Women's Trans-National, three consecutive Oklahoma Junior Championships (1960–62), and the 1965 Oklahoma Women's Amateur.

Terri Thompson—Thompson, a two-time All-American at Tulsa (1991–92), qualified for three U.S. Women's Opens as an amateur and won the 1988 Women's Western Junior. Before joining the LPGA Tour in 1994, she played on the European, Asia, and Swedish tours.

Chris Tidland—Tidland, a four-time All-American at OSU (1992–95), won three times as a collegian (including a share of the 1995 Big Eight individual title) and played on OSU's 1995 NCAA championship team. He qualified for the 2000 U.S. Open at Pebble Beach.

Mark Tinder—Tinder earned All-American honors at Oral Roberts in 1979.

Dick Turner—Turner was Missouri Valley Conference individual champion for OSU in 1948.

Greg Turner—Turner was a two-time All-American at OU (1983–84), winner of the 1984 Oklahoma Amateur, and winner of five European Tour events.

Bob Tway—Tway, a three-time first-team All-American at OSU (1979–81) and winner of the 1979 Big Eight title, holed out a bunker shot at the seventy-second hole of the 1986 PGA Championship at Inverness, Ohio, to win by two strokes over Greg Norman. Born in Oklahoma City, Tway won six times as a collegian and was named college golf's 1981 player of the year. He played on two OSU national championship teams (1978, 1980). Including the major championship, Tway won seven PGA Tour events during his first eleven years on Tour. He also won the 1978 Trans-Mississippi Amateur, the 1980 Southern Amateur, the 1980 Georgia Open, and two Oklahoma Opens. While winning at Kickingbird in 1985, Tway shot 198, to match Gil Morgan for low fifty-four-hole total in Oklahoma Open history.

Jim Unruh—A three-time captain for Tulsa, Unruh won thirty-three matches during his collegiate career and was the first golfer inducted into the TU Athletic Hall of Fame.

Bo Van Pelt—Van Pelt was a two-time All-American at OSU (1997– 98).

Scott Verplank—As a four-time All-American at OSU (1983–86) and Haskins Award winner, Verplank was NCAA runner-up as a freshman, then won nine tournaments in his collegiate career, including the 1984 Big Eight Conference Championship and the 1986 NCAA Championship, and was named Big Eight Athlete of the Year in 1986. Verplank also won the 1984 U.S. Amateur (at Oak Tree in Edmond), the 1984 Western Amateur, the 1984 and 1985 Sunnehanna Amateur, four consecutive LaJet Amateurs (1982–85), and three Texas Amateurs in four years (1982, 1984–85). Verplank was a member of the 1983 OSU NCAA Championship team. At the 1985 Western Open, Verplank defeated Jim Thorpe in a playoff to become the first amateur to win a PGA Tour event in thirty-one years. He turned professional in 1986 and joined the "Oak Tree Boys" (see chapter 8) in Edmond. Two years after winning the 1988 Buick Open, Verplank was hospitalized for complications from diabetes. Also in 1990 he began experiencing right elbow pain and underwent surgery to remove bone spurs in 1991. Additional elbow surgery to increase blood flow kept Verplank off the PGA Tour for much of 1992 and all of 1993. In 1994 Verplank played half a year on the Tour with a medical exemption and retained his card for 1994 and 1995. However, following a third surgery,

Verplank was nonexempt in 1996, but he came back strongly, winning the 1997 PGA Tour National Qualifying Tournament and earning over $3 million on Tour in 1998–2000.

Jim Vickers—Vickers, an OU All-American and four-year letterman from Wichita, won the 1952 NCAA Championship at the Purdue University Golf Course in West Lafayette, Indiana.

Ernie Vossler—After winning four PGA Tour events from 1958 to 1960, Vossler, a Texas native, became head professional at Oklahoma City's Quail Creek Country Club in 1961. In the early 1970s, Vossler formed a partnership with Oklahoma Citian Joe Walser. Together they built three championship courses at Oak Tree in Edmond and brought the 1988 PGA Championship to Oak Tree Golf Club. Vossler won the South Central PGA Championship in 1966.

Grant Waite—Waite, a three-time All-American at OU (1985–87), is a native of Palmerston North, New Zealand, and won the Australian Junior twice. He won the Big Eight individual title in 1985. In 1993, Waite held off Tom Kite to win the PGA Tour's Kemper Open.

Rocky Walcher—Walcher, a native of Carnegie, Oklahoma, won eight times in college at Southwestern Oklahoma State. He has had six holes in one and captured the 1996 Nike Omaha Classic.

Craig Walker—Walker won the South Central PGA Championship in 1998.

Joyce Wallace—Wallace won three Oklahoma Women's Amateurs and placed second at the 1932 Women's Trans-National.

Jeff Walser—In 1980, Walser was an All-American at OSU and played on the Cowboys' national championship team.

Joe Walser—Walser, an Oklahoma Citian who played at OSU in 1952–54, won the 1952 Oklahoma Amateur, the 1953 Missouri Valley Conference title, and the 1959 Oklahoma Open. Walser later founded Edmond's Oak Tree Golf Club with Ernie Vossler.

Margaret Ward—Ward, an Ardmore native, won the 1975 Oklahoma Junior Girls'. She then went on to play at OU, where she was named to the all-conference team in 1978. Ward played fifteen seasons on the LPGA Tour. In 1988 she finished second at the Ocean State Open.

Brian Watts—Watts, a Texas state high school champion at Carrollton and four-time All-American at OSU, won the 1986 Big Eight Conference individual title, the 1986 Trans-Mississippi, and 1987 NCAA individual title. He won nine tournaments while at OSU. An accomplished international player, in 1993 Watts won the Asian Tour Order of Merit and was given a one-year exemption on the Japanese PGA Tour, where he won ten times in five years, earning more than $4 million. Playing out of Oak Tree in Edmond, Watts moved steadily up in the Sony World Rankings, then burst onto the world stage by finishing second to Mark O'Meara in the 1998 British Open at Royal Birkdale.

Amy Weeks—Weeks was Big Eight Conference champion for OSU in 1995. She succeeded Ann Pitts as OSU women's golf coach in 2000.

Tammy Welborn-Fredrickson—Welborn was an All-American at Tulsa in 1984.

Kevin Wentworth—Wentworth, a four-time All-American at OSU (1988–91) and two-time NCAA Central Region champion, led the Cowboys to the 1991 NCAA team championship. Wentworth won a total of seven collegiate tournaments, including back-to-back Big Eight championships (1989–90). In 1990, Wentworth received college golf's Ben Hogan Award for academic and athletic excellence. As a pro, Wentworth won the 1992 St. Louis Open and 1997 Philippines Open. He plays left-handed.

Leif Westerberg—Westerberg, a four-time All-American at OSU (1994–97), played on OSU's 1995 NCAA championship team. In 1997, he won the inaugural Big 12 Conference individual title and was voted the Big 12 player of the year.

Lindsey Wetzel—Wetzel won the inaugural Big Eight Conference individual crown for OU in 1976.

Sherry Wheeler—Wheeler, a native of Muskogee, won the 1957 Western Junior and back-to-back Southwestern Amateurs (1960–61). She was runner-up to Judy Eller at the 1958 U.S. Girls' Junior and runner-up in 1959 at the Women's Trans-Mississippi Amateur. Wheeler, an Arizona State graduate, turned pro in 1962 and competed in twenty-six LPGA events in 1963. An automobile accident cut short her playing career.

David White—White, a 1990 All-American at OSU, played on OSU's national championship team of 1987 and was runner-up medalist at the 1990 Big Eight Conference Championship.

George Whitehead—Whitehead, long-hitting pro at Tulsa's Indian Hills Country Club (later Spunky Creek), won the 1942 Oklahoma Open at Oakhurst Country Club in Tulsa. At the time he was the reigning Tulsa PGA District champion, the state PGA Match Play champion, and runner-up in the 1942 Oklahoma PGA. Whitehead won four South Central PGA Championships between 1934 and 1945.

Lanny Whiteside—A 1996 OSU graduate, Whiteside won the 1997 Colorado Women's Open.

Margaret Williford—Williford won three consecutive Oklahoma Women's Amateurs (1951–53) and a fourth in 1958.

Jim Wilson—Wilson was an All-American at Oral Roberts in 1983.

Francis "Bo" Wininger—Nicknamed "Bwana" for his love of the hunt, Wininger came to the Oklahoma City area from California and played for four years at OSU (1947–50) for Labron Harris Sr., winning the 1948 Oklahoma Amateur and back-to-back Missouri Valley championships (1949–50). Wininger later turned professional and had success on the PGA Tour, winning six times between 1955 and 1963. Half of Wininger's PGA wins came in Louisiana: the 1955 Baton Rouge Open and back-to-back New Orleans Opens (1962–63). He also won consecutive South Central PGA Championships in 1962–63.

Mark Witt—Witt, winner of the 1974 Oklahoma Amateur, was a 1975 All-American at OU.

Willie Wood—Wood, a four-time All-American at OSU (1980–83), played on OSU NCAA championship teams as a freshman and senior. He won the 1977 U.S. Junior, the 1978 PGA Junior, and the 1979 Western Junior. He won eight collegiate events at OSU, including the 1982 Big Eight individual medal. Wood, a two-time winner of the Oklahoma Open (1990, 1995), was medalist at the 1983 PGA Tour qualifying tournament and won the 1996 Deposit Guaranty Golf Classic.

Jim Woodward—Woodward, who played at OSU from 1976–79, won the 1975 Oklahoma State High School championship, the 1975 Texas-Oklahoma Junior, the 1978 Oklahoma Amateur, and the 1978 Southern Amateur. He was a team member during two of OSU's NCAA Championship years (1976, 1978). As a professional, Woodward won the 1986 and 1988 California State Opens. He finished second at the 1990 Canadian Open and tied for seventeenth at the 1987 U.S.

Open. At the 1992 Byron Nelson Classic in Dallas, Woodward birdied the first two holes of the final round, to take the lead at twelve under. But the round was rained out and so were Woodward's birdies. Everyone's scores reverted to the third-round totals, where Woodward finished fifth, one stroke behind Billy Ray Brown, who won a four-way playoff. Woodward received a medical exemption for the 1994 PGA Tour, after fracturing his kneecap during the final round of the 1993 Houston Open. Woodward won the South Central PGA Championship in 1987 and 1997.

Jimmy Wright—Wright, the first three-time All-American at OSU (1959–61), won the 1961 Oklahoma Amateur and two Big Eight individual titles (1959–60).

David Yates—Yates, OU men's golf coach from 1982 to 1985, led the Sooners to an eighth-place NCAA finish in 1983 and to third place in 1984. He coached Sooner greats Andrew Magee, Grant Waite, and Greg Turner.

Patsy Zimmer—Zimmer was Big Eight Conference champion for OSU in 1977.

Jim Zimmerman—Zimmerman was All-American at OU in 1973.

OKLAHOMA OPEN, 1910–1999

DATE	CITY	COURSE	WINNER	SCORE
05-23-10	Tulsa	Tulsa CC	William Nichols	169
06-04-11	Muskogee	Muskogee Town & CC	William Nichols	153
06-16-12	Tulsa	Tulsa CC	Chester Nelson	n/a
06-01-13	Oklahoma City	Oklahoma City G & CC	Chester Nelson	157
06-14-14	Bartlesville	Oak Hill CC	William Nichols	152
05-23-15	Oklahoma City	Oklahoma City G & CC	Chester Nelson	153
06-18-16	Muskogee	Muskogee Town & CC	William Nichols	141
06-10-17	Oklahoma City	Oklahoma City G & CC	J.G. "Jock" Collins	153
09-22-18	Oklahoma City	Oklahoma City G & CC	Jack Taylor	161
10-07-19	Muskogee	Muskogee Town & CC	John Gatherum	152
11-15-20	Tulsa	Tulsa CC	Bill Mehlhorn	152
06-12-21	Oklahoma City	Oklahoma City G & CC	Sandy Baxter	156
06-11-22	Oklahoma Cit	Lakeside G & CC	Phil Hessler	145
*6-03-23	Tulsa	Tulsa CC	Bill Mehlhorn	310
*6-15-24	Ardmore	Dornick Hills CC	William Creavy	302
06-13-25	Tulsa	Tulsa CC	Ed Dudley	151

(a) denotes amateur   * Oklahoma Open as official PGA event

DATE	CITY	COURSE	WINNER	SCORE
06-09-26	Oklahoma City	Oklahoma City G & CC	Ed Dudley	148
05-29-27	Tulsa	Tulsa CC	Dick Grout	152
06-02-28	Oklahoma City	Lakeside G & CC	Harold Long	146
05-18-29	Ardmore	Dornick Hills CC	Dick Grout	150
06-08-30	Oklahoma City	Twin Hills G & CC	Clarence Clark	149
09-13-31	Tulsa	Tulsa CC	Emmett J. Rogers (a)	298
10-10-32	Oklahoma City	Twin Hills G & CC	James Gullane	304
08-06-33	Bartlesville	Hillcrest CC	James Gullane	296
08-19-34	Catoosa	Indian Hills CC	Jug McSpaden	289
08-11-35	Oklahoma City	Oklahoma City G & CC	Walter Emery (a)	285
08-09-36	Tulsa	Oakhurst CC	Clarence Yockey	294
07-11-37	Oklahoma City	Oklahoma City G & CC	Jack Malloy (a)	292
07-31-38	Catoosa	Indian Hills CC	Billy Simpson (a)	294
10-08-39	Oklahoma City	Lincoln Park GC	Zell Eaton	296
09-29-40	Bartlesville	Hillcrest CC	Billy Simpson (a)	148
08-17-41	Tulsa	Oakhurst CC	Buddy Poteet	146
10-11-42	Tulsa	Oakhurst CC	George Whitehead	149
1943–1945	No Oklahoma Opens (World War II)			
10-18-46	Oklahoma City	Oklahoma City G & CC	Raymond Gafford	136
08-29-47	Tulsa	Oaks CC	George Getchell	141
09-23-48	Tulsa	Tulsa CC	Jimmie Gauntt	140
10-18-49	Catoosa	Indian Hills CC	Tex Consolver	145
10-20-50	Muskogee	Muskogee CC	Chuck Klein	135
1951–1952	No Oklahoma Opens (Korean War)			
09-11-53	Enid	Oakwood CC	Labron Harris Sr.	138
10-14-54	Enid	Oakwood CC	Jimmie Gauntt	212
09-29-55	Tulsa	Southern Hills CC	Jimmie Gauntt	209
10-04-56	Bartlesville	Hillcrest CC	Jimmie Gauntt	211
10-03-57	Oklahoma City	Twin Hills G & CC	Johnny Palmer	209
09-18-58	Muskogee	Muskogee CC	Buster Cupit	208

(a) denotes amateur   * Oklahoma Open as official PGA event

DATE	CITY	COURSE	WINNER	SCORE
09-08-59	Enid	Oakwood CC	Joe Walser Jr.	206
09-11-60	Ardmore	Dornick Hills CC	Jimmie Gauntt	210
09-28-61	Enid	Oakwood CC	Buster Cupit	210
10-04-62	Oklahoma City	Lincoln Park GC	Babe Hiskey	215
10-24-63	Muskogee	Muskogee CC	Labron Harris Jr. (a)	203
10-01-64	Shawnee	Elks CC	Jerry Pittman	208
10-14-65	Burneyville	Turner Resort Course	Buster Cupit	216
11-10-66	Muskogee	Muskogee CC	Bob Dickson (a)	142
09-29-67	Enid	Oakwood CC	Jamie Gough (a)	210
09-27-68	Ardmore	Dornick Hills CC	Grier Jones	201
10-02-69	Ardmore	Dornick Hills CC	Chris Gers	210
10-08-70	Ardmore	Dornick Hills CC	Chris Gers	138
10-07-71	Ardmore	Dornick Hills CC	Bob Dickson	207
10-05-72	Ponca City	Lakeside GC	Don Maddox	209
10-04-73	Ponca City	Lakeside GC	Spike Kelley	211
10-10-74	Ponca City	Lakeside GC	Bobby Stroble	206
10-09-75	Ardmore	Dornick Hills CC	Danny Edwards	207
10-07-76	Oklahoma City	Twin Hills G & CC	Mark Hayes	214
10-06-77	Oklahoma City	Twin Hills G & CC	Danny Edwards	216
10-04-78	Broken Arrow	Indian Springs CC	Lindy Miller	219
09-28-79	Edmond	Kickingbird GC	Danny Edwards	205
10-02-80	Edmond	Kickingbird GC	Jaime Gonzalez	204
09-24-81	Edmond	Kickingbird GC	Gil Morgan	198
10-14-82	Edmond	Kickingbird GC	Doug Tewell	205
10-12-83	Edmond	Kickingbird GC	Tom Jones	205
09-13-84	Edmond	Kickingbird GC	Kenny Huff	207
09-14-85	Edmond	Kickingbird GC	Bob Tway	198
09-12-86	Edmond	Oak Tree CC	Lindy Miller	209
09-18-87	Edmond	Oak Tree CC	Bob Tway	209
09-16-88	Edmond	Oak Tree CC	Mark Hayes	208

350 (a) denotes amateur   * Oklahoma Open as official PGA event

DATE	CITY	COURSE	WINNER	SCORE
09-16-89	Edmond	Oak Tree CC	Doug Martin	205
09-23-90	Edmond	Oak Tree CC	Willie Wood	205
09-22-91	Edmond	Oak Tree CC	Jim Kane	203
08-30-92	Edmond	Oak Tree CC	Bryan Norton	202
08-25-93	Edmond	Oak Tree CC	Mark Hayes	200
08-26-94	Edmond	Oak Tree CC	David Edwards	201
08-27-95	Edmond	Oak Tree CC	Willie Wood	202
08-25-96	Edmond	Oak Tree CC	David Edwards	128
08-24-97	Edmond	Oak Tree CC	Gil Morgan	201
08-30-98	Edmond	Oak Tree CC	Kevin Dillen	200
08-29-99	Edmond	Oak Tree CC	Todd Hamilton	198
08-27-00	Edmond	Oak Tree CC	John Bizik	204

Dates are final round.

LOWEST TOTALS:

36 holes—128; David Edwards, Oak Tree Country Club (1996)

54 holes—198; Gil Morgan, Kickingbird Golf Course (1981);
        Bob Tway, Kickingbird Golf Course (1985)

72 holes—285; Walter Emery (a), Oklahoma City Golf &Country Club (1935)

(a) denotes amateur   * Oklahoma Open as official PGA event

CHRONOLOGY, COURSES, AND WINNERS
IN OKLAHOMA TOURNAMENT GOLF

TOURNAMENT CHRONOLOGY, 1923–2001

DATE	TOURNAMENT	COURSE	WINNER	SCORE
06-03-23	Oklahoma Open*	Tulsa CC	Bill Mehlhorn	310
06-15-24	Oklahoma Open*	Dornick Hills CC	William Creavy	302
11-28-26	Oklahoma City Open	Lakeside/Ok. City G & CC	Al Espinosa	297
10-23-27	Oklahoma City Open	Lakeside/Ok. City G & CC	Harry Cooper	283
11-04-28	Oklahoma City Open	Lakeside/Ok. City G & CC	Horton Smith	288
10-27-29	Oklahoma City Open	Oklahoma City G & CC	Craig Wood	298
06-07-30	Women's Trans-National	Tulsa CC	Mrs. Hulbert Clarke (a)	6 & 5
09-06-30	Southwest Inv. Am.	Oklahoma City G & CC	Byron Nelson (a)	7 & 6
06-25-34	Trans-Miss. Amateur	Oklahoma City G & CC	Gus Moreland (a)	1 up
07-15-34	Western Amateur	Twin Hills G & CC	Zell Eaton (a)	4 & 3
10-23-35	PGA Championship	Twin Hills G & CC	Johnny Revolta	5 & 4
10-17-37	Oklahoma Four Ball	Oklahoma City G & CC	Harry Cooper and Horton Smith	66
06-11-38	Women's Trans-National	Oakhurst CC	Patty Berg (a)	6 & 5
07-16-39	Western Amateur	Oklahoma City G & CC	Harry Todd (a)	2 & 1
06-23-40	Trans-Miss. Amateur	Southern Hills CC	Arthur Doering (a)	6 & 5

(a) denotes amateur   * Oklahoma Open as official PGA event   ** Formerly Turner Resort Course (Burneyville)

DATE	TOURNAMENT	COURSE	WINNER	SCORE
09-16-45	Tulsa Open	Southern Hills CC	Sam Snead	277
09-28-46	U.S. Women's Amateur	Southern Hills CC	Babe Zaharias (a)	11 & 9
06-26-49	Women's Western Open	Oklahoma City G & CC	Louise Suggs	5 & 4
06-08-52	Ardmore Open	Dornick Hills CC	Dave Douglas	279
05-10-53	Ardmore Open	Dornick Hills CC	Earl Stewart Jr.	282
08-01-53	U.S. Junior Amateur	Southern Hills CC	Rex Baxter Jr. (a)	2 & 1
09-19-53	U.S. Amateur	Oklahoma City G & CC	Gene Littler (a)	1-up
05-09-54	Ardmore Open	Dornick Hills CC	Julius Boros	279
09-26-54	LPGA Ardmore Open	Dornick Hills CC	Patty Berg	299
04-03-55	LPGA OK City Open	Lincoln Park GC	Louise Suggs	229
09-25-55	Women's Trans-National	Twin Hills G & CC	Polly Riley (a)	11 & 9
06-24-56	Trans-Miss. Amateur	Oklahoma City G & CC	Charles Coe (a)	11 & 9
09-23-56	Oklahoma City Open	Twin Hills G & CC	Fred Hawkins	279
10-22-56	LPGA Lawton Open	Lawton Municipal	Betty Dodd	214
04-21-57	LPGA Lawton Open	Lawton Municipal	Marlaze Hagge	216
05-11-58	LPGA Lawton Open	Lawton Municipal	Beverly Hanson	212
06-15-58	U.S. Open	Southern Hills CC	Tommy Bolt	283
09-01-58	LPGA Opie Turner Open	Falconhead Resort**	Mickey Wright	222
05-11-59	Oklahoma City Open	Twin Hills G & CC	Arnold Palmer	273
09-27-59	LPGA Opie Turner Open	Falconhead Resort	Betsy Rawls	221
06-12-60	Oklahoma City Open	Twin Hills G & CC	Gene Littler	273
08-19-60	U.S. Girls' Junior	Oaks CC	Carol Sorenson (a)	2 & 1
08-27-60	U.S. Women's Amateur	Tulsa CC	JoAnne Gunderson (a)	6 & 5
05-07-61	Waco Turner Open	Falconhead Resort	Butch Baird	281
08-27-61	Trans-Miss. Amateur	Twin Hills G & CC	Herb Durham (a)	38 holes
10-07-61	U.S. Senior Amateur	Southern Hills CC	Dexter Daniels (a)	2 & 1
05-20-62	LPGA Muskogee Open	Muskogee CC	Patty Berg	290
08-26-62	Oklahoma City Open	Quail Creek G & CC	Doug Sanders	280
05-06-62	Waco Turner Open	Falconhead Resort	Johnny Pott	276
05-19-63	Oklahoma City Open	Quail Creek G & CC	Don Fairfield	280

(a) denotes amateur   * Oklahoma Open as official PGA event   ** Formerly Turner Resort Course (Burneyville)   **353**

DATE	TOURNAMENT	COURSE	WINNER	SCORE
05-19-63	LPGA Muskogee Open	Muskogee CC	Mickey Wright	285
05-05-63	Waco Turner Open	Falconhead Resort	Gay Brewer	280
05-03-64	Waco Turner Open	Falconhead Resort	Pete Brown	280
05-17-64	LPGA Muskogee Open	Muskogee CC	Mickey Wright	213
05-18-64	Oklahoma City Open	Quail Creek G & CC	Arnold Palmer	277
05-16-65	LPGA Muskogee Open	Muskogee CC	Susie Maxwell	213
09-05-65	Oklahoma City Open	Quail Creek G & CC	Jack Rule	283
09-18-65	U.S. Amateur	Southern Hills CC	Bob Murphy (a)	291
05-29-66	Oklahoma City Open	Quail Creek G & CC	Tony Lema	271
05-28-67	Oklahoma City Open	Quail Creek G & CC	Miller Barber	278
08-05-67	U.S. Junior Amateur	Twin Hills G & CC	John Crooks (a)	2 & 1
07-??-68	Trans-Miss. Amateur	Southern Hills CC	William Hyndman (a)	2 & 1
09-22-68	National Team Champ.	Twin Hills/Quail Creek	Bobby Nichols and George Archer	265
07-05-70	U.S. Women's Open	Muskogee CC	Donna Caponi	287
07-19-70	Trans-Miss. Amateur	Oklahoma City G & CC	Allen Miller (a)	4 & 3
08-16-70	PGA Championship	Southern Hills CC	Dave Stockton	279
06-24-73	NCAA Championship	Stillwater CC	University of Florida; Ben Crenshaw, University of Texas (a)	1,149 282
07-14-74	Trans-Miss. Amateur	Cedar Ridge CC	Tom Jones (a)	3 & 2
07-12-75	Western Junior	Stillwater CC	Britt Harrison (a)	2 & 1
08-23-75	Women's Trans-National	Oaks CC	Beverley Davis (a)	4 & 3
06-19-77	U.S. Open	Southern Hills CC	Hubert Green	278
06-16-79	AIAW Championship	Stillwater CC	Southern Methodist; Kyle O'Brien, SMU (a)	1,208 292
09-21-80	PGA Cup Matches	Oak Tree GC	United States	15-6
07-18-82	Trans-Miss. Amateur	Oklahoma City G & CC	John Sherman (a)	4 & 3
08-08-82	PGA Championship	Southern Hills CC	Raymond Floyd	272
07-31-83	U.S. Women's Open	Cedar Ridge CC	Jan Stephenson	290

354 (a) denotes amateur   * Oklahoma Open as official PGA event   ** Formerly Turner Resort Course (Burneyville)

DATE	TOURNAMENT	COURSE	WINNER	SCORE
06-17-84	Roy Clark Senior PGA	Tulsa CC	Miller Barber	212
09-02-84	U.S. Amateur	Oak Tree GC	Scott Verplank (a)	4 & 3
05-24-87	Silver Pages Classic	Quail Creek G & CC	Chi Chi Rodriguez	200
10-15-87	U.S. Women's Mid-Amateur	Southern Hills CC	Cindy Scholefield (a)	6 & 5
06-26-88	U.S. Women's Publinx	Page Belcher GC	Pearl Sinn (a)	4 & 3
06-26-88	S'western Bell Classic	Quail Creek G & CC	Gary Player	203
08-14-88	PGA Championship	Oak Tree GC	Jeff Sluman	275
05-28-89	S'western Bell Classic	Quail Creek G & CC	Bobby Nichols	209
06-10-89	NCAA Championship	Oak Tree GC	University of Okla;	1,139
			Phil Mickelson,	
			Ariz. St. (a)	281
05-13-90	S'western Bell Classic	Quail Creek G & CC	Jimmy Powell	208
07-15-90	Trans-Miss Amateur	Oklahoma City G & CC	Bobby Godwin (a)	5 & 4
08-11-91	Ben Hogan Tulsa Open	GC of Oklahoma	Frank Conner	210
07-25-92	Southern Amateur	Oak Tree CC	Justin Leonard (a)	274
08-23-92	Ben Hogan Tulsa Open	GC of Oklahoma	Steve Lowery	213
08-14-94	PGA Championship	Southern Hills CC	Nick Price	269
10-29-95	Tour Championship	Southern Hills CC	Billy Mayfair	280
10-28-96	Tour Championship	Southern Hills CC	Tom Lehman	260
05-22-99	NCAA Women's Champ.	Tulsa CC	Duke;	
			Grace Park,	
			Ariz. St. (a)	212
07-11-99	Trans-Miss Amateur	Oklahoma City G & CC	Mike Podolak (a)	22 holes
07-19-99	Women's Trans-National	Oak Tree CC	Kellee Booth (a)	5 & 4
06-25-00	PGA Club Pro Champ.	Oak Tree CC	Tim Thelen	214
06-17-01	U.S. Open	Southern Hills CC	???	???

(a) denotes amateur   * Oklahoma Open as official PGA event   ** Formerly Turner Resort Course (Burneyville)

Oklahoma Courses Hosting Open, Professional Tour, Major Amateur Championships, 1910–2003

Cedar Ridge Country Club (Tulsa)—1974 Trans-Mississippi Amateur; 1983 U.S. Women's Open

Dornick Hills Country Club (Ardmore)—1924, 1929, 1960, 1968–1971, 1975 Oklahoma Open; 1952–54 Ardmore Open; 1954 LPGA Ardmore Open

Elks Country Club (Shawnee)—1964 Oklahoma Open

Falconhead Resort & Country Club (formerly Turner Resort Course, Burneyville)—1958–59 LPGA Opie Turner Open; 1961–64 Waco Turner Open; 1965 Oklahoma Open

Golf Club of Oklahoma (Broken Arrow)—1991–92 Ben Hogan Tulsa Open

Hillcrest Country Club (Bartlesville)—1933, 1940, 1956 Oklahoma Open

Indian Springs Country Club (Broken Arrow)—1978 Oklahoma Open

Karsten Creek Golf Club (Stillwater)—2003 NCAA Championship

Kickingbird Golf Course (Edmond)—1979–85 Oklahoma Open

Lakeside Golf & Country Club (Oklahoma City)—1922, 1928 Oklahoma Open; 1926–28 Oklahoma City Open

Lew Wentz Lakeside Golf Course (Ponca City)—1972–74 Oklahoma Open

Lawton Public Golf Course (Lawton)—1956–58 LPGA Lawton Open

Lincoln Park Golf Course (Oklahoma City)—1939, 1962 Oklahoma Open; 1955 LPGA Oklahoma City Open

Muskogee Golf & Country Club—1911, 1916, 1919, 1950, 1958, 1963, 1966 Oklahoma Open; 1962–65 LPGA Muskogee Civitan Open; 1970 U.S. Women's Open

Oak Hill Country Club (Bartlesville)—1914 Oklahoma Open

Oakhurst Country Club (Tulsa)—1936, 1941–42 Oklahoma Open; 1938 Women's Trans-National

Oaks Country Club (Tulsa)—1947 Oklahoma Open; 1960 U.S. Girls' Junior; 1975 Women's Trans-National

Oak Tree Country Club (Edmond)—1986–present Oklahoma Open; 1992 Southern Amateur; 1999 Women's Trans-National

Oak Tree Golf Club (Edmond)—1980 PGA Cup Matches; 1984 U.S. Amateur; 1988 PGA Championship; 1989 NCAA Championship; 2000 PGA Club Professional Championship

Oakwood Country Club (Enid)—1953–54, 1959, 1961, 1967 Oklahoma Open

Oklahoma City Golf & Country Club—1913, 1915, 1917–18, 1921, 1926, 1935, 1937, 1946 Oklahoma Open; 1926–29 Oklahoma City Open; 1930 Southwest Invitational Amateur; 1934, 1956, 1970, 1982, 1990, 1999 Trans-Mississippi Amateur; 1937 Oklahoma Four Ball; 1939 Western Amateur; 1949 Women's Western Open; 1953 U.S. Amateur

Page Belcher Golf Course (Tulsa)—1988 U.S. Women's Amateur Public Links

Quail Creek Golf & Country Club (Oklahoma City)—1962–67 Oklahoma City Open; 1968 PGA National Team Championship; 1987 Senior PGA Silver Pages Classic; 1988–90 Senior PGA Southwestern Bell Classic

Southern Hills Country Club (Tulsa)—1940, 1968 Trans-Mississippi Amateur; 1945 Tulsa Open; 1946 U.S. Women's Amateur; 1953 U.S. Junior Amateur; 1955 Oklahoma Open; 1958, 1977, 2001 U.S. Open; 1961 U.S. Senior Amateur; 1965 U.S. Amateur; 1970 PGA Championship; 1982 PGA Championship; 1987 U.S. Women's Mid-Amateur; 1994 PGA Championship; 1995–96 Tour Championship

Indian Hills Golf Course—(formerly Spunky Creek Country Club, Indian Hills Country Club and Rollingwood Hills Country Club, Catoosa)—1934, 1938, 1949 Oklahoma Open

Stillwater Country Club—1973 NCAA Championship; 1975 Western Junior; 1979 Association of Intercollegiate Athletics for Women National Championship

Tulsa Country Club—1910, 1912, 1920, 1923, 1925, 1927, 1931, 1948 Oklahoma Open; 1930 Women's Trans-National; 1960 U.S. Women's Amateur; 1984 Roy Clark Senior PGA Classic; 1999 NCAA Women's Championship

Twin Hills Golf & Country Club (Oklahoma City)—1930, 1932, 1957, 1976–77 Oklahoma Open; 1934 Western Amateur; 1935 PGA Championship; 1955 Women's Trans-National; 1956, 1959–60 Oklahoma City Open; 1961 Trans-Mississippi Amateur; 1967 U.S. Junior Amateur; 1968 PGA National Team Championship

OKLAHOMAN WINNERS OF MAJOR PROFESSIONAL AND AMATEUR CHAMPIONSHIPS

Jody (Rosenthal) Anschutz—1984 British Women's Amateur; 1987 du Maurier Classic

Susie Maxwell Berning—1965 Women's Western Open; 1968, 1972, 1973 U.S. Women's Open

Tommy Bolt—1958 U.S. Open; 1969 PGA Seniors' Championship

Heather Bowie—1997 NCAA Championship

Michael Bradley—1983 PGA Junior Championship

Keefe Carter—1925 Western Amateur

Mrs. Hulbert Clarke—1930 Women's Trans-National Amateur

Charles R. Coe—1947, 1949, 1952, 1956 Trans-Mississippi Amateur; 1949, 1958 U.S. Amateur; 1950 Western Amateur

David Dawley—1991 PGA Junior Championship

Bob Dickson—1967 U.S. Amateur; 1967 British Amateur

Dale Douglass—1986 U.S. Senior Open

Zell Eaton—1934 Western Amateur

David Edwards—1978 NCAA Championship

Dave Eichelberger—1999 U.S. Senior Open

Walter Emery—1933 NCAA Championship

Larry Field—1976 PGA Junior Championship

Kathy (Baker) Guadagnino—1980 Women's Western Amateur; 1982 NCAA Championship; 1985 U.S. Women's Open

Hunter Haas—1999 U.S. Amateur Public Links

Labron E. Harris Jr.—1962 U.S. Amateur

Mark Hayes—1977 Players Championship

Charles Howell—2000 NCAA Championship

Betty Jameson—1937, 1940 Women's Trans-National Amateur; 1939, 1940 U.S. Women's Amateur; 1940, 1942 Women's Western Amateur; 1942, 1954 Women's Western Open; 1947 U.S. Women's Open

Grier Jones—1968 NCAA Championship

Tom Jones—1974 Trans-Mississippi Amateur

Nancy Lopez—1972, 1974 U.S. Girls' Junior; 1976 NCAA Championship; 1976 Women's Trans-National Amateur; 1976 Women's Western Amateur; 1978, 1985, 1989 LPGA Championship

Doug Martin—1984 U.S. Junior Amateur

Marnie McGuire—1986 British Women's Amateur

Melissa McNamara—1988 NCAA Championship

Cathy Mockett—1984 U.S. Girls' Junior; 1990 U.S. Women's Amateur Public Links

Earl Moeller—1953 NCAA Championship

Brian Montgomery—1986 U.S. Junior Amateur; 1986 PGA Junior Championship

Orville Moody—1969 U.S. Open; 1989 U.S. Senior Open;1989 Senior Players Championship

Gil Morgan—1997, 1998 Tradition; 1998 Senior Players Championship

E. J. Pfister—1988 NCAA Championship

Tracy Phillips—1980 PGA Junior Championship

Robert H. ("Skee") Riegel—1946, 1948 Trans-Mississippi Amateur; 1947 U.S. Amateur; 1948 Western Amateur

Jo Jo Robertson—1995, 1997 U.S. Women's Amateur Public Links

Kelly Robbins—1995 LPGA Championship

Jeannie Thompson—1962 Women's Trans-National Amateur

Bob Tway—1978 Trans-Mississippi Amateur; 1986 PGA Championship

Doug Tewell—2000 PGA Seniors' Championship

Scott Verplank—1984 U.S. Amateur; 1984 Western Amateur; 1985 Western Open (as amateur); 1986 NCAA Championship

Jim Vickers—1952 NCAA Championship

Brian Watts—1986 Trans-Mississippi Amateur; 1987 NCAAChampionship

Willie Wood—1977 U.S. Junior Amateur; 1978 PGA Junior Championship

USGA Championships in Oklahoma 1946–2001

DATE	TOURNAMENT	COURSE	WINNER	SCORE
09-28-46	U.S. Women's Amateur	Southern Hills CC	Babe Zaharias (a)	11 & 9
08-01-53	U.S. Junior Amateur	Southern Hills CC	Rex Baxter Jr. (a)	2 & 1
09-19-53	U.S. Amateur	Oklahoma City G & CC	Gene Littler (a)	1 up
06-15-58	U.S. Open	Southern Hills CC	Tommy Bolt	283
08-19-60	U.S. Girls' Junior	Oaks CC	Carol Sorenson (a)	2 & 1
08-27-60	U.S. Women's Amateur	Tulsa CC	JoAnne Gunderson (a)	6 & 5
10-07-61	U.S. Senior Amateur	Southern Hills CC	Dexter Daniels (a)	2 & 1
09-18-65	U.S. Amateur	Southern Hills CC	Bob Murphy (a)	291
08-05-67	U.S. Junior Amateur	Twin Hills G & CC	John Crooks (a)	2 & 1
07-05-70	U.S. Women's Open	Muskogee CC	Donna Caponi	287
06-19-77	U.S. Open	Southern Hills CC	Hubert Green	278
07-31-83	U.S. Women's Open	Cedar Ridge CC	Jan Stephenson	290
09-02-84	U.S. Amateur	Oak Tree GC	Scott Verplank (a)	4 & 3
10-15-87	U.S. Women's Mid-Amateur	Southern Hills CC	Cindy Scholefield (a)	6 & 5
06-26-88	U.S. Women's Publinx	Page Belcher GC	Pearl Sinn (a)	4 & 3
06-17-01	U.S. Open	Southern Hills CC		

Regional Champions

South Central PGA Section Champions

1924	Ed Dudley	1942	Floyd Farley	1960	Buster Cupit
1925	William Creavy	1943	(No tournament)	1961	Pete Fleming
1926	Dick Grout	1944	William Oliver	1962	Francis "Bo" Wininger
1927	James Gullane	1945	George Whitehead	1963	Francis "Bo" Wininger
1928	James Gullane	1946	Tex Consolver	1964	Chris Gers
1929	Clarence Clark	1947	Jimmie Gauntt	1965	Charles Rotar
1930	Clarence Clark	1948	Morrie Gravatt	1966	Ernie Vossler
1931	Bob Higgins	1949	Jimmie Gauntt	1967	Larry Fryer
1932	Bob Higgins	1950	Jimmie Gauntt	1968	George McKeown
1933	James Gullane	1951	Ted Gwin	1969	Richard Crawford
1934	George Whitehead	1952	Dick Metz	1970	Jerry Abbott
1935	Francis Scheider	1953	E. J. "Dutch" Harrison	1971	Richard Crawford
1936	George Whitehead	1954	Labron Harris Sr.	1972	David Lee
1937	Floyd Farley	1955	Jimmie Gauntt	1973	Art Proctor
1938	Ed Stanard	1956	Jimmie Gauntt	1974	Dick Goetz
1939	Buddy Poteet	1957	Buster Cupit	1975	Labron Harris Jr.
1940	Frank Higgins	1958	Ted Gwin	1976	Jimmie Bullard
1941	George Whitehead	1959	Buster Cupit	1977	Jerry Jones

1978	Doug Tewell	1986	Steve Ball	1994	Tim Fleming
1979	Bob Ralston	1987	Jim Woodward	1995	Rod Nuckolls
1980	Chris Cole	1988	Andy Schaben	1996	Bob Ralston
1981	Dick Goetz	1989	Bob Ralston	1997	Jim Woodward
1982	Bob Ralston	1990	Art Romero	1998	Craig Walker
1983	Art Proctor	1991	Dave Bryan	1999	Tim Fleming
1984	Don Maddox	1992	Jeff Combe	2000	Pat McTigue
1985	Bob Ralston	1993	Glen Day		

OKLAHOMA MEN'S AMATEUR MATCH PLAY CHAMPIONS

1910	Harry Gwinnup	1926	Keefe Carter	1942	Dee Replogle
1911	Harry Gwinnup	1927	William Nichols	1943–45	(No tournaments)
1912	Harry Gwinnup	1928	Lee Pendergraff	1946	George Coleman
1913	Akra West	1929	Walter Critchlow	1947	Ken Rogers
1914	Frank Moore	1930	Keefe Carter	1948	Bo Wininger
1915	George Frederickson	1931	Henry Robertson	1949	Dee Replogle
1916	Harry Gwinnup	1932	Emmett Rogers	1950	John Garrison
1917	C. R. Hoffer	1933	Henry Robertson	1951	Charles Stohland
1918	Edward Bates	1934	Charles Reasor	1952	Joe Walser
1919	Gustave Mattson	1935	Earl Berryhill	1953	Leonard Young
1920	James Kennedy	1936	Walter Emery	1954	Ben Dickson
1921	James Kennedy	1937	Paul Jackson	1955	Ab Justice
1922	James Kennedy	1938	Guy Underwood	1956	Harold Corbett
1923	James Kennedy	1939	Walter Emery	1957	Bob Goetz
1924	Keefe Carter	1940	Emmett Rogers	1958	Glen Fowler
1925	William Nichols	1941	John Stammer	1959	Glen Fowler

1960	Glen Fowler	1974	Mark Witt	1988	Andre Bossert
1961	Jim Wright	1975	Bill Detournillon	1989	Joe Nick
1962	Labron Harris Jr.	1976	Craig Strothers	1990	Matt Gogel
1963	Hugh Edgmon	1977	Jeff McMillian	1991	Bill Brafford
1964	George Hixon	1978	Jim Woodward	1992	Joe Nick
1965	Bob Dickson	1979	Jim Kane	1993	Joe Nick
1966	Bob Dickson	1980	Jim Kane	1994	Lance Combrink
1967	Mark Hayes	1981	Jeff McMillian	1995	Buddy Hamilton
1968	Mike Holder	1982	Bill Brafford	1996	Dax Johnston
1969	Jay Friedman	1983	Jim Kelson	1997	Bob Mase
1970	Jay Friedman	1984	Greg Turner	1998	Brian McGreevy
1971	Mark Hayes	1985	Fred Lutz	1999	Randy Robinson
1972	Henry DeLozier	1986	Kyle Flinton	2000	Tripp Davis
1973	Dave Barr	1987	Kurt Nelson		

OKLAHOMA WOMEN'S AMATEUR CHAMPIONS

1915	Mrs. Arthur Will	1925	Mrs. Hulbert Clarke	1935	Estelle Drennan
1916	Mrs. Sam Harris	1926	Estelle Drennan	1936	Mrs. Dean Stacy
1917	Mrs. A. R. Lingafelt	1927	Estelle Drennan	1937	Jenny Grout
1918	(No tournament)	1928	Estelle Drennan	1938	Joyce Wallace
1919	Mrs. A. T. Allison	1929	Estelle Drennan	1939	Pat Grant
1920	Mrs. Arthur Will	1930	Joyce Wallace	1940	Pat Grant
1921	Mrs. Carl Wells	1931	Patti Blanton	1941	Pat Grant
1922	Mrs. Kent Shartel	1932	Patti Blanton	1942	Pat Grant
1923	Mrs. J. P. Solomon	1933	Joyce Wallace	1943–45	(No tournaments)
1924	Mrs. Hulbert Clarke	1934	Estelle Drennan	1946	Pat Grant

1947	Patti Blanton	1965	Jeannie Thompson	1983	Melissa McNamara
1948	Patti Blanton	1966	Linda Morse	1984	Leslie Core
1949	Pat Grant	1967	Lucy Beeler	1985	Lee Ann Hammack
1950	Al Rumbaugh	1968	Dale Fleming McNamara	1986	Patty McGraw Coatney
1951	Margaret Williford	1969	Dale McNamara	1987	Shelly Duncan
1952	Margaret Williford	1970	Teresa Weinshelbaum	1988	Patty McGraw Coatney
1953	Margaret Williford	1971	Mary Alice Hines	1989	Sheila Luginbuel
1954	Betsy Cullen	1972	Dale Fleming McNamara	1990	Patty McGraw Coatney
1955	Betsy Cullen	1973	Louise Blumenthal	1991	Patty McGraw Coatney
1956	Dale Fleming	1974	Linda Morse	1992	Michele Gard
1957	Dale Fleming	1975	Dale Fleming McNamara	1993	Rachel Preble
1958	Margaret Williford	1976	Teresa Weinshelbaum	1994	Sheila Luginbuel Dills
1959	Dale Fleming	1977	Patty McGraw	1995	Sheila Luginbuel Dills
1960	Beth Stone	1978	Linda Brown	1996	Sheila Luginbuel Dills
1961	Betsy Cullen	1979	Patty McGraw Coatney	1997	Ashley Wilkerson
1962	Linda Melton Morse	1980	Patty McGraw Coatney	1998	Bonnie Hanlin
1963	Susie Maxwell	1981	Patty McGraw Coatney	1999	Bonnie Hanlin
1964	Linda Morse	1982	Lee Ann Hammack	2000	Natasha Rowe

OKLAHOMA MEN'S AMATEUR STROKE PLAY CHAMPIONS

1989	Sean Collard	1993	Tim Graves	1997	Billy Brown
1990	Joe Nick	1994	Joe Nick	1998	Brad Golden
1991	Chris Edgmon	1995	Fred Lutz	1999	Billy Brown
1992	Joe Nick	1996	Joe Nick	2000	(tie) Gary Cowan
					Mike Hughett

OKLAHOMA SENIOR WOMEN'S AMATEUR CHAMPIONS

Year	Champion	Year	Champion	Year	Champion
1977	Anne Gookin	1985	Lucy Beeler	1993	Sharon Garner
1978	Lucy Beeler	1986	Canceled (rain)	1994	Mary Lou Scharf
1979	Jarita Askins	1987	Jeanette Brown	1995	Audrey Olson
1980	Joyce Wallace	1988	Rose Mary Fox	1996	Mary Lou Scharf
1981	Jarita Askins	1989	Mary Lou Scharf	1997	Dena Nowotny
1982	Lucy Beeler	1990	Mary Lou Scharf	1998	Lee Ellen Thurman
1983	Mary Lou Scharf	1991	Dena Nowotny	1999	
1984	Lucy Beeler	1992	Dena Nowotny		

OKLAHOMA SENIOR MEN'S AMATEUR CHAMPIONS

Year	Champion	Year	Champion	Year	Champion
1963	Everett Watkins	1976	Stormy Williams	1989	
1964	Len Gold	1977		1990	
1965	Ed Hamilton	1978	Jack Shelton	1991	
1966	F. Hixon	1979	Jack Shelton	1992	
1967	Harold DeLong	1980		1993	
1968	Gerald Hefley	1981	Jack Shelton	1994	Charles Hill
1969		1982	Bob Dirk	1995	Roger Brown
1970	Gerald Hefley	1983		1996	Roger Brown
1971	Gerald Hefley	1984	Jim Unruh	1997	
1972	Bill Winslow	1985	Jim Unruh	1998	
1973	E. H. Masonhall	1986	Roger Little	1999	Roger Brown
1974	O. T. McCall	1987	Ronnie Holder	2000	John Walker
1975	Stormy Williams	1988	El Collins		

Note: Blanks indicate information not located.

OKLAHOMA WOMEN'S MID-AMATEUR CHAMPIONS

1996   Mary Lou Scharf
1997   Sheila Dills
1998   Jo Glenn
1999   Patty McGraw Coatney

OKLAHOMA MEN'S MID-AMATEUR CHAMPIONS

1984	Joey Dills	1990	Fred Lutz	1996	James Reid
1985	Jim Young	1991	Mel Huffaker	1997	Tim Graves
1986	Fred Lutz	1992	Joe Nick	1998	Tripp Davis
1987	Bob Mase	1993	Jim Hayes	1999	Ricky Lutz
1988	Tom Merry	1994	Gary Cowan	2000	Mike Hughett
1989	Gary Cowan	1995	James Reid		

OKLAHOMA JUNIOR GIRLS' AMATEUR CHAMPIONS

1950	Ann Ervine	1958	Patty David	1966	Teresa Weinshilboum
1951	JoAnn Grimes	1959	Patty David	1967	Teresa Weinshilboum
1952	Sue Gail Dillman	1960	Jeannie Thompson	1968	Jonya Stapp
1953	Betsy Cullen	1961	Jeannie Thompson	1969	Teresa Weinshilboum
1954	Betsy Cullen	1962	Jeannie Thompson	1970	Pam Hiti
1955	Jill Kreager	1963	Sherry Taylor	1971	Joannie Gardner
1956	Beth Stone	1964	Susan Basolo	1972	Patty Livingston
1957	Beth Stone	1965	Susan Basolo	1973	Brenda Moyers

1974	Holly Pryor	1983	Julie Rieger	1992	Sarah Warwick
1975	Margaret Ward	1984	Sheila Luginbuel	1993	Stacy Prammanasudh
1976	Patty McGraw	1985	(No Tournament)	1994	Stacy Prammanasudh
1977	Linda Brown	1986	Julie Rieger	1995	Stacy Prammanasudh
1978	Linda Brown	1987	Jennifer French	1996	Stacy Prammanasudh
1979	Adele Lukken	1988	Alycya Rambin	1997	Stacy Prammanasudh
1980	Adele Lukken	1989	Tascha Rinehart	1998	Brooke Fincher
1981	Melissa McNamara	1990	Michele Gard	1999	Amy Lee
1982	Melissa McNamara	1991	Kerri Prammanasudh	2000	Danielle Miron

OKLAHOMA JUNIOR BOYS' AMATEUR CHAMPIONS

1963	David Hines	1976	Jeff McMillian	1989	Craig Cozby
1964	Jim Deaton	1977	Jody Myers	1990	Dustin York
1965	Mark Adkins	1978	Gavin Goss	1991	Shannon Friday
1966	Mark Hayes	1979	Mark Fuller	1992	Chance Cozby
1967	Bob Karlovich	1980	Darrin Hoedebeck	1993	Tom Zeiders
1968	Randy Boyce	1981	Rick Pedersen	1994	Andy Crabtree
1969	Joey Dills	1982	Kevin Whipple	1995	Tosh Hays
1970	Bob Small	1983	Jeff Oakes	1996	Vaughn Marshall
1971	Teddy Mitchell	1984	Brian Montgomery	1997	Matt Larson
1972	Steve Walser	1985	Curtis Wangrud	1998	Andy Hayes
1973	David Edwards	1986	Derrick Bandelier	1999	Mick Morgan
1974	Mike Lawson	1987	Craig Cozby	2000	Zac Reynolds
1975	Jeff McMillian	1988	Richard Barnett		

ACKNOWLEDGMENTS

James Achenbach, Mike Adams, John Albertson, David Aldrich, Mike Allen, David Anderson, Bart Antle, Sally Antrobus, Jim Apfelbaum, Ricky Arnett, Tommy Askew, Ralph Baker, Joe Balander, Mark Baldree, Al Barkow, Ralph Barrera, Bill Barrett, Brian Basore, Bill Bass, Ken Beaty, Steve Becker, Lucy Beeler, Mike Beltz, Jason Benson, Jimmy Benson, William M. "Mac" Bentley, Eric Bergquist, Charles Bishop, Sam Blair, Frank Boggs, Tommy Bolt, Dean Boortz, Marci Bozarth, Jackson Bradley, Brian Branch, LaDonna Brauchle, Gay Brewer, George Bridges, John Bridges, Mark Brooks, Rod Brooks, Bill Brogden, Joyce Brown, Les Brown, Patrick Brown, Dave Bryan, Rachel Bryson, Rich Buchanan, Lee Buddrus, Dan Burke, Bill Burford, Bob Burns, President George H. W. Bush, David Buxton, Rosemary Buxton, Jack Burke, Robin Burke, Steve Buzzard, Carol Campbell, Earl Campbell, Kit Campbell, Len Casteel, Mike Chandler, Billy Clagett, Jim Clayton, Beth Cleckler, Susanne Clement, Ed Clements, Bob Close, Dave Cody, Rick Coe, Frank Conner, Bill Connors, Charles Coody, Cotton Cook, Jerry Cozby, Buster Creagh, Ben Crenshaw, Russell Crockett, Marion Milroy, "Doc" Curry, Jim Danky, Steve Darby, Eddy Davis, Jeff Davis, Jed Day, Bob Dickson, Alex Dingman, Bill Dixon, Joan Dixon, Frank Doane, Lynne Dobson, Ochirkhu Dorjisurung, Danny Douglas, Marvin Douglas, Dale Douglass, Jerry Drake, Charles Dorton, Terry Dungee, Jim Durham, Danny Edwards, Fran Elliott, Mal Elliott, Sharon Ellzey, Jake Engel, Angela Enright, John Erickson, Bob Estes, Tom Faires, Kim Fajt, Mark Fajt, Taylor Fajt, Floyd Farley, Doug Ferguson, U. C. Ferguson, John Fields, Cindy Figg-Currier, Art Finley, Keith Flowers, Elliot Foster, Denne Freeman, Earnest Fox, Steve Fromholz, Siegel Fry, Steve Fry, Bobby Galvez, Troy Gann, Jimmie Gauntt, Sand Gibbs, Gordon Gibson, Bob Goldman, Spec Goldman, Keith Good, Ross Goodner, Kevin Gracie,

Tara Gravel, Glenn Greenspan, Jackie Greer, Bob Hadden, Martha Hall, Will Hancock, George Hannon, Tommy Hargett, Dennis Hargrove, Mike Hargrove, Martin Hart, Mark Hayes, Mickey Herskowitz, Bob Hersom, Dave Hill, Gary Holaway, Doug Holloway, Mary Alice Holman, Ray Holman, Charles Howard, John Hudson, Martha Hummer, David Humphrey, Bob Hurt, Alsie Hyden, Mr. Henry P. Iba, Warren Igleheart, Bill Inglish, Chester F. "Jiggs" Jackson, Marty Javors, Raymond Jenkins, Tom Jenkins, J. J. Jennings, Rand Jerris, Chuck Johnson, Curt Johnson, David Johnson, Mary Johnston, Jenk Jones Jr., Tom Jones, Mike Kelley, Doug Kennemer, Tom Kensler, Leslie King, Tom Kite, Gib Kizer, John Klein, Mike Klemme, Ellen Knighton, Jeff Knighton, Randy Krehbiel, Phil Krick, Kelli Kuehne, Jim Lassiter, John Leach, Martha Leach, Jim Lefko, Jeff Leicht, Gustaveous Erasmus Lemon, Anna Lemon, Chrys Lemon, Fay Lemon, Gabriel Lemon, Glen E. Lemon, Helaine Lemon, Jacqueline Lemon, Jim Lemon, Laura Lemon, Leslie Holman Lemon, Lucia Licavoli-Lemon, Marcus Lemon, Susan Lemon and Colton Edwards, Martin Lemon, Mary Lou Lemon, Michael Lemon, R. M. Lemon, Robert D. Lemon, Robyn Lemon Sellers, Justin Leonard, Janice Littlefield, Gene Littler, Tony Longoria, Annie Love, Ken MacLeod, Steve Madden, Mark Maguire, Marty Malin, Steven Margolin, Jack Marr, General Marshall, Edmund Martin, Duffy Martin, Juanita Martin, Jeff Martin, Guy Mason, Joyce Mason, Ralph Maxfield, Gail Mayfield, George McCall, Kevin McCalla, Bill McCallie, Buford McCarty, Jack McClellan, Mike McClure, Mike McGettrick, Terry McGowan, Jim McGuire, Kenny McGuire, Pat McKamey, Matt McKay, Jeff McMillian, Mike McGraw, Dale McNamara, Bertha Means, Volney Meece, Mark Metcalf, Philip Miranda, Leon "Spanky" Moody, Lloyd Moody, Betty Moody, Lucille (Moody) Reed, Reggie (Moody) Harrison, Orville Moody, Richard Monroe, Bill Moretti, Dale Morgan, Lloyd Morrison, Mike Morrissey, Ken Mossberg, Floyd Moten, Fred Mueller, Pat Murphy, Laura Lynn Neal, Byron Nelson, Willie Nelson, Jody Noll, Cindy Nunn, Lucy Nunn, Ron Nunn, Harry Nunnelly, Jerry O'Brien, Dan O'Kane, Jack O'Leary, Rob Ormand, Volma Overton Jr., Volma Overton Sr., Dee Paige, Robert L. "Bobby" Parker Jr., Risa Parker, Russ Pate, Brent Peck, Harvey Penick, Tinsley Penick, Bill Penn, John Carlo Peracuti, Ed Perales, Cary Petri, Ed Petri, Randy Petri, Dirk Peterson, Buddy Phillips, Mary Ann Phillips, Randy Phillips, Ron Pinckard, Turk Pipkin, Ann Pitts, Tommy Pletcher, Charles

Prather, Lisa Dunn Prather, Ron Prather, Mike Prusinski, Barbara Puett, Roane Puett, Greg Quadlander, Charlie Randle, Tony Ragsdale, Judy Rankin, Mike Ray, Michael Reisor, Wayne Reisor, Jim Reid, Sonny Rhodes, Ty Rickman, Gary "Dude" Riley, Robert Rivera, David Roberts, Steve Robertson, Diana Rogers, Garry Rogers, Arnilius Johnson, Jenny Rogers Johnson, Shakira Johnson, Julia Rogers, Kevin Rogers, John Rohde, Elliot Rowan, Lee Rowan, Lorne Rubenstein, Cindy Rugeley, Jim Ryan, Curt Sampson, Tom Sanders, Ray Sanchez, Doug Sanders, Bill Sansom, Scott Sayers, Barbara Schlief, Randy Seirer, John Sellers, Barbara Sessions, Don Sessions, Scott Sessions, Danny Shackelford, Otis Shearer, Dave Sheinin, Allen Shelley, Bud Shrake, Curtis Short, Wes Short, Charles Sifford, Steve Sigler, Bob Simmons, Ron Simon, Calvin Sinnette, Dave Sittler, Val Skinner, Phil Slack, Dennis Smith, Grace Morgan Smith, Jeff Smith, Natha Smith, J. H. Smith Sr., Jimmy Smith, Larry Smith, Martha Walker Smith, Parker Smith, Richard Smith, Shirley Smith, Wayne Smith, Vernon Snell, Walter Snow, Lee Spencer, Katherine Staat, Jim Stafford, Fred Standley, Alice Stanton, Will Stephens, Dave Stockton, Clarence E. "Bill" Stumbaugh, Emil Susanj, Al Swihart, Bubba Sykes, Sally Sykes, Larry Terry, Kyley Tetley, Adam Thrasher, Barry Thompson, Peter Thomson, Diane Thorp, John Tomicki, Don Tom Kalski, Sally Tomlinson, Dan Torluemke, Bobby Trader, Larry Trader, Berry Tramel, Jack Treece, John Triplett, Carl Turner, Lori Turner, Ralph Turtinen, Terry Tush, Marjorie Urban, Omar Uresti, Marsha Van Hooser, Vance Van Hooser, Steve Veriato, Scott Verplank, Roll Wagner, Susan Wagner, Victor Wallace, Susan Watkins, Chris Watt, Justice Joseph M. Watt, Susan Hergert Weaver, Amy Weeks, Kimberly Wiar, Duke Webb, Don Webster, Pat Weis, Camille Wheeler, Ray White, Robert White, Joan Whitworth, Karen Wieder, Patsy Willcox, Jep Wille, Bob Williams, George Williams, Brian Williamson, Jeff Wilson, Ken Wilson, Greg Wooldridge, Lu Ellyn Wright, Margaret Wright, Eric Yeager, Guy Yocom.

Full references for books consulted are in the bibliography; articles consulted are not included there but are cited in full in these notes.

CHAPTER 1: FIRST TEE

1. Sutphen, *Harper's Official Golf Guide 1901*, 254.
2. Norman E. J. Findlay,"Guthrie Golf Course May Be First: Historian Researches Country Club," *Guthrie Daily Leader*, May 25, 1980.
3. Kerr and Gainer, *Story of Oklahoma City*, 536–37.
4. Wilbur Johnson, *Daily Oklahoman*, May 11, 1958.
5. Jim Hamilton, *Daily Oklahoman*, Dec. 31, 1985.
6."Recreation in Indian Territory," *Sturm's Statehood Magazine* vol. 1, no. 2 (Oct. 1905): 2.
7. Douglas *History of Tulsa*, 506
8."Recreation in Indian Territory," 3.
9. Cornish and Whitten, *Architects of Golf*, 38.
10. Findlay, "Guthrie Golf Course."
11. Frank Boggs,"Golf, Mr. Jackson Very Good Friends," *Daily Oklahoman*, Oct. 19, 1966.
12. While Tulsa Country Club, Dornick Hills, and Oklahoma City Golf and Country Club had bermudagrass greens by 1922, Oklahoma's thirty other golf courses did not. Sand greens or compressed cottonseed-hull greens were common at courses throughout the southwestern United States before affordable irrigation. Sand was usually mixed with oil and used as a putting surface. However, if the sand was too fine, or if light fuel oil was used, greens could wash away during heavy rainfall. Instead, coarser sand and heavy residuum from oil refineries or cleanings from old fuel-oil supply tanks generally worked better, according to a May 1998 communique from Susanne Clement, librarian/curator of the Golf Course Superintendents Association of America (e-mail, May 14, 1998).
13. Bob Hersom,"Once upon a Time at Lincoln Park: It Will Be 50 Years Since PGA Hall of Famers Played Course," *Daily Oklahoman*, Feb. 24, 1987.
14. Hersom,"Once upon a Time."

15. John Rohde,"Hall of Famer: Ferguson Honored for More than Longevity,"*South Central Golf,* Aug. 1996, 25.

16. Rohde,"Hall of Famer: Ferguson,"25.

17. Rohde,"Hall of Famer: Ferguson,"25.

18. Ron Fimrite,"A Mad Master," *Sports Illustrated Golf Plus,* Aug. 1997.

19. Frank Hannigan,"Tillie Leaves A Legacy," *Golf Digest,* Aug. 1977.

20. Ken MacLeod,"Job Well Done: Crummett Stands Tall at Oaks," *South Central Golf,* Dec. 1996, 13.

21. Ken MacLeod,"Touches of Genius," *South Central Golf,* Aug. 1994, 17.

22. Charles Evans,"Perry Duke Maxwell,"in *Chronicles of Oklahoma* (Oklahoma Historical Society) vol. 31, no. 2 (summer 1953): 133.

23. O. B. Keeler,"The Story of the Augusta National,"(originally written March 15, 1940), in *Records of the Masters Tournament 1934–1993,* 57.

24. Mac Bentley, *Daily Oklahoman,* May 23, 1983.

CHAPTER 2: OKLAHOMA OPEN

1. Mac Bentley,"OGA Helps Steer State Golfers on Right Course," *Daily Oklahoman,* Dec. 6, 1989.

2. Mac Bentley,"Oklahoma Open Has Come a Long Way," *South Central Golf,* Sept. 1995, 8.

3. Ray Soldan,"He Took the Long Route," *Daily Oklahoman,* July 6, 1983.

4. Bob Hersom,"Tway's Par Enough in Oklahoma Open," *Daily Oklahoman,* Sept. 15, 1985.

5. Wlliam Voigt Jr., *Tulsa Daily World,* Aug. 6, 1933.

6. Nelson *Byron Nelson: The Little Black Book,* xi.

7. Elliott, *100 Years of Kansas Golf,* 100.

8. Anthony DeGiusti,"City's Grout Family Won Top Billing in State's Golf History," *Daily Oklahoman,* Dec. 4, 1985.

9."Grout Rallies to Annex Open Title," *Tulsa World,* May 30, 1927.

10. Vernon Snell,"Okmulgeean Turns in Card of 150 to Cop Golf Title," *Daily Oklahoman,* May 18, 1929.

11. Nelson, *How I Played the Game,* 26.

12."To Nicklaus, Grout Was a Golf Pro's Pro," *Daily Oklahoman,* May 14, 1989.

13."To Nicklaus."

14. Barkow, *Gettin' to the Dance Floor,* 3.

15. Charles Price,"My All-Star Golf Team," *Golf,* Jan., 1975.

16. Barkow, *Gettin' to the Dance Floor,* 10.

17. Barkow, *Gettin' to the Dance Floor,* 7.

18. Barkow, *Gettin' to the Dance Floor,* 12.

19. Barkow, *Gettin' to the Dance Floor*, 10.
20. "Tournament at Country Club," *Tulsa World*, May 24, 1910.
21. "Golf Match Is Won by Nichols," *Daily Oklahoman*, June 5, 1911.
22. "Frederickson Head of Country Club," *Daily Oklahoman*, July 8, 1911.

CHAPTER 3: THE MAN

1. Wally Wallis, "Golfing Greats No Strangers Here," *Daily Oklahoman*, June 5, 1960.
2. "Joplin Pro Has 288," *Tulsa World*, Nov. 5, 1928.
3. "New Jersey Pro Shoots 298," *New York Times*, Oct. 28, 1929.
4. "Texas Sharpshooters Set Qualifying Pace," *Daily Oklahoman*, Sept. 2, 1930.
5. Bus Ham, "Finals of the Southwest Tourney Here Today," *Daily Oklahoman*, Sept. 5, 1930.
6. Nelson and Dennis, *Shape Your Swing*, 12–13.
7. Nelson and Dennis, *Shape Your Swing*, 13.
8. Nelson, *Little Black Book*, 15.
9. Vernon B. Snell, "Johnny Sinks Sphere from Every Angle," *Daily Oklahoman*, Oct. 24, 1935.

CHAPTER 4: SOUTHERN HILLS

1. Ken MacLeod, "USGA Opens Arms to Southern Hills," *South Central Golf*, July 1996.
2. USGA press release, June 14, 1996.
3. John Rohde, "State Pride Retained in PGA Site Switch," *South Central Golf*, June 1994, 14.
4. Rohde, "State Pride Retained," 14.
5. "Southern Discomfort," *Golf*, Aug. 1994, 38.
6. Jack Berry, "Major Congratulations to PGA, USGA," *Golf Writers Association of America Newsletter*, July–Aug. 1994, 1.
7. Glenda Carlile, "Heroines of Oil," *Oklahoma Today*, July–Aug., 1997, 78.
8. Ralph Marsh, "Return to Tulsey Town: The Oil Capital of the World Turns 100," *Oklahoma Today*, July–Aug. 1997, 70.
9. "Masterpiece: Southern Hills Stands Test of Time," in *PGA Tour Championship Issue*, Tulsa: South Central Publications, 1996, 18.
10. Mac Bentley, "A True Legend: Pioneer Golf Course Architect's Work Brings Game's Great Golfers to Oklahoma," *Daily Oklahoman*, May 23, 1993.
11. Dan O'Kane, "In Due Course: Pro Golf Has a Long, Respected History on Tulsa Fairways," *Tulsa World*, July 15, 1997.

12. Zaharias and Paxton, *This Life I've Led,* 140–41.
13. Zaharias and Paxton, *This Life I've Led,* 141.
14. Clay Henry, "Winters Led the Way," *South Central Golf,* Aug. 1994, 34.
15. Henry, "Winters Led the Way," 34.
16. Blackie Sherrod, "Some Hither, Others Yon," *Dallas Morning News,* Sept. 14, 1997.
17. Ken MacLeod, "Caddie Was Stockton's 'Best Friend' at Crucial Time," *South Central Golf,* Aug. 1994, 42.
18. MacLeod, "Caddie Was Stockton's 'Best Friend,'" 42.
19. Richard Mudry, "Green Played On—and Won—Despite Death Threat in 1977," *Golfweek,* June 7, 1997, 24.
20. Mudry, "Green Played On," 26.
21. Rohde, "State Pride Retained," 14.
22. Ken MacLeod, "Southern Hills Again Proves Open Quality," *South Central Golf,* Dec. 1995, 14.

CHAPTER 5: BURNEYVILLE

1. Hamilton, Bill, "Turners Spent Millions Sponsoring Ardmore Golf Tournament," *Daily Ardmoreite,* July 7, 1968, 6-A.
2. John Merwin, "The Last Prospectors," *D Magazine,* July 1976, 60.
3. John Cronley, "Once Over Lightly," *Daily Oklahoman,* May 12, 1953.
4. Barbara Sessions, "Golf's Giveaway Man: Falconhead Resort Owes All to Eccentric Waco Turner," *Oklahoma Living,* Sept. 1998, 18–19.
5. Wally Wallis, "Stewart's 135 Tops Oliver by One Stroke at Ardmore," *Daily Oklahoman,* May 9, 1953.
6. Cronley, "Once Over Lightly," *Daily Oklahoman,* May 12, 1953.
7. Wally Wallis, "The Golf Shop," *Daily Oklahoman,* May 10, 1953.
8. Barkow, *Golf's Golden Grind,* 165–66.
9. Sessions, "Golf's Giveaway Man," 20.
10. Tom Archdeacon, "Pete Brown Open's Roots Are on Highway 51," *Dayton Daily News,* July 2, 1995.
11. "Pete Brown: A Golf Champion at Last," *Sepia,* July 1964, 63.
12. Archdeacon, "Pete Brown Open's Roots."
13. Ron Cross, "Brown Scores First in Waco Turner Open," *Daily Ardmoreite,* May 4, 1964.
14. Gary Nuhn, "Brown Led Way for Tiger, Too," *Dayton Daily News,* April 17, 1997.
15. Nuhn, "Brown Led Way."
16. Archdeacon, "Pete Brown Open's Roots."
17. Nuhn, "Brown Led Way."
18. "PGA Purses Skyrocket but 'Poor Boys' Lose Turner," *Golf World,* Dec. 16, 1964.

19. Vernon B. Snell, "Sportsmanship Award Suggested for Turners by State PGA President," *Oklahoma City Times*, Oct. 1, 1954.

CHAPTER 6: QUAIL CREEK

1. Wilbur Johnson, "Gauntt Says 'Give me 280,'" *Daily Oklahoman*, Sept. 16, 1956.
2. Wally Wallis, "Palmer Drew Notice Here in '53 Meet," *Daily Oklahoman*, June 3, 1960.
3. Sanders and Pate, *Action on the First Tee*, 99.
4. Wally Wallis, "Open Starts Today," *Daily Oklahoman*, Aug. 23, 1962.
5. Wally Wallis, "Youth, Southpaw Add Zest to City Open," *Daily Oklahoman*, May 12, 1963.
6. Wallis, "Youth."
7. Ron Nance, "It's a Happy Fairfield Who Leads City Open," *Daily Oklahoman*, May 19, 1963.
8. Wally Wallis, "Fairfield Birdies 18th for Crown," May 20, 1963.
9. John Cronley, "Once Over Lightly," *Daily Oklahoman*, May 14, 1964.
10. Wally Wallis, "Wininger Fires 70, Remains 1–Up," Sept. 4, 1965.
11. Doug Todd, "Rodgers' Play Isn't Wreckless," *Daily Oklahoman*, Sept. 5, 1965.
12. Doug Todd, "Don't Mention Drouth to Lema," *Daily Oklahoman*, May 27, 1966.
13. Wally Wallis, "Pott's 69 Retains Four-Stroke Edge," *Daily Oklahoman*, May 28, 1966.
14. Doug Todd, "Weiskopf Happy Dropout," *Daily Oklahoman*, May 29, 1966.
15. Doug Todd, "Lema, Writers Gulp Champagne," *Daily Oklahoman*, May 30, 1966.
16. Sommers, *Golf Anecdotes*, 273.
17. Wade, *"And Then Jack Said to Arnie,"* 11–12.
18. Barry McDermott, "The Extraordinary Mr. X," *Sports Illustrated*, Sept. 17, 1984, 73.
19. McDermott, "The Extraordinary Mr. X," 74.

CHAPTER 7: WOMEN

1. Harrell Butler, "Host Pro Gives Tips on Best Way to Watch Western Open," *Daily Oklahoman*, June 19, 1949.
2. Laymond Crump, "Riley Upsets the Babe, 3 & 1," *Daily Oklahoman*, June 24, 1949.
3. Sampson, *Texas Golf Legends*, 64.
4. Craig Dolch, "Hall of Famer Betty Jameson," *Palm Beach Post*, May 9, 1999.
5. *LPGA Media Guide*, 1998, 14.
6. Dolch, "Hall of Famer Betty Jameson."
7. Wally Wallis, "Berg Captures Ardmore Crown," *Daily Oklahoman*, Sept. 27, 1954.
8. Wallis, "Berg Captures Ardmore Crown."

9. Tom Wright, "Lawton Open Champ Learned Golf at Fort Sill," *Lawton Constitution*, Oct. 23, 1956.

10. Lew Johnson, "Column," *Lawton Constitution*, April 23, 1957.

11. Sommers, *Golf Anecdotes*, 188.

12. Johnson, "Column."

13. Vernon Snell, "Creed Leading at Burneyville," *Daily Oklahoman*, Aug. 31, 1958.

14. Wally Wallis, "Patty Berg Looks Ahead to More Winning Years," *Daily Oklahoman*, May 20, 1962.

15. "Wright 'Given' 2-Stroke Lead at Muskogee," *Daily Oklahoman*, June 19, 1963.

16. John Rohde, "Ferguson Is Local Golf Icon," *Daily Oklahoman*, June 9, 1996.

17. Rohde, "Ferguson."

18. Lincoln A. Werden, "Mrs. Berning Cards 71 to Win U.S. Open," *New York Times*, July 8, 1968.

19. Steve Cady, "Mrs. Berning Praised by Caddie," *New York Times*, July 3, 1972.

20. Lincoln A. Werden, "Mrs. Berning Recaptures U.S. Open Golf Crown," *New York Times*, July 3, 1972.

CHAPTER 8: MODERN

1. Mac Bentley, "Oklahoma City Is Going, Going Golf," *Daily Oklahoman*, July 10, 1994.

2. Jim Stafford, "Empire Builder: Duffy Does It His Own Way," *South Central Golf*, May 1994, 24.

3. Stafford, "Empire Builder," 24.

4. Stafford, "Empire Builder," 24.

5. Green, *Panhandle Pioneer,* 232.

6. John Rohde, "Mantle Hit Ball Out of Sight on Golf Course Too," *South Central Golf*, July 1996, 7.

7. Jenk Jones Jr., "A Goat Ranch No More," *South Central Golf*, Oct. 1995, 10.

8. Mac Bentley, "Norman Seniors Qualify for Open," *Daily Oklahoman*, June 25, 1995.

9. Bob Hurt, "Quail Creek, Vossler Won't Forget Slap in Face by PGA," *Daily Oklahoman*, Aug. 18, 1970.

10. Tom Kensler, "Made for a Major: Snubbing Inspiration for Oak Tree," *Daily Oklahoman*, July 31, 1988.

11. Dye and Shaw, *Bury Me in a Pot Bunker*, 117.

12. Tom Kensler, "Oak Tree among World's Best Courses," *Daily Oklahoman*, Aug. 14, 1983.

13. Kensler, "Oak Tree."

14. Tom Kensler and Volney Meece, "Age Given No Respect at Oak Tree," *Daily Oklahoman*, Aug. 29, 1984.

15. John Rohde, "Dye: Golf Genius or Gremlin?" *Daily Oklahoman*, July 31, 1988.
16. Rohde, "Dye."
17. Mac Bentley, "PGA Event to Feed Passion for Golf," *Daily Oklahoman*, April 29, 1990.
18. Tom Kensler, "Sooners Coast to 19-Stroke Victory," *Daily Oklahoman*, June 11, 1989.
19. Bentley, "PGA Event."
20. Mac Bentley, "Around Oklahoma: Familiar Name Active Again in Building Golf Courses," *South Central Golf*, June 1994, 6.
21. Ken MacLeod, "Stonebriar Set for Bartlesville," *South Central Golf*, May 1997, 21.
22. Ken MacLeod, "New Kid on the Block," *South Central Golf*, March 1994, 17.
23. Ken MacLeod, "Battle Creek a Beauty to Brooks," *South Central Golf*, May 1997, 22.
24. Frank Boggs, "Errant Putts Foil Hayes' Hopes for Masters: Lead Catastrophe on 18 Spoils Good Round," *Daily Oklahoman*, April 10, 1982.
25. Ken MacLeod, "Matching Maxwell No Picnic," *South Central Golf*, July–Aug. 1997, 3.

CHAPTER 9: VARSITY

1. Jenk Jones Jr., "Golden Touch: McNamara Has Put University of Tulsa Golf on the Map," *South Central Golf*, May 1995, 17.
2. Jones, "Golden Touch," 17–18.
3. Jones, "Golden Touch," 18.
4. Wade, *And Then Arnie Told Chi Chi*, 129.
5. John Klein, "Women's College Golf Hits Big Time," *Tulsa World*, Oct. 6, 1998.
6. Randy Krehbiel, "$1 Million Donated for OU Golf Course," *Tulsa World*, July 16, 1996.
7. Mac Bentley, "Renovated OU Course Will Get Best of Both Worlds," *South Central Golf*, May 1995, 7.
8. Mac Bentley, "Maxwell Endorses Renovation," *Daily Oklahoman*, April 4, 1993.
9. Brian McCallen, "New Challenges: University of Oklahoma GC," *Golf*, Dec. 1997, 98.
10. Ken MacLeod, "Sooner Course Draws Raves," *South Central Golf*, Sept. 1996, 15.
11. John Rohde, "Coe Honored as OU's 'Greatest': New Center Named after Former Sooner Golfer," *Daily Oklahoman*, Sept. 5, 1998.
12. Wally Wallis, "Labron Harris Sr. Named 'Sportsman of the Month,'" *Daily Oklahoman*, July 28, 1963.
13. Bob Hersom, "Eichelberger Credits OSU For Success," *Daily Oklahoman*, Aug. 3, 1982.
14. John Klein, "Holder's Life a Hole-in-One Dream," *Tulsa World*, May 24, 1997.
15. Klein, "Holder's Life."
16. Ken MacLeod, "OSU Beauty: Jones Leaves Golf Club to Rejoin Holder," *South Central Golf*, Aug.–Sept. 1993, 21.
17. MacLeod, "OSU Beauty," 21.

CHAPTER 10: OKLAHOMA AND THE USGA

1. Tom Kensler, "Love Is U.S. Open Title," *Daily Oklahoman*, Aug. 1, 1983.

2. Gordon White, "Jan Stephenson Leads by Two," *New York Times*, July 31, 1983.

3. Kensler, "Love Is."

4. Kensler, "Love Is."

5. Tom Kensler, "Verplank Flies to Top on Flock of Birdies," *Daily Oklahoman*, Sept. 3, 1984.

6. Joe McLaughlin, "Orville Moody Is Man 'Three Back of Barber,'" *Houston Chronicle*, June 15, 1969.

7. McLaughlin, "Orville Moody Is Man."

8. Jack Gallagher, "'I Can Win,' Says Orville: Moody Not Afraid of Open Pressure," *Houston Post*, June 15, 1969.

9. Jack Agness, "Moody Marches Off with U.S. Open Crown, $30,000," *Houston Post*, June 16, 1969.

10. Agness, "Moody Marches Off."

11. Jack Gallagher, "Moody Loot May Top Million," *Houston Post*, June 16, 1969.

12. Gallagher, "Moody Loot."

13. John Hollis, "A Putt Happiness for Moody Caddy," *Houston Post*, June 16, 1969.

14. Hollis, "A Putt Happiness."

15. Lorne Rubenstein, "A Great Amateur—Bob Dickson," *Golf Journal*, June 1995, 39; reprint, www.usga.org.

16. Rubenstein, "A Great Amateur," 40.

EPILOGUE

1. Randy Ellis, "State Mounts Drive to Bring Its Golf Courses Up to Par," *Daily Oklahoman*, Nov. 20, 1989.

Allis, Peter. *The Who's Who of Golf*. Englewood Cliffs, N.J.: Prentice-Hall, 1983.

American Annual Golf Guide and Year Book. Vols. 1–14. New York: Golf Guide Publishing Company, 1916–31.

Apfelbaum, Jim. *Golf on $30 A Day (or Less): A Bargain Hunter's Guide to Great Courses and Equipment*. New York: Villard Books, 1995.

Barkow, Al. *Gettin' to the Dance Floor: The Early Days of American Pro Golf*. London: Heinemann Kingswood, 1986.

———. *Golf's Golden Grind: The History of the Tour*. New York: Harcourt Brace Jovanovich, 1974.

———. *The History of the PGA Tour*. New York: Doubleday, 1989.

Bischoff, John Paul. *Mr. Iba: Basketball's Aggie Iron Duke*. Norman: Oklahoma Heritage Association, 1980.

Cayleff, Susan E. *Babe: The Life and Legend of Babe Didrikson Zaharias*. Urbana: University of Illinois Press, 1995.

Cornish, Geoffrey S., and Ronald E. Whitten. *The Architects of Golf: A Survey of Golf Course Design from Its Beginnings to the Present, with an Encyclopedic Listing of Golf Course Architects and Their Courses*. New York: Harper Collins, 1993.

———. *The Golf Course*. New York: Rutledge Press, 1981.

Cotton, Henry. *A History of Golf Illustrated*. Philadelphia: J. B. Lippincott, 1975.

Cross, George Lynn. *Presidents Can't Punt: The OU Football Tradition*. Norman: University of Oklahoma Press, 1977.

Doak, Tom. *The Confidential Guide to Golf Courses*. Chelsea, Mich.: Sleeping Bear Press, 1996.

Dobereiner, Peter. *The World of Golf: The Best of Peter Dobereiner*. New York: Atheneum, 1981.

Donovan, Richard E., and Joseph S. F. Murdoch. *The Game of Golf and the Printed Word 1566–1985: A Bibliography of Golf Literature in the English Language*. Endicott, N.Y.: Castalio Press, 1987.

Douglas, Clarence B. *The History of Tulsa, Oklahoma: A City with Personality*. Chicago: S. J. Clarke, 1921.

Dye, Pete, with Mark Shaw. *Bury Me in a Pot Bunker: Golf through the Eyes of the Game's Most Challenging Course Designer*. Reading, Mass.: Addison-Wesley, 1995.

Elliot, Len, and Barbara Kelly. *Who's Who in Golf*. New Rochelle, N.Y.: Arlington House, 1976.

Elliott, Mal. *100 Years of Kansas Golf*. Wichita: Elfco Publishing, 1996.

Ferber, Edna. *Cimarron*. Garden City, N.Y.: Doubleday, 1929.

Flaherty, Tom, *The U.S. Open (1895–1965): The Complete Story of the United States Championship of Golf*. New York: E. P. Dutton, 1966.

Fraser's International Golf Yearbook. New York: Fraser, 1923–37.

Garrity, John. *America's Worst Golf Courses: A Collection of Courses Not up to Par*. New York: Macmillan, 1994.

Gibson, Nevin H. *The Encyclopedia of Golf with the Official All-Time Records*. New York: A. S. Barnes, 1958.

Golf Book of Records: History and Statistics of World-Wide Golf. Ed. Douglas C. Billian. Atlanta: Billian, 1989.

Golf Digest Retirement Planner. Ed. Mike O'Malley. Trumbull, Conn.: New York Times Magazine Group, 1997.

Golf Digest's 4200 Best Places to Play, 2nd edition. New York: Fodor's Travel Publications, 1995.

Golf Magazine's Encyclopedia of Golf: The Complete Reference, 2nd edition. New York: Harper Collins, 1993.

Golfer's Digest: First Anniversary Deluxe Edition. Chicago: Golf Digest Publications, 1966.

Graffis, Herb. *The PGA: The Official History of the Professional Golfers' Association of America*. New York: Thomas Y. Crowell, 1975.

Green, Donald E. *Panhandle Pioneer: Henry C. Hitch, His Ranch, and His Family*. Norman: University of Oklahoma Press, 1979.

Kerr, W. F., and Ina Gainer. *The Story of Oklahoma City, Oklahoma: The Biggest Little City in the World*. Chicago: S. J. Clarke, 1922.

Leighton, Beach. *Mr. Dutch: The Arkansas Traveler*. Foreword by Bob Hope. Champagne, Ill.: Sagamore Publishing, 1991.

Lema, Tony, with Bud Harvey. *Champagne Tony's Golf Tips*. New York: Simon and Schuster, 1967.

LPGA Media Guide. Daytona Beach, Fla.: LPGA Communications Department, 1998.

MacKenzie, Alister. *The Spirit of St. Andrews*. Chelsea, Mich.: Sleeping Bear Press, 1995.

Martin, Harry B. *Fifty Years of American Golf*. New York: Dodd, Mead, 1936.

Masters Media Guide 1999. Augusta, Ga.: Augusta National, 1998.

Masters Tournament Scoring Records and Statistics 1934–1998. 31st edition. Comp. Bill Inglish. Augusta, Ga.: Augusta National, 1993.

McCord, Robert. *The Best Public Golf Courses in the United States, Canada, the Caribbean and Mexico*. New York: Random House, 1993.

McReynolds, Edwin C. *Oklahoma: A History of the Sooner State*. Norman: University of Oklahoma Press, 1964.

Mehlhorn, Bill, with Bobby Shave. *Golf Secrets Exposed*. Miami: M and S Publishing, 1984.

Nelson, Byron. *Byron Nelson: The Little Black Book*. Arlington, Tex.: Summit, 1995.

———. *How I Played the Game*. Dallas: Taylor Publishing, 1993.

Nelson, Byron, with Larry Dennis. *Shape Your Swing the Modern Way*. Norwalk, Conn.: Golf Digest, 1976; reprint New York: Ailsa, 1985.

Nelson, Kevin. *The Greatest Golf Shot Ever Made*. New York: Simon and Schuster, 1992.

Nichols, Bobby. *Never Say Never: The Psychology of Winning Golf*. New York: Fleet, 1965.

Penick, Harvey, with Bud Shrake. *And If You Play Golf, You're My Friend: Further Reflections of a Grown Caddie*. New York: Simon and Schuster, 1993.

———. *For All Who Love the Game: Lessons and Teachings for Women*. New York: Simon and Schuster, 1995.

———. *The Game for a Lifetime: More Lessons and Teachings*. New York: Simon and Schuster, 1996.

———. *Harvey Penick's Little Red Book: Lessons and Teachings from a Lifetime in Golf.* New York: Simon and Schuster, 1992.

Peper, George, with Robin Macmillan, Jim Frank, and the editors of *Golf Magazine. Golf in America: The First One Hundred Years.* New York: Harry N. Abrams, 1988.

Records of the Masters Tournament 1934–1993. Augusta, Ga.: Augusta National, 1993.

Sampson, Curt. *Texas Golf Legends.* Lubbock: Texas Tech University Press, 1993.

Sanders, Doug, with Russ Pate. *Action on the First Tee: How to Cash in on Your Favorite Sport.* Dallas: Taylor Publishing, 1987.

Sifford, Charlie, with James Gullo. *Just Let Me Play: The Story of Charlie Sifford, the First Black PGA Golfer.* Latham, N.Y.: British American Publishing, 1992.

Sinnette, Calvin H. *Forbidden Fairways: African Americans and the Game of Golf.* Chelsea, Mich.: Sleeping Bear Press, 1998.

Snead, Sam, with Al Stump. *The Education of a Golfer.* New York: Simon and Schuster, 1962.

Sommers, Robert T. *Golf Anecdotes.* New York: Oxford University Press, 1995.

Spalding's Athletic Library Official Golf Guide. New York: American Sports Publishing, 1895, 1897–31.

Sports Illustrated Golf Lessons From the Pros. Englewood Cliffs, N.J.: Prentice-Hall, 1961.

Stricklin, Art. *Shell's Golf Guide to Austin–San Antonio.* Houston: 21st Century Media, 1994.

Suggs, Louise. *Golf For Women.* New York: Cornerstone Library, 1960.

Sutphen, William G. Van Tassel. *Harper's Official Golf Guide 1901: A Directory af All Golf Clubs and Associations in the United States, Together With Statistical Tables, the Rules of Golf and Other General Information.* New York: Harper's, 1901.

Wade, Don. *And Then Arnie Told Chi Chi: More Than 200 of the Best True Golf Stories Ever Told.* Chicago: Contemporary Books, 1993.

———. *And Then Fuzzy Told Seve: A Collection of the Best True Golf Stories Ever Told.* Chicago: Contemporary Books, 1996.

———. *And Then Jack Said to Arnie: A Collection of the Greatest True Golf Stories of All Time.* Chicago: Contemporary Books, 1991.

Wilson, Mark (comp. and ed.), with Ken Bowden. *The Best of Henry Longhurst.* New York: Golf Digest, 1978.

Wind, Herbert Warren. *The Story of American Golf: Its Champions and Championships.* New York: Alfred A. Knopf, 1975.

The World Atlas of Golf: The Great Courses and How They Are Played. Ed. Pat Ward-Thomas. London: MitchellBeazley, 1976.

Zaharias, Babe Didrikson, with Harry Paxton. *This Life I've Led: My Autobiography.* New York: A. S. Barnes, 1955.

Barnett, Pam, 188–89
Barnsdall Oil Co., 93
Barr, Dave, 312
Barrett, Bill, 37, 228
Barrett, Sharon, 243, 273, 312
Bartlesville, Okla., 92, 231, 235, 255
Bartley, Jenny, 312
Barton, Russ, 188
Basolo, Susan, 185
Battle Creek, Mich., 53
Battle Creek Golf Club, 233–34, 240
Bauer, Alice, 23, 178
Baxter, A. D. (Mr. and Mrs.), 162
Baxter, Rex Jr., 267
Baxter, Sandy, 19, 312
Bayer, George, 159
Bayou de Siard Country Club, 172
Bean, Andy, 105
Beaumont, Tex., 96
Beaumont Country Club, 18
Beautell, Sara, 312
Beavers Bend State Park Golf Course, 212, 232
Beck, Tommy, 148
Beggs, Okla., 218
Begwin, Jim, 312
Bell, Judy, 178, 270, 273
Bell, Ricky, 227–28, 312
Bellflower, Calif., 276
Belmar Golf Club, 233
Beman, Deane, 268, 279
Bench, Johnny, 169, 312
Benedict, Kevin, 236
Ben Hogan Tulsa Open, 218
Benson, Vic, 271
Bentgrass, 8
Bentley, Mac, 6, 229
Benz, Amy, 288
Berg, Patty, 174, 176, 179–80, 182–84, 271
Berning, Dale, 187–88, 190
Berning, Robin, 188, 190
Berning, Susie Maxwell, 24–25, 123, 182, 185–
    90, 269, 272, 276–77, 313
Berra, Yogi, 217
Berry, Robert W., 99
Besselink, Al, 114
Bethlehem, Pa., 286
Bethpage Black, 87
Beverly Country Club, 187

Bibb, Boyd, 236
Biddick, Dottie, 183
Big Eight Conference, 259
Bigham, George, 115, 313
Big Seven Conference, 251
Big Twelve Conference, 261
Bixby, Okla., 232
Bizik, Vince, 236
Black Thursday, 77
Blakeney, Bert, 20
Blakeney, Paul, 20
Blalock, Jane, 273
Blancas, Homero, 169
Blanchard, Barbara, 283
Bland, Charlie, 236
Blanton, Patti, 173, 313
Blevins, Lynn, 251, 313
Bliss, Don, 313
Blumenthal, Joan, 313
Bob Jones Award, 128, 286, 288
Boden, Maria, 313
Boggs, Frank, 4, 19
Boiling Springs State Park Golf Course, 217, 232
Bolt, Tommy, 99–101, 114, 151–52, 154, 277, 286,
    313–14
Bonallack, Michael, 103, 247
Booher, Don, 236
Boren, David, 252
Boros, Julius, 119, 152, 279
Bossert, Andre, 314
Bothell, Wash., 283
Bowens, Howard, 6
Bowie, Heather, 314
Boyd, Michael, 314
Boyer, Joe, 236
Brackenridge Park, 26
Bradley, Jackson, 101–102
Bradley, Michael, 259, 314
Bradley, Pat, 273
Branch, Brian, 17
Bratton, Alan, 259, 288, 314
Breault, Ann, 177
Bredemus, John, 74
Brent Bruehl Memorial Course, 236
Brewer, Gay, 121, 123, 152, 156, 165, 268
Brigman, Jaxon, 314
Brink, Maria, 315
Bristow, Okla., 287